CHANGE YOUR
BRAIN,
CHANGE YOUR
PAIN

Mark Grant, MA

First published in 2009 by:
Mark Grant
Wyong Medical Centre
Margaret Street
Wyong NSW 2259
Australia
www.overcomingpain.com

Editing, design and typesetting by Sunset Digital Pty Ltd, Brisbane, Queensland.
www.sunsetdigital.com.au

Printed and bound in Australia by:
BookPOD, Vermont South, Victoria
www.bookpod.com.au

All figures are original and were prepared by Garth Andries.

ISBN: 978-0-646-51471-0

Publisher's note:
*This publication is designed to provide accurate and authoritative
information in regard to the subject matter covered. It is sold with
the understanding that the publisher is not engaged in rendering
psychological, financial, legal or other professional services.*

Dedicated to my darling wife Ana

Acknowledgments

Books have always been a part of my life. When I was a young boy I loved nothing more than to escape into a good book. Later, books became a source of knowledge as I traveled through high school and university. As an adult I have found books to be a great source of wisdom when faced with different crises and challenges in life.

After everything books have given me, I'm very happy to have created a book of my own, one that I hope will open up as many doorways for others as books have for me. But I didn't really create this book by myself. I have to acknowledge the generous support and advice of my friends and colleagues, an early mentor Doug Sotheren, as well as Albert Zbik, Dr G. David Champion, Jeff Zeig, Joseph Riordan and Uri Bergmann. I also thank the anonymous reviewers whose sharp critiques spurred me on to improve the text.

This book is built on the work of others, and I have to acknowledge an intellectual debt to Dr Milton Erickson, whose ability to see into people and whose simple wisdom remain my benchmarks; Francine Shapiro, PhD, whose determination and insight continues to transform psychotherapy; Bruce Eimer, PhD, who got me started on EMDR and pain; Bessel van der Kolk, whose research into the effects of trauma helped me understand the effects of stress on mind and body; Michael White, for showing that nothing is ever quite what it seems and that the stories we have about ourselves are changeable; and also, all those "explorers" in the EMDR community, and the researchers involved in developing a neuroscientific approach to understanding and treating human problems.

I thank my patients, whose stories continue to touch, educate and amaze me. I thank my parents for their conscious and unconscious contributions to my development. I am particularly appreciative of my father for passing on to me his sense of humor and stubborn determination, and my mother for the gifts of creativity and curiosity.

I reserve my greatest thanks for my wife, whose grace and compassion are complemented by her roles as colleague, collaborator, sounding-board and cheerleader during the several years it took to complete this book.

The root of all health is in the brain
The trunk of it is in emotion
The branches and leaves are the body
The flower of health blooms
When all parts work together.

Kurdish Folk Wisdom

The systematic training of the mind—the cultivation of happiness, the genuine inner transformation by deliberately selecting and focusing on positive mental states, and challenging negative mental states—is possible because of the very structure and function of the brain . . . our brains are adaptable.

Dalai Lama[1]

If I had to live my life again I would have made a rule to read some poetry and listen to some music at least once a week; for perhaps the parts of my brain that have atrophied could thus have been kept active.

Charles Darwin, 1887

---

[1] *The art of happiness. A handbook for Living*, New York: Riverhead Books (1998).

Contents

PART TWO: CHANGE YOUR BRAIN, CHANGE YOUR PAIN

Introduction

Pain is an unavoidable part of life and, for one in five people, a major part of life. Despite its physical connotations, pain is rarely just a physical problem. At least 50 per cent of people with physical pain also suffer from emotional pain, such as stress, anxiety and depression. Because of the overlap between physical and emotional pain, the term is increasingly used to refer to both. It's also been discovered that pain is in the brain as much as in the body. Although the brain has long been regarded as a passive recipient of experience, we now know that the brain not only receives pain signals, it is also modified by pain and it is capable of modifying pain. Without your brain you wouldn't feel pain, and without your brain you couldn't *not* feel pain. This discovery has led to the development of new ways of treating pain, based on changing the brain activity that maintains pain. This book is about those techniques, and how to use them to "change your brain, change your pain".

Traditionally, physical and emotional pain were viewed as separate problems, treatable by different methods. In recent years health professionals have accepted that physical and emotional pain are connected and that they need to be treated in a unified way. Pain is also increasingly seen as a problem that involves the mind and the body, which has prompted greater acceptance of the role of thoughts and feelings in pain. One of the most exciting developments has been increased understanding of the role of the brain in pain. Neuroscientists have uncovered the brain activity that maintains physical and emotional pain. They have also discovered that the same areas of the brain are involved in physical pain as emotional pain. The other important discovery is neuroplasticity—the brain's capacity to be changed by experience. Neuroplasticity is the key to understanding pain that cannot be explained in terms of physical pathology.

The type of experience that has the greatest impact on the brain is severe stress. Severe stress has been found to trigger changes in brain chemistry, structure and functioning. For example, adult survivors of childhood abuse and neglect have reduced brain volume. Chronic pain sufferers have decreased gray matter and decreased levels of neurotransmitters associated with emotional regulation. People who have suffered severe stress tend to react abnormally to later stress, including increased risk of anxiety, depression and chronic pain, regardless of whether the stressor was physical or mental. They also respond less well to normally effective treatments such as drugs, surgery and counselling. Increased understanding of the effects of stress on the brain, together with neuroplasticity, has revolutionized both our understanding of pain and our approach to overcoming pain.

The key to overcoming pain lies in learning how to change the brain activity that maintains physical and emotional pain. This requires investing a little time in learning about the brain, which is arguably just as important to know how to look after as the body is. The brain is the center of the human nervous system and essential to experience. Everything we experience goes through our brains. The brain is organized in a hierarchical fashion, with the lower areas responsible for processing sensory-emotional information and the upper areas responsible for interpreting and deciding how to respond to events. Generally speaking, your brain processes sensory information in an "upward" direction from the brain-stem to the neocortex. Your brain is also divided into left and right hemispheres, with each side responsible for different tasks. Good brain functioning requires a smooth flow of information in all directions. Anything which disrupts the normal flow of information between the different areas of the brain causes problems.

Most people who have suffered severe stress are unaware of any connection between their physical and emotional pain. For example, more than 50 per cent of depressed people's first visit to a medical practitioner is for a physical symptom.[1] There is also a tendency to ignore or deny emotional pain; downplaying the effects of stress is better than feeling vulnerable or defeated. The adult survivor of abuse or neglect can start their own family and appear to have overcome their "bad start" in life. The war veteran can don civilian clothes, get a job and appear to have left the horrors of combat behind. The benefit of this denial is that it helps us believe that we have triumphed over past adversity. No one wants to admit that they are still suffering because of something that happened 20 years ago. The problem is that it leaves the physical and emotional effects of stress unacknowledged and unresolved. Behind the façade of normalcy, problems such as anxiety and depression, ill-health and chronic pain all remind us that, ultimately, "the body remembers". The inescapable conclusion is that if we are to have any hope of overcoming pain, we need to understand how our nervous system works and how it is affected by stress.

Understanding how your brain works and is affected by stress is the key to overcoming physical and emotional pain. Severe stress changes the structure and functioning of the brain in ways that predispose us to pain. Healing pain requires restoring normal brain functioning including emotional connectedness, responsivity and regulation. This requires five sensory-emotional strategies, each of which addresses a particular effect of stress, namely:

1 safety and support.
2 reconnecting with your feelings
3 learning how to control stressful feelings and pain
4 changing your thinking
5 building resilience.

These strategies are also organized in the same bottom–up order in which your nervous system processes information. Safety is a basic need without which the lower sensory areas of the brain would remain in a state of arousal and closed to new information. Safety is a prerequisite for learning how to control stressful feelings and pain. The most effective way to change stressful feelings and pain is to stimulate the non-rational lower areas of the brain where pain is mainly "stored". Activities that enhance brain connectivity and information flow are also beneficial. These include loving relationships, and interesting and enjoyable activities — anything that stimulates different feelings to those associated with pain. Over time, these kinds of activities stimulate neural repair and re-wiring, and changes in the brain activity that is maintaining the pain. Changing your thinking and resilience involves higher-order mental processes such as monitoring your thinking, goal-setting and self-actualization.

The nature and sequencing of the above strategies is based on the phase-oriented approach to the treatment of post-traumatic stress disorder, which simply means that the problem is broken down into different parts which are addressed in order of priority. For example, you have to be emotionally stable before you can confront your pain. You have to learn how to regulate negative feelings and emotions if you are to have any hope of overcoming past trauma. One approach which incorporates all of these elements in an effective way is eye movement desensitization and reprocessing (EMDR). EMDR derives its name from a procedure wherein clients engage in a dual attention exercise involving stimulated bilateral eye movements and focusing on their problem. When integrated with other treatment elements (as above), this procedure has been found to reduce physical and mental distress, and improve coping. Since its inception as a treatment for post-traumatic stress disorder (PTSD), EMDR has been applied to a range of other somatic and emotionally-based problems. The method's unique combination of sensory inputs, focused attention and cognitive re-appraisal makes it the most brain-smart psychological treatment method around.

Do you need this book?

This book is for you if you suffer from persistent physical and/or emotional pain which is not adequately explained or managed by current medical methods. Associated with this you may also have:

- endured severe stress prior to your pain and/or injury, (e.g. childhood emotional neglect, family instability, physical or sexual abuse, combat experience, prolonged life instability, etc.)
- experienced a physical injury, resulting in pain and disability, which is causing stress or depression.

Mental health professionals should also find this book a useful tool for understanding chronic pain and the effects of stress on mind and body, as well as how to treat these problems more effectively.

How will this book help you?

You may think that you have not been affected by early stress in your life, or that you have been able to escape your past unscathed. Extensive research suggests that no matter how "successful" you are, it is very difficult to go through severe stress without some physical and mental ill-effects — so whether your pain was triggered by a physical injury or illness, and has persisted beyond the normal healing timeframe, or whether it started after a period of severe stress, you need to understand the role of the different physical, mental and emotional factors.

Change Your Brain, Change your Pain will teach you how to neutralize the physical, mental and emotional effects of severe stress that maintain pain. The first half of the book explores the similarities and overlap between physical and emotional pain, including changes to brain structure and functioning. The second half of the book describes a range of techniques designed to reverse the sensory-emotional effects of stress which maintain pain.

Chapter 1 consists of a brief review of what we know about pain and the brain, including how stress affects the brain, plus five things that you can do right now to start changing the brain processes that are maintaining your pain. The aim of Chapter 1 is to orient you to the notion that pain is as much in your brain as your body, and how and why this is so.

Stress can be both a precipitating factor *and* a response to pain, particularly after a serious injury. Chapter 2 describes the normal emotional responses to injury and pain and what they mean. In this chapter you will learn that anxiety, anger and depression are normal and potentially adaptive responses to injury and pain. Chapter 2 will help you understand *why* you feel anxious, angry or depressed, and the role that these feelings play in pain.

Chapter 3 explores the relationship between stress, pain and the brain more deeply. Here you will learn how your brain works, including how it communicates with your body. You will see that there is a kind of bio-chemical feedback loop between your brain and your body which transmits information back and forth, sometimes in the absence of external stimuli. You will learn how stress affects your brain and your thoughts, feelings and behaviors, and how those effects can maintain and exacerbate pain. Although this chapter contains a lot of terms that may be new to the lay reader, you have to remember that understanding any complex system requires becoming familiar with the terminology. Give yourself time to absorb this information, and don't be worried if you don't understand everything at first—you can always re-read it later.

Whether you realize it or not, the way you think about pain and your theories about pain determine how you deal with it. If your theories about pain are wrong, chances are the way you cope with pain is going to be wrong. In Chapter 4 you will find an explanation for your pain, including the role of the brain in pain and how physical and emotional pain overlap. You'll also learn how memory and neuroplasticity maintain pain and how they can be harnessed to change pain. This will give you a theoretical basis for the five sensory-emotional strategies that follow. The chronic pain stress risk factors questionnaire will enable you to evaluate which types and effects of stress are involved in your pain, and consequently which self-help strategies you need to focus on most.

In Chapters 5 through 12, you will learn the five sensory-emotional strategies for overcoming pain. Chapters 5 and 6 cover safety and support, and reconnecting with your feelings. These are two basic types and effects of stress which are often associated with chronic pain. Without them you will find it difficult to succeed in implementing the pain-control strategies that follow. Chapters 7, 8 and 9 describe a range of strategies for changing the sensory-emotional processes that maintain your pain. Some of these, such as relaxation, exercise and sleep management, will be familiar. Others, such as bilateral stimulation, are new. This is where you will need the CD at the back of the book. The CD contains four tracks of evocative words, music and bilateral stimulation, designed to evoke your inner pain resources. You will need a set of headphones and some uninterrupted time. The more often you listen to the CD, the more relaxed you will learn to feel. Chapter 10 is about how to change your thinking, particularly negative, self-defeating attitudes. Chapter 11 is about building resilience. Resilience is not a pain-management strategy *per se*, but it is an important buffering factor against stress and pain. Some types of pain are too intense to overcome on your own. Chapter 12 is about how EMDR treatment can help overcome pain, particularly pain associated with psychological trauma.

The strategies in this book differ from those associated with mainstream approaches to the treatment of pain. Instead of being told that you should ignore your pain (when it lacks a medical diagnosis), you will be encouraged to understand

and respect it. Instead of being encouraged to ignore your feelings about your pain, you will be taught how to deal them. Instead of being told that you alone are responsible for your pain, you will be encouraged to share the burden of it with others. Instead of being pressured into reducing your medication and increasing your levels of physical activity, you will be shown how to discover the right levels of these vital self-help strategies. Some professional readers will no doubt find these ideas challenging, but pain sufferers should find them liberating and useful.

How to use this book

This book is designed to be both an instructional and a practical tool. You should begin by reading it and reflecting on the content. At this stage, feel free to read the chapters in any order you like. You will find a lot of new ideas and insights, some of which will have an immediate impact on how you feel about yourself and your coping; others may take a little longer to integrate. You may find it helpful to share this information with your loved ones or therapist. "Jessie" felt that her family didn't accept how her chronic pain condition made her feel, but after she showed them the chapter about normal emotional reactions to injury and pain they became less judgmental and more tolerant.

Before you try to apply the self-help strategies contained in the second half of the book, you should complete the questionnaire in Chapter 4. This will guide you regarding which self-help strategies you need to concentrate on most. Each strategy is accompanied by exercises to help you learn the skill. You don't have to stop reading and complete the exercises immediately you come upon them, but you should attempt the exercise(s) at some stage. Although you may wish to move backwards and forwards between the different strategies, remember that they are designed to build on one another. If you find yourself having difficulty with a particular strategy, you may need to go back and ensure that you have adequately mastered an earlier skill-set.

Caveats

A few caveats. You will notice that this book uses the term "pain" to refer to both physical and emotional pain. This is not meant to imply that physical pain is the same as emotional pain. Physical pain and emotional pain *are* different, and there is plenty of information about how to treat them as such. However, physical pain and emotional pain also have many similarities including overlapping physical, emotional and neurological processes. Any pain that is not purely based on physical pathology is likely to involve some combination of the above factors.

Change Your Brain, Change Your Pain is aimed at people who suffer from overlapping physical and emotional pain and want to learn a unified way of healing both. This is the kind of pain meant where the term is used in this book. The challenge, and the key to successful treatment, is knowing how and when to separate physical from mental pain, and how and when to view them in a unified way. You should find this book helpful in this regard. If your pain is predominantly physical, you should of course pursue all reasonable medical treatment options.

As this book is primarily designed for a non-professional audience, I have tried to keep the brain stuff as simple as possible. Inevitably it will be overwhelming to some, and not enough for others. The aim is to give you enough information to understand how your brain might be maintaining your pain and how you can change that. You don't need to understand all the brain stuff, but it's there because it's impossible to understand chronic pain without it. Having said that, the description of the brain processes involved in physical and emotional pain will almost certainly be out of date by the time this book is printed—this is such a rapidly developing area—however, I am confident that the five sensory-emotional strategies described in this book will become more popular as more research is conducted.

Finally, although this book is about addressing the contribution of stress to pain, you should never ignore the possibility that there may be a physical cause for your pain. For example, many women who were sexually abused experience vaginal pain during intercourse. For some women this is a psychosomatic reaction, but for other women it may be a manifestation of a medical condition, such as vulvadynia. Even then, childhood abuse may have acted as a prediposing factor for this condition. As always, understanding pain requires careful examination of all causal factors—so try to get out of the habit of "either-or" thinking when trying to understand your pain.

The strategies in this book may not "cure" your pain, but with understanding, patience and disciplined application of the sensory-emotional strategies contained herein, you can feel better.

Mark Grant
Sydney
June 2009

PART ONE

Pain and your brain

1

Pain, stress and your brain

No brain, no pain.
Anonymous

Pain hurts. It's a mixture of unpleasant physical and emotional feelings which take away your ability to participate in and enjoy life. Physically, pain takes away your ability to feel comfortable in your own body. Emotionally, pain takes away your ability to feel happy. Chronic physical or emotional pain leads to anxiety, depression, and even post-traumatic stress disorder. Because of how it affects us, there is no problem more urgent than pain. Chronic pain is also a very difficult problem to overcome. We may seek help from a doctor or therapist, but traditional treatments are often ineffective. Chronic pain doesn't even make sense in terms of our usual understanding of pain. Two areas of scientific inquiry have started unlocking the mystery of pain: one is stress research and the increase in knowledge about how stress affects the nervous system; the other is neuroscience and the expansion in knowledge about how the brain works. Discoveries from these fields have led to the development of new healing strategies based on changing the brain processes that maintain pain.

Although we are used to thinking of pain as a physical problem, and increasingly an emotional problem, it also helps to be able to think of pain as a brain problem. Why? Firstly, your brain is responsible for regulating all the symptoms of your body, including heart-rate, temperature, mood, sleep, etc. Secondly, your brain acts as a kind of experiential decoder of everything that happens to you. It tells you whether something is good or bad, friend or foe, edible or poisonous. Based on its interpretation of events, your brain guides you on how to respond. But your brain does more than passively receive information; your brain is also altered by what you experience—what scientists call neuroplasticity. Examples of neuroplasticity include the discovery that the area of the brain responsible for memory and navigation is larger in London taxi drivers.[1] Adults who were abused as children have been found to have smaller hippocampi.[2]

The types of experience that most affect the brain are those that threaten your physical or mental health—accidents, injuries, family problems and so on. These sorts of events trigger a strong reaction in the brain and, over time, affect its structure and functioning. Prolonged severe stress impairs your brain's ability to regulate your body and cope with pain. For example, the more stress you experience, the more sensitive your brain becomes to pain. There's nothing strange about this—just think about how much better you cope with physical pain or stress when you feel relaxed compared with when you feel tired or depressed. Fortunately, neuroplasticity works both ways: what has been learned can be unlearned; what has been missed can be recovered. But first you have to understand how your brain works and the nature of the relationship between your body and your mind.

From your body to your brain

How does pain get into your brain? Pain begins in your body. Physical pain is a product of nerve signals stimulated by tissue damage, which travel from the body to the brain. Your brain responds by signaling the muscles to tighten and protect the injured part of your body. It also guides you to "rest and protect" the injured area. Over time the damaged tissue heals, the central nervous system ceases to send out signals, and the pain goes away. This kind of pain, which is how most of us think about pain, is known as acute pain. Acute pain is time-limited, consistent with the injury that caused it, and generally manageable. Pain that persists beyond normal healing time-frames—chronic pain—is different. Chronic pain usually starts with an injury or illness, but is greater than would be expected for the injury that caused it, and it doesn't respond to normally effective treatments. Chronic physical pain comes in many different forms, including:

- arthritis
- back pain
- cancer
- complex regional pain syndrome
- fibromyalgia
- sciatica
- somatization disorder
- migraine pain.

Chronic pain involves a different mix of physical and mental symptoms than acute pain. Some types of chronic pain are mainly physical in origin. For example, arthritis pain is mainly understood in terms of physical pathology—damage to the joints of the body. Other types of pain involve both physical and mental factors. Complex regional pain syndrome (or reflex sympathetic dystrophy) is caused by a disturbance of the sympathetic nervous system—the network of nerves located along the spinal cord which controls bodily functions such as the opening and closing of blood vessels and sweat glands. Fibromyalgia involves increased sensitivity to pain, including touch (known as allodynia) and fatigue in muscles and tendons. In addition to physical pathology, complex regional pain syndrome and fibromyalgia are thought to be maintained by a genetic predisposition to stress. Chronic pain is also processed differently in your brain, with greater involvement of areas of the brain involved in memory and emotion than for acute pain.

Migraine pain is thought to be caused by hypersensitivity in the brain. In *The Migraine Brain*, neurologist Carolyne Bernstein proposes that the brain cells of migraine sufferers are more easily aroused by stimuli such as fatigue, stress, temperature changes and certain foods. Bernstein bases her model on research wherein migraine sufferers were found to have brain abnormalities including thickening of the somatosensory cortex—the area of the brain that relays pain and sensation. Other research has found structural impairments in the brains of chronic pain sufferers which affect the brain's ability to maintain itself in a balanced state while they are performing mentally demanding tasks. Bernstein concludes that one of the causes of migraines is that the brains of people who have migraines are different and function differently. The question is: what causes the brain to behave in this way, and what can you do about it?

Pain, stress and your brain

Stress is the feeling of tension we get when faced with an event that we feel unable to control or cope with. The term actually comes from the Latin word "stringer" which means to draw tight. In terms of normal, everyday stress, there are basically two types of stress—acute stress and chronic stress. Acute stress is triggered by short-term challenges, such as temporary unemployment, illness, or running to escape a mugger. Acute stress involves a temporary state of heightened arousal producing increased adrenalin, constriction of the arteries (to maximize blood pressure), metabolism of glucose and fat into energy, etc. These changes, which produce a surge in energy and alertness, are short-lived and dissipate once the stressor has passed. Acute stress is often referred to as the "fight-or-flight" response or the "rabbit in the headlights" look (or deer or fox depending on the types of wild animals where you live). With the exception of life-threatening events (see below), acute stress doesn't normally have any long-term effects.

Chronic stress is triggered by more severe forms of adversity, such as being raised in an emotionally unstable family, significant rejection, abuse or criticism during childhood, chronic illness, having to live or work in unsafe conditions, etc. One of the most common and damaging types of chronic stress is physical abuse and/or emotional neglect in childhood. Emotional abuse means being subject to criticism or ridicule by our parents, being manipulated and/or being held responsible for things that are outside our control. Emotional neglect means not receiving adequate love and affection because mom and dad were either not around or because they were unable to show love. Emotional abuse and neglect tend to occur in families where there was mental illness, alcoholism or drug abuse, intergenerational abuse or neglect, violence and instability; however, they can also occur in apparently normal families where everything may appear happy on the surface but there is no real intimacy. In such cases, emotional neglect can be subtle; we may believe we were loved because our physical needs were taken care of, but maybe we were never (or rarely) touched, held or told we were loved.

Another type of stress comes from experiencing (or witnessing) life-threatening situations such as motor vehicle accidents, physical or sexual abuse during childhood, rape, assault, war combat, or even being diagnosed with a life-threatening illness. The event must also have involved feelings of intense fear, helplessness or horror, although sometimes these feelings may not have occurred until some time later. Post-traumatic stress disorder (PTSD) involves more severe symptoms than those of normal stress, including nightmares and flashbacks, avoidance, numbness, trembling and catatonia. PTSD can also involve re-experiencing symptoms, wherein the sufferer actually re-lives the traumatic event in their body. These re-living symptoms can incorporate physical pain, making PTSD the most potent form of stress in terms of causing pain. PTSD-like symptoms can also result from non–life-threatening stressors such as emotional abuse and neglect, workplace bullying, the unexpected death of a loved one, or being sued. Of course, these effects are increased when traumatic stress is combined with chronic stress.

Why all this talk about stress? Because after physical injury, it is the second leading cause of chronic pain. In one of the largest investigations of its kind, a study of 9508 adult members of a health plan in the USA found that people who had suffered severe stress were more than twice as likely to have health problems (e.g. heart disease, diabetes, fractures and occupational health problems) compared with people who had not.[3] These researchers also found that the more stressful events a person has experienced, the greater their risk of pain and illness. Stressed people experience greater levels of pain than non-stressed people with similar injuries, and they don't respond as well to normally effective medical interventions.[4] Stressed people are more likely to be injured at work and experience greater levels of disability than non-stressed people.[5] Stressed people are more likely to have complications following surgery.[6] Stressed people are even more at risk of the common cold![7]

The predisposing effects of stress on pain are potentially felt from infancy; if your mother was stressed while you were in the womb, or your birth was marred by complications or post-natal problems, you may be more vulnerable to pain. Researchers have found that premature infants who were subject to painful medical procedures became more sensitive to pain than normal babies.[8] The types of stress most likely to lead to pain include:

- early childhood adversity (e.g. physical or sexual abuse, witnessing domestic violence, having a parent with a mental illness, family instability, etc.[9,10])
- emotional abuse and/or neglect[11,12]
- traumatic stress (e.g. accidents, surgery, diagnosis of a life-threatening illness, abortion, combat trauma, exposure to political violence[13–18]).

Stress is involved in just about every type of chronic pain, including fibromyalgia, gastrointestinal problems, headaches, and chronic widespread pain. Conditions such as diabetes, heart disease, bladder problems, immune disorders, digestive and genitourinary disorders, irritable bowel syndrome, skin problems and increased risk of fractures have all been linked to PTSD.[19,20] PTSD is also more common among sufferers of fibromyalgia, reflex sympathetic dystrophy, chronic fatigue syndrome, and temporomandibular disorders.[21,22]

Severe stress is also more common than is generally thought; emotional stress such as anxiety and depression affects 20 per cent of people in many countries. Even traumatic stressors, which used to be considered unusual, have been found to occur in over 50 per cent of people, with problems such as child abuse and neglect affecting around 25 per cent of children in developed nations.[23] Chronic pain is also stressful; it robs us of the ability to feel comfortable in our own bodies, and it takes away our ability to live in the present and plan for the future. The stress from chronic pain can take various forms including negative feelings (anxiety, depression), memories (of past pain) and thoughts ("I can't stand this anymore."). The stress caused by chronic pain has long been thought to explain the additional suffering associated with this problem. The more stressed we feel, the less well we cope and the more we hurt.

Although some people still get hung up about the mention of psychological factors in relation to pain, the idea that stress is involved in pain is not new. The nineteenth century psychiatrist Pierre Janet described stress as "a disease which modifies the whole organism".[24] Sigmund Freud was also famous for suggesting that physical pain could be a symptom of emotional hurt.[25] Over 40 years ago, the International Association for the Study of Pain actually re-defined pain as "... an unpleasant sensory *and emotional* experience associated with actual or potential tissue damage ..." (italics mine). Accepting that stress is part of your pain doesn't mean that you're crazy; it's just a different, and more useful, way of thinking about your pain. When your pain isn't responding to medical treatment, your only hope may be to learn how to change whatever neurological and psychological factors are contributing to your pain.

Stress and pain

The key to understanding chronic pain lies in understanding human needs and functioning, and how stress affects your brain. Basically stress is anything that threatens your ability to satisfy your survival needs. Stress impacts upon your nervous system, leading to increased arousal and alertness. Some amount of stress is to be expected as part of life, but we are not meant to exist in a permanent state of arousal. Severe stress causes permanent biochemical imbalances, sleeping problems, anxiety and depression, and increased sensitivity to pain. It's also been discovered that severe stress changes the way your brain processes information, including delayed reaction times, concentration and memory problems, impaired decision-making, etc. Stress, pain and your brain are thus an overlapping cause-and-effect system wherein stress impacts on your nervous system, which impacts upon your health, which affects how you feel, and so on. Viewed this way, stress is involved in pain at all levels of human functioning, including physical, emotional and social. Experts have come up with five main types and effects of stress which lead to pain:

1 lack of safety and support
2 emotional disconnection
3 increased physiological arousal
4 negative thinking
5 trauma (pain memories).

It doesn't take much to figure out how these factors might lead to pain. For example, lack of safety and support, such as unresolved post-traumatic stress or inadequately managed pain, means you can never relax, which causes tension, which exacerbates pain. Emotional disconnection makes it harder to regulate negative feelings associated with stress and pain, leaving you more vulnerable to these problems. Increased physiological arousal involves biochemical imbalances among other things, including increased levels of substance P, a neurotransmitter which increases your perception of pain. Stress-related sleeping problems cause fatigue, which also increases your sensitivity to pain. Traumatic stress involves significant physiological and emotional changes, wherein pain can occur as part of an unresolved traumatic memory. Severe stress also triggers changes in brain structure and functioning, such as decreased communication between the left and right hemispheres, and decreased ability of the brain to regulate itself. We will look more closely at the mechanisms by which the effects of stress lead to pain in the following three chapters.

How to use your brain to change your pain

Knowing how your brain works, and how the effects of stress on your brain can maintain pain, opens the way to new methods of controlling pain. They involve strategies which are specifically designed to target the different types and effects of stress, and neutralize the learned sensory-emotional patterns that maintain stress and pain. These strategies take advantage of neuroplasticity — your brain's capacity to be changed by experience. These strategies are also designed to work *with* your nervous system in terms of how it processes information to release stress and pain. Based on what we know about stress, pain and the brain, there are five basic strategies for overcoming pain:

1   safety and support
2   reconnecting with your feelings
3   learning how to control stressful feelings and pain
4   changing your thinking
5   building resilience.

It should not seem strange to think of pain as being maintained by changes in the brain and to use this as a basis for treatment. We are all amateur neuropsychologists. We smoke and drink to calm ourselves down; we take stimulants to perk ourselves up. We take antidepressants to correct the chemical imbalance that is supposedly causing our depression. If we are really smart, we exercise to increase our endorphins (natural pain-relieving chemicals) and/or meditate to reduce our levels of stress hormones. Most of these strategies are pursued with, at best, only a vague understanding of how what we are doing might be helping the mental and emotional processes that maintain physical and emotional pain. Knowing how we work, and how stress affects us, enables us to take a much more intelligent approach to overcoming pain.

Safety and support

People mainly tend to think of pain management in terms of getting rid of the hurt; however, there are certain conditions you must satisfy in order to be able to do this. Imagine you fell and sprained your ankle, but then you noticed a gang of thugs coming toward you. What would be your first concern? You would want to get out of danger first. So the first priority is to deal with any clear and present danger, or threats to your safety and well-being. If you suffer from chronic pain, this might mean reviewing your pain-management strategies to ensure you have adequate control over your pain. If you are unsure about your diagnosis, it might mean seeking further investigations. If you live or work in an unsafe place, it might mean taking action to make your living conditions safer. Take a moment to think about what situations or events make you feel threatened or unsafe. What is stopping you from overcoming that threat? Is there anything more you need to do to protect yourself? The more safe you feel, the less stressed you will feel. The less stressed you feel, the less pain you will feel.

Reconnecting with your feelings

The next step is to reconnect with your feelings. Many sufferers of stress and pain have either never learned to feel, or they have disconnected from their feelings as a way of coping. Although emotional disconnection starts out as an attempt to cope with stress, over the long term it actually perpetuates the problem. There are a number of reasons for this. Feelings are necessary for integrating experience; without feelings we cannot learn and change. Being connected with your feelings also gives you more control over them; when you feel depressed you can pull yourself out of it by doing or thinking of something that makes you feel happy.

Reconnecting with your feelings means developing "emotional intelligence." Emotional intelligence begins by paying attention to your body and learning how to recognize the physiological signs of different emotional states. The more "in tune" you are with your feelings, the more able you will be to manage pain and stress. For example, take a moment to focus on how you are feeling right now. Notice any feelings of stress, fatigue, sadness, etc. Without judging or analysing, just notice your pain. If you can do this, you will notice that just the act of not judging your pain takes away some of its sting. Next, again without judging or analysing, try to interpret what your body is signaling through those feelings. Now, think about how you can give yourself what you need to alleviate that pain, even if it's only out of your memory or imagination.

Changing your pain

Once you are stable and able to listen to your feelings, you are ready to learn how to change your pain directly. Based on what we know about how the brain processes information, the most direct and powerful way to change your pain is to direct your attention *away* from your pain and *toward* something that makes you feel different, preferably happier or more relaxed. It could be a memory of happier times; it could be playing with your pet dog, or listening to music. When you concentrate on something pleasant, you change the way your brain perceives the pain. Joanne felt overwhelmed by her pain and the future seemed hopeless. However, when she remembered how she and her husband renovated the old house they'd bought as their first home, it brought back feelings of efficacy and joy, which made her feel less overwhelmed by her pain.

Another strategy for changing how you feel is dual attention stimulus. Dual attention stimulus is a treatment element of eye movement desensitization and reprocessing (EMDR), a memory processing treatment developed by Francine Shapiro, PhD. We will talk about EMDR in more detail later, but for now all you need to know is that dual attention stimulus (DAS) involves focusing on the pain or stress while simultaneously concentrating on an external bilateral stimulation (Bls). This unique combination of stimuli has been found to reduce the physical and mental distress associated with stress and pain. If you have ever had the experience of paying attention to a neutral, bilateral stimulus while simultaneously recalling or thinking about something stressful, you have had some experience of this technique. An example would be tapping your knees while waiting for a job interview, or going for a walk (especially on a beach) when feeling stressed. You might recall feeling somehow calmed by the bilateral stimulus provided by tapping or walking.

The next time you feel bothered by pain, instead of avoiding or resisting it, try "just noticing" it in a detached way and at the same time hum, tap yourself, or focus on rhythmical sounds such as rain, a recording of ocean waves, or the bilateral stimulation track (Track 4) on the CD that comes with this book. Initially, do this for about 30 seconds to a minute, then take a deep breath and re-focus your attention back on the pain. *Don't try to make anything happen while focusing on the Bls; just pay attention to it and let whatever happens happen.* If you really pay attention to the Bls, you will almost certainly notice either a difference in the intensity of your pain, or a change in how you perceive your pain—it will seem further away and less important.

Changing your thinking

Stress and pain can trigger negative attitudes and beliefs, which can reinforce emotional and behavioral aspects of these problems. Negative thoughts are self-defeating attitudes and beliefs, such as "I'm bad", "I'm weak", "I'm helpless", etc. Such beliefs are often unconscious, meaning that we don't necessarily go through life having those thoughts "out loud"; however, we may feel anxious, helpless and/or inadequate, and negative emotions tend to incorporate negative attitudes and beliefs about ourself. Negative attitudes and beliefs can also be reflected in our behavior, such as when we fail to take action to help ourself, or when we engage in self-destructive behavior such as overworking, or abusing drugs or alcohol. Negative thinking can contribute to pain by making us believe we are weak, that things will never change, or that only bad things ever happen.

Changing your thinking can lead to more effective coping and decision-making. Changing your thinking is not an abstract, intellectual exercise. Changing your thinking is an aspect of emotional intelligence. For example, Harry felt overwhelmed and depressed as a result of not being able to work because of chronic pain, but when a friend pointed out to him that at least he was now able to spend more time with his young children when they most needed him, it made him feel less depressed.

Harry's children were the most important thing in his life, and he had to admit that since he had been at home his relationship with his children had improved. As a result of feeling less depressed, Harry's thinking changed; he realized that he could still make a contribution, and this made Harry feel better about himself.

Changing your thinking means more than just "happy talk"; it involves stimulating new emotional responses by changing attention, perception and behavior. Although it's normal to feel sad and anxious about having chronic pain, you need to be able to put aside these feelings sometimes and think about those aspects of your life or yourself that have survived the pain. Examples include personal qualities such as courage, persistence, caring for others; or relationships such as being a parent, sibling or friend. Honestly ask yourself what those enduring qualities or relationships say about you as a person. Then, the next time you feel overwhelmed by negative thoughts, remember those qualities and what they say about you.

Building resilience

Some people are able to withstand adversity, injury and/or pain and move on with seemingly few problems. This ability to "bounce back" from adversity is known as resilience. Resilience comes from a combination of personal and social qualities including temperament, family background, education and cultural factors. Resilient individuals tend to possess many of the above-mentioned stress-management skills including emotional regulation skills, a positive attitude and an ability to transform negative events into useful learning. Although resilience is hereditary to some degree, it can also be learned. Resilience can be developed through building and maintaining strong family and/or community ties, having goals, knowing how to turn problems into strengths, etc. Resilience doesn't alleviate pain and stress directly, but it creates a powerful buffer against these problems, and a strong foundation from which to build coping strategies.

After social support, perhaps the best thing you can do to increase your resilience is to find some means of transforming your painful circumstances into something useful. While he was temporarily disabled as a result of a fractured spine, Rodney taught himself memory techniques out of a paperback a friend gave him. By the time Rodney was back on his feet, he could remember over 1000 items of information, a skill that enabled him to earn a living as a memory expert. Instead of focusing on the negative effects of your pain, remember some past achievements and what they say about you. Think about what you can still do that is purposeful and meaningful.

Five things you can do right now to start feeling better

The aim of the preceding five strategies is to neutralize the processes that maintain stress and pain. At the heart of this approach is a belief that your nervous system either knows or has the capacity to learn how to feel better. It's important to remember too that you are not really meant to be in a constant state of pain or stress and that you have the capacity to learn how to overcome these problems. So to summarize, here are five things you can do immediately to start reversing the brain activity/processes that are maintaining your pain.

1 **Detachment:** Learn how to separate how you think from how you feel. Pain is unpleasant. It can make you feel stressed, anxious and depressed. While perfectly normal, these reactions can also exacerbate pain by feeding negative emotions into an already unpleasant sensory experience. Imagine your breath as a conduit to your pain and that with each inward breath you make contact with your pain, and with each outward breath you let go of your pain, a bit at a time.

2 **Stop thinking:** Learn how to live in the now and accept reality without judging it. Pain triggers negative thinking, worry and doubt. While worry is an understandable reaction to a threat such as pain, after a while it only clouds your judgment and adds to your anxiety. Isn't your current pain enough to deal with without adding to it by worrying about tomorrow? When you stop worrying about your pain, you remove a significant component of emotional distress.

3 **Make friends with your feelings:** Learn how to absorb feelings—not just pain but *all kinds* of feelings. Pain starts out as a warning signal, to alert you to injury and prompt you to take action such as resting or protecting the injured area. In that way pain is your friend. Pain can persist for many reasons including undiagnosed pathology, emotional distress and biochemical imbalances. Maybe you need to learn how to manage stress better, deal with depression or get more sleep. Find out what's maintaining your pain and what action or skills are needed to address it.

4 **Focus your attention on something else:** Pain can dominate your mind. Although pain is important, after a certain time focusing on it just makes you feel worse. There are many other things you can pay attention to that will make you feel less pain and stress: your breathing, a happy memory, a physical stimulus such as tapping, a beach or a waterfall. Without denying the reality of your pain, shift your attention to remembering or doing something that triggers different feelings to those associated with the pain.

5 **Review your levels of safety and support:** Sharing your feelings, whether negative or positive, with someone close is one of the most powerful long-term antidotes to chronic physical and emotional pain. Shared

emotion stimulates the same parts of the brain as those involved in physical pain, in a positive way. Seek out someone you feel close to and have a conversation.

Don't worry if you aren't sure how to put all of the above strategies into practice yet. You will find more detailed information and exercises in the second half of the book which will help you develop the skills necessary to implement them.

Conclusion

The aim of this chapter has been to introduce you to the notion that your pain is in your brain as much as it is in your body, particularly if you have suffered severe stress. You should now have a rough understanding of the five main physical and emotional effects of stress and how they lead to pain. You have been introduced to a new way of managing pain, in the form of five strategies designed to neutralize the pain-maintaining effects of stress on your brain, plus five practical steps that you can implement immediately to start feeling better. Obviously there are no quick or easy solutions to chronic pain and stress, so the rest of this book is about how to apply these five strategies in more detail. But before that we need to look a little more deeply at how stress affects your brain, and the role of memory and emotional functioning in maintaining pain. Understanding the causes of a problem makes it easier to know how to overcome it.

2

Emotional aspects of pain

*One's suffering disappears when one lets oneself
go, when one yields—even to sadness.*

Antoine de Saint-Exupéry*

Chronic pain hurts, both physically and emotionally. The emotional pain that we feel when we have been hurt physically is an inseparable element of pain. Any significant illness or injury involves emotion, including depression, anger and shame. These emotions become part of our pain experience, as well as influencing how we cope. Many people are confused about the role of emotion following injury and pain. Emotions such as anxiety and depression are often regarded as "bad", and a sign that we are not coping. But emotions are a response to events. Most emotions that people have following injury and pain are actually normal and necessary. For example, although depression is often regarded as a sign of not coping, it can also be a way of conserving scarce energy in times of ill-health.[1] Depressed people are less active. Depression generally passes when a person starts to feel better. Understood this way, negative emotions can be seen as part of an adaptive survival response, rather than as a sign of weakness. Understanding the role of emotion following injury and pain is essential for coming to terms with what has happened and moving on.

* *Southern Mail*, 1929, translated from French by Curtis Cate.

Normal emotional reactions to injury and pain

Elizabeth Kubler-Ross originally suggested that negative life-events cause predictable emotional responses. In her classic book about death and dying, Kubler-Ross defined bereavement as an emotional process involving five distinct stages: denial, anger, bargaining, depression and acceptance.[2] Kubler-Ross felt that each emotional stage represented part of an evolving attempt to come to terms with the loss. Kubler-Ross's ideas have helped thousands of people understand and move through the emotional pain of grief. Victims of injury and pain are also grappling with loss: loss of control; lost working capacity; and lost ability to enjoy family and recreational activities. Not surprisingly, victims of injury and pain experience very similar emotions to those associated with grief.

Many people's first reaction to injury or pain is denial; they don't want to believe what has happened. Denial can take the form of ignoring the pain, not seeking medical help soon enough following injury, or minimizing the severity of the injury ("it's just a scratch"). Denial is usually followed by fear/anxiety as the pain persists and the realization dawns that there really is something wrong. Fear eventually triggers more active attempts to manage the problem, such as protecting the injury and seeking medical help. If the injury or pain doesn't respond to medical treatment, fear turns into anxiety, and anxiety turns into depression.

Depression is one of the most common emotional reactions to injury and chronic pain. Depression involves feelings of helplessness and hopelessness, and the feeling that there is nothing you can do.[3,4] Depression is also often associated with anger and guilt. Anger is a defensive emotion—it stimulates aggressive behavior toward the things or people that we feel are hurting us. Guilt is a form of emotional self-punishment as a result of feeling that we are failing in our social obligations. Guilt can come from a reduced ability to work or contribute to one's family or society after pain and injury. Depression is where many people get stuck. Only after a long and painful struggle, sometimes to the point of wondering if life is worthwhile, do people reach acceptance. Acceptance doesn't mean that you like what has happened, but that you accept your injury and its consequences and have let go of the past (wishing it had never happened, etc.). Acceptance leads to reduced anxiety, depression and anger, and better coping.

The emotional stages of injury and pain are slightly different to Kubler-Ross's stages of grief. There are actually six primary emotional reactions to injury and pain: denial, anxiety, depression, anger, shame and acceptance. Each emotional stage involves particular thoughts, perceptions and behaviors, reflecting whatever aspect of injury and pain you are struggling with. Although we talk about these emotions as occurring in stages, in reality, they are not experienced so separately, but blend with each other through the daily experience of struggling to cope with injury and pain. Table 2.1 summarizes the six most common emotional reactions to injury and pain, including the thoughts and behaviors that go with them.

Table 2.1   The normal emotional stages of injury and pain

Emotion	Thought	Behavior
1. Denial	"It's probably nothing serious." "I'll be all right."	Ignore the pain. Keep going as though nothing has happened. Not seeking medical help. Not following medical advice/ treatment
2. Fear/anxiety	"Something's wrong." "What's going to happen?" "Will I be able to cope?"	Rest/seek medical help. Worry/preoccupation. Avoidance.
3. Depression	"What is the use?" "It's hopeless." "I'm weak/inadequate." "Why bother?"	Reduced participation in physical activities, even enjoyable ones. Social withdrawal. Sleeping problems.
4. Anger	"It's not fair." "Why me?" "Nobody cares."	Impulsive or compulsive behaviors. Aggressive behavior. "Overreacting" to things. Self-destructive behavior (e.g. abusing drugs or alcohol).
5. Shame	"I'm bad." "I'm unlovable." "I'm worthless." "I'm a failure."	Social withdrawal. Decreased confidence and assertiveness. Self-destructive behavior (e.g. abusing drugs or alcohol).
6. Acceptance	"What has happened has happened." "It's not my fault." "I deserve help." "It is up to me." "I can cope."	Being less focused on the past Having more realistic expectations of self Maintaining appropriate levels of physical activity. Using medication more appropriately. Reduced mental and emotional stress Increased feelings of peace and calmness

Roughly speaking, the six emotional stages of coping with injury and pain occur in the above order; most people feel anxious before succumbing to depression; anger is often felt before acceptance. Each emotion represents a different stage on your healing journey. Of course, life is not so black and white, and most people experience a mixture of feelings, often in a single day. Nevertheless, there is a certain order and logic to your feelings about your pain. You can judge what emotional stage you are in by identifying which emotion you experience most. For example, if you feel depressed most of the time, that's probably the emotional stage you are at.

For victims of earlier stress or trauma, injury and pain can also place an intolerable strain on maladaptive but previously effective coping mechanisms such as workaholism, perfectionism and other-centeredness. The adult who was unloved as a child may be suddenly confronted with feelings of inadequacy as a result of losing their ability to "earn" love through doing things for others. The workaholic who avoids their feelings by keeping busy may suddenly find themselves confronted by feelings of anxiety and sadness which they previously avoided through activity. The loss of physical functioning can be quite traumatic and invariably triggers feelings of vulnerability, anxiety and depression. This collapse of normal emotional homeostasis can heighten the sense of crisis associated with the emotional effects of injury and pain. As one chronic pain sufferer said, "I've been through cancer and four ectopic pregnancies, but none of it compares to this."

Victims of stress, injury and pain often feel confused and ambivalent about their emotional reactions. No one likes to feel angry or depressed, or out of control of their emotions. Feeling out of control of your emotions is stressful and can add to the feelings of loss of control associated with injury and pain. Understanding the different emotions associated with injury and pain can relieve distress and improve coping.

Denial

The first reaction to pain is often denial. Denial means being unwilling or unable to accept something we don't like. Denial is what psychologists call a defense mechanism; it protects us against unpleasant events. When Jenny, a factory worker, first noticed pain in her lower back, she ignored it—with a family to support, Jenny simply couldn't afford to take time off. When Leo, a construction worker, developed tingling and shooting pains in his arms, he continued working, hoping that it was just a strain. Leo was afraid of getting in trouble with the foreman and losing his job. The problem with denial is that it is not solving the problem, merely concealing it.

Denial doesn't mean we don't know that there is pain or disability. We may know we have pain, but we refuse to make any changes or take any steps to adapt to the pain—that is denial. We may know that we cannot live, love and play normally because of our pain, but refuse to acknowledge how these losses make us feel— that is denial. To live in denial is to avoid reality. Denial is most commonly used by people who were raised without proper love and security. Abused or neglected children quickly realize that it's not safe to show feelings of vulnerability, so that by the time they reach adulthood they are adept at presenting a calm exterior, regardless of what is going on inside. Denial can "sabotage" our ability to respond appropriately to injury and pain, by creating a false sense of security. Because they ignored the initial warning signs, Jenny and Leo both developed serious injuries and chronic pain.

Denial can be unwittingly reinforced by well-meaning medical practitioners who give unrealistic indications of how long an injury will take to heal. When your doctor tells you it's "only a strain" and that you'll be better in two weeks, you want to believe him. Some doctors dismiss pain when they can't determine the cause. This often causes confusion and self-doubt, further undermining the individual's ability to accept reality. Denial can also be reinforced by cultural factors; many societies encourage a stoic, non-complaining attitude toward pain. The popularity of entertainment heroes such as Rocky, the Terminator and even Hannibal Lecter stems in part from their ability to ignore pain and suffering (theirs or others).

Fear/anxiety

Fear/anxiety comes when the reality that there is something wrong hits home. Fear is an initial response to a clear and present danger, and usually generates some sort of behavioral response (i.e. fight or flight). Anxiety tends to be triggered by a future, often less-specific threat. Emotionally, anxiety involves apprehension and dread. Behaviorally, anxiety generates scanning of the environment and the body. Anxiety also tends to follow fear: for example, your doctor finds a benign lump in your breast and tells you it will have to be removed, which stimulates fear. After the lump has been removed, you find that you feel relieved, but you also worry more about the possibility of getting sick again (anxiety). Both anxiety and fear involve increased physiological arousal: with fear the arousal may be more intense and of shorter duration; with anxiety the arousal tends to be less severe, but more prolonged.

When associated with injury or pain, anxiety is generally a response to the threat these problems pose to our well-being and functioning. Injury and pain rob us of the ability to make plans and achieve our goals. Pain levels can change from day to day, hour to hour, making it hard to commit to work schedules or planned activities. Injury also robs us of the ability to perform physical activities necessary for work, love and play. The longer the injury and pain persist, the more anxiety can build up; if anxiety becomes too great, panic attacks can occur.

Anxiety is thought to have its origins in childhood. Freud felt that anxiety originated from the overwhelming experience of birth, and the helplessness of infancy. Evolutionary psychologists believe that anxiety is "hard-wired" into us as part of an adaptive survival response.[1] Certainly one of the most basic childhood fears is the fear of pain. Young children lack the ability to separate how they feel from how they think, or the mental capacity to reassure themselves that the pain is only temporary. Ideally, as they mature, children learn how to cope with unpleasant emotions and pain. However, children who were neglected or abused may never have learned how to regulate their emotions. Even people who were fortunate enough to receive normal love struggle to cope with the challenge of serious injury and pain. We will look at various ways of managing anxiety in Part Two.

Depression

Depression is the most common emotional response to injury and pain. Depression is a state of sadness or despair. Depression can also involve irritability, sleeping problems, and decreased energy and motivation. Depression occurs when we feel defeated by negative events or circumstances. Depression comes from feeling that there's nothing we can do that will make any difference. Depression is a heavy, draining emotion that takes away energy, spontaneity and joy. There is a feeling of "what's the use?" Behaviorally, depressed people feel less able to interact with the world and other people. Depression shrinks your world. Depression stimulates a withdrawal from normally enjoyable recreational activities, hobbies, sports and social pursuits. There may also be avoidance of responsibilities such as parenting, domestic duties and work.

Depression tends to come after anxiety and feels quite different from anxiety. As stress expert Robert Sapolsky describes it, "If anxiety is a crackling, menacing bushfire, depression is a suffocating heavy blanket thrown on top of it."[5] Unlike anxiety, depression evolves slowly and its effects are more subtle. Depression may be present long before it is recognized as a problem. Depression gradually gnaws away at your ability to feel, to laugh, plan for and enjoy life. It's often only when we find ourselves yelling at our children or spouse, or avoiding our friends, that we realize there is a problem.

Depression can be a serious mental illness, but it's also a normal reaction to problems such as injury, disability and chronic pain. Depression is your nervous system telling you, "I don't know how to cope with this situation." Depression can have several adaptive effects. First, it is telling you that whatever you have been doing to try to overcome the problem is not working and that you need to try something different. Many people seek outside help at this stage. Depression can also be a way of saving energy; the decreased activity associated with this emotion acts to conserve scarce energy resources for healing and coping with injury and pain.

The withdrawal that depression stimulates is normal. Think of what an animal does when it is hurt: it retreats to its cave or lair to rest and lick its wounds until it feels strong enough again to face the world. Human beings also need to be able to rest and recover when they are hurt. Unfortunately, because of the demands of modern life, we often ignore this basic need and deny ourselves the resting space necessary for healing. Interestingly, the thing that gives us the ability to do this is our frontal cortex or thinking brain, the part of our psyche which enables us to override distressing emotions.

Depression can also be part of a grieving process for the lost activities and opportunities caused by your injury and pain. Injury and pain undermine your ability to participate in the three main activities of life: work, love and play. Injury and pain also create a negative sensory-feedback loop which damages your sense of self. The constant sensory feedback that we get from our bodies is a major part of our sense of self. Pain impairs your sense of self—if you cannot take care of yourself, work, or play with your children, who are you?

> Joanne succumbed to depression after she had to give up her job as a nursing aide due to a back injury. Joanne loved her work and derived much of her sense of self from it. Helping sick people made her feel needed and useful, and she enjoyed being able to care for vulnerable people and help them get well. A significant element of Joanne's work was performing physical tasks such as lifting patients, changing beds, cleaning up, etc. Joanne felt proud of her physical strength; she often lifted patients unaided, saving time and money when the unit was understaffed. Joanne's injury and pain took away her ability to perform the physical aspects of her work and, with it, a significant part of who she thought she was. She felt useless and, worse, that she was a burden to her team-mates.

Joanne's depression was actually a manifestation of her grief, resulting from the loss of the part of her identity that was based on work.

As is often the case with emotions, the problem with depression is that it does not get talked about enough. For the sufferer, depression may be regarded as a sign of failure or weakness. To those around them, including treating professionals, depression tends to be regarded as a separate problem, rather than a response to challenging circumstances. As you will learn in the second half of this book, the key to dealing with depression is to recognize it, accept it and act on it.

Anger

In addition to depression, anger is also a very common emotional response to injury and pain. While anxiety stimulates protective behavior, anger stimulates defensive behavior. Anger stimulates the fight part of the "fight or flight" response. As a response to injury and pain, anger energizes you to resist the effects of these problems. Anger stimulates aggressive behavior to ward off danger and restore control, safety and security; however, if not understood and acted on appropriately, anger can be destructive and exacerbate feelings of frustration and helplessness.

Anger is primarily a physiological response, but it may also involve a *belief* that you have been mistreated or wronged and that this should be righted. Anger may be directed at yourself ("it's all my fault") or others ("they did this to me!"). Like all emotions, anger needs to be acted on. When anger is suppressed or internalized, it has an exacerbating effect on stress and pain.[6] Chronic pain sufferers who have internalized anger have increased pain. Unexpressed anger is often associated with chronic pain conditions such as fibromyalgia and low back pain.[7,8] Unexpressed anger can turn inwards and lead to a "why bother" attitude. Anger and hostility can also alienate family and friends, thereby undermining social support networks.

Anger management problems can be caused by cultural factors, shame, and a desire to avoid upsetting those around us. Anger management problems can also be caused by alexithymia: when people fail to recognize and express what they are feeling. Regardless of the cause, unexpressed anger builds up until it gets triggered by some relatively minor upset. When anger is expressed in an uncontrolled way, it can be destructive; but anger is a perfectly normal and even necessary emotional response to pain and stress since it energizes us to ward off the threatening circumstances. Once understood and discharged appropriately, anger can become a healing resource.

> As a result of a head-on car collision, Brian suffered serious leg injuries and needed a wheelchair. Soon after he'd come home from the hospital, Brian's wife had to travel overseas to be with her terminally ill father. Brian was left to cope with his pain and disability on his own. After about two weeks of being at home alone, struggling just to cook and care for himself while stuck in a wheelchair, Brian became deeply depressed. Some days he would sit at the kitchen table thinking, "This isn't my life." Thoughts of suicide entered his head. Although Brian didn't really want to die, he couldn't think of any other way out. Brian also felt angry: he had lived a good life; he didn't deserve this. He also felt angry at the person who caused the accident.
>
> Then, one day as he was sitting at the kitchen table feeling resentful, Brian thought, "To hell with this — I'm sick of sitting here like a dummy." He thought about his wife. He knew she was due back in two weeks and he thought what a surprise it would give her if he could meet her at the airport. But to do this he would have to be out of the wheelchair, a seemingly impossible task. Then Brian remembered what he had learned about setting goals as a pilot in the air force. There they taught you that if you broke a problem down into small steps and stuck at it, you could overcome even the biggest obstacles. Brian realized this was how he had to approach his injury and pain: one step at a time. For the rest of that day, Brian just walked up and down the hallway of his home, forcing himself to keep walking despite the searing pain in his legs. Brian repeated this routine every day, gradually building his strength and tolerance levels.
>
> When Brian's wife arrived home two weeks later, he was able to be there to meet her at the airport. The look of surprise on his wife's face when she saw him made all the pain worthwhile. But Brian's best reward was the feeling that he had not let this problem beat him.

Brian's story demonstrates how depression and anger can be transformed into a resource for overcoming injury and pain. Many depressed people are really angry at themselves and harbour self-destructive fantasies in the form of suicidal thoughts. The trick is to be able to take this energy and channel it into something positive. Perhaps Kevin Costner's character from the movie *The Upside of Anger* summed it up when he said:

> The . . . upside of anger is the person you become. Hopefully someone that wakes up one day and realizes they are not afraid of the journey. Someone that knows the truth is at best, a partially told story. That anger, like growth, comes in spurts and starts and in its wake leaves a new chance of acceptance and the promise of calm.

Understanding and accepting your anger will enable you to transform its energy into a powerful resource for overcoming your injury and pain.

Guilt and shame

Injury and pain can also trigger feelings of guilt and shame.[6] Guilt is the feeling we get when we see ourselves as having failed in our social or moral obligations. Guilt comes from the feelings that we have let ourselves or others down. Part of the "price" of belonging to social units such as families, organizations and societies is this sense that we should all contribute or, at least, carry our own weight. Guilt comes when we can't contribute and we feel as if we have let others down. Closely related to guilt is shame, which has more to do with how we see our self. Having a physical injury can make you feel like "damaged goods". Your body is damaged; your body is part of you; therefore you are damaged. This can also translate into feelings of disgust, self-loathing and worthlessness — feelings that can be unwittingly reinforced each time a physician throws up his hands in frustration or each time a social obligation is missed.

Where there is *guilt* there must be *punishment*. People who feel guilty are more likely to hold unconscious negative self-beliefs such as "I'm bad", "I don't deserve to be loved" and/or no one can love me". These negative feelings and attitudes can stimulate self-neglect and even self-harm such as drug or alcohol abuse, excessive physical activity, insufficient physical activity, emotional outbursts, etc. These behaviors only exacerbate pain and suffering. Despite their destructive consequences, guilt and shame are normal emotional responses to injury and pain. We all want to feel useful, whole and able to connect normally with others — when we can't, we have to blame someone.

Guilt and shame must be resolved if they are not to become part of the problem. The antidote to guilt is to let go of self-blame, and acknowledge the grief we feel about not being able to live life normally. The concept of forgiveness is relevant. To forgive means to "give up", to let go. The word forgiveness comes from the root word "give". Forgiveness means letting go of hurt, resentment, self-blame and guilt. Forgiveness is an act of imagination. It challenges you to create a better future, based on the possibility that you have a choice about whether to hang on to the past or let it go. Researchers have found that chronic pain sufferers who practice forgiveness have lower levels of pain, anger and psychological distress.[9]

Although we tend to think of forgiveness as something we do to others, forgiveness can also be something we give to ourselves. Forgiveness frees you from anger and depression, and brings peace and freedom. Non-forgiveness keeps you in the struggle, whether with yourself or another person. Old wounds have a drawing power and pull our attention to them over and over, taking energy and preventing us from healing. There is no future in the past. The key to forgiveness is acceptance.

Acceptance

Acceptance is the final emotional stage of coping with injury and pain. Acceptance means accepting things as they are, without judging them. It means living in the present with "what is" rather than "what was" or how you wish things could be. Acceptance means being at peace with what has happened. Acceptance is the day you realize that you can survive despite not being able to wrestle with your son or work in your chosen career. Acceptance doesn't mean that you like what has happened, but that you are willing to face the physical and emotional reality of your stress and pain.

Accepting unpleasant events, including pain, is a more effective coping strategy than trying to control them. Accepting your pain reduces the anxiety, fear, depression, and even the pain itself, as well as stimulating better coping.[10] Accepting what you can't change often paves the way for changing what you can.

> A few years ago a young man named Aron Ralston was hiking in the American wilderness when he fell down a cliff. When the dust settled, Aron found himself perched on a narrow ledge, with a large boulder resting on his right arm. No matter how hard he pulled and twisted, Aron could not free himself from that rock. For five long days and nights he remained trapped, becoming weaker and more dehydrated by the day. Aron knew that if he couldn't find a way to free himself soon, he would die. Aron even thought about cutting his arm off, but he couldn't bring himself to do it. In those five long days Aron experienced denial, fear, anger and depression. At one point he blamed the rock for falling on his arm. At another point he felt angry and blamed himself for taking unnecessary risks. But mostly he felt like a helpless victim of his circumstances.
>
> Then on the sixth night, delirious from dehydration and lack of sleep, Aron had a dream. In the dream he saw himself entering a room in which he found a young boy. Somehow he knew the child was his own future son. Aron rushed to scoop the child into his left arm, using his handless right arm to balance him, and they laughed

together as he swung him up on his shoulder. When Aron awoke from the dream he knew what he had to do to free himself from his predicament. Over the next few hours he was able to do the unthinkable and he hacked the trapped arm off with a pen-knife, thereby freeing himself to find help and survive.[11]

In a somewhat compressed way, Aron's story demonstrates one individual's journey through the emotional stages of injury and pain, from his initial disbelief to his ultimate acceptance of his situation and what he had to do to free himself. In Aron's case, acceptance came as a result of a dream wherein he could see himself as a person who did not have two arms—a way of viewing himself which he could never have imagined consciously. Through acceptance, Aron integrated what had happened and his feelings about it, leading to his discovery of a tough but life-saving option. Like many chronic pain sufferers, it was not the situation that kept Aron trapped for those six days—it was his view of himself.

The goal of accepting and dealing with our emotions is acceptance. Acceptance is an emotional state where we are able to face our problems calmly and squarely. Although we may know consciously that we are hurt and in pain, acceptance is more than that. Acceptance is being at peace with "what is", whether we like it or not. Acceptance doesn't come all at once, but as a result of having the courage to have our feelings, no matter how painful, and learn from them. In the process, we often have to let go of cherished beliefs and self-concepts. Even after reaching acceptance, you may still experience occasional feelings of denial, anxiety, depression, anger and guilt, but generally less often and less strongly. Acceptance doesn't mean not feeling. Acceptance does not cure pain, but it does reduce emotional stress and facilitate more adaptive coping.

3

How stress leads to pain

Your pain is the breaking of the shell that encloses your understanding.

Kahlil Gibran

Where does pain come from? Why does pain persist? Most people have some understanding of the processes involved in physical pain, but there is very little information about the contribution of non-physical factors to pain. As we have seen, pain is an inextricable web of physical and emotional reactions. Physical pain involves both nociception *and* anxiety, anger, shame and depression. Emotional pain involves both feelings *and* physical sensations including headaches, nausea, and vague aches and pains. Although the link between physical and emotional pain is increasingly accepted, the processes underlying this connection have long remained mysterious. But in the last decade or so, thanks to new brain scanning technology, we have begun to understand the invisible processes that link the mind and the body, and stress and pain. Stress researchers have identified the stress-induced changes in brain chemistry, structure and functioning that maintain physical and emotional pain. This has illuminated the processes by which physical pain leads to emotional pain and vice-versa.

How do you work?

Most people have a rough idea of how their body works, including the main organs and what they do. We know that our heart pumps blood throughout the body. We know that our lungs bring oxygen into the body. We know that we must maintain these organs in good working order if we are to survive; however, few people know how their brain is constructed, which is just as essential to survival. The human brain is where your mind and your body meet, and the center of your nervous system. Think of your nervous system as a kind of information processor wherein everything that happens to you (sensory input) gets transformed into "information" (feelings and thoughts) which your brain processes in a way that helps you adapt to the demands of life. For example, when learning to walk as a child you often fell and scraped your knee; eventually you "learned" to pay more attention to how you walk. You might have also learned something about attachment, when your mother empathized with your suffering (hopefully). As you will discover later, these early communications with parents and loved ones are vital sources of learning in terms of how you respond to the world and manage your feelings and needs. All feelings, including pain and stress, are part of your nervous system's attempt to adapt to life — whether it's alerting you to injury or energizing you to fight off danger.

Your nervous system processes information in a particular way, according to its structure. The structure includes your *body*, which is equipped with five *senses*, through which you perceive the world. Your senses (taste, touch, smell, hearing and sight) send messages to your brain which interprets that information and generates an appropriate response, i.e. *behavior*. Your brain processes sensory data ("information") through a combination of emotional responses, thoughts and memories. *Emotions* are a kind of raw, uncensored response to external stimuli; they tell you immediately whether something is good or bad, dangerous or safe. *Thoughts* enable you to analyse the situation more deeply and decide how to respond. Thoughts are based on past experience, knowledge and *memories*. Thoughts, feelings and memories, which are physically rooted in the brain, are collectively known as the *mind*. The mind is divided into two parts, the conscious and the unconscious, with each part being responsible for different aspects of mental activity. Thoughts occur in the conscious mind, while emotions occur in the unconscious. There is a kind of separation between the conscious and the unconscious mind, meaning that most people are not readily aware of the goings-on of their unconscious mind.

An easy way to understand your brain is to imagine it as being divided into top and bottom and left and right with each part responsible for processing different aspects of experience. Vertically, your brain is divided into three levels. At the bottom is the brain stem, where your spinal cord enters your brain. Most information which enters the brain gets routed though the thalamus, a kind of relay station. Just above the brain stem is the cerebrum which consists of four lobes: the frontal lobe, the parietal lobe, the occipital lobe and the temporal lobe. These lobes are responsible for different aspects of thinking, feeling and responding.

Within the cerebrum, the anterior cingulate cortex (ACC), the amygdala and the insula are important for emotions. The ACC is responsible for emotional processing, attention and correcting mistakes. The amygdala is mainly responsible for survival emotions, such as fear. The ACC and the amygdala are involved in the expression of negative emotions associated with physical pain. Another important organ is the insula. The insula is responsible for social emotions (e.g. disgust, pride, guilt and empathy) and also the feeling and anticipation of pain. The insula is a sort of receiving zone that reads the physiological state of the entire body and then generates subjective feelings that can bring about actions (e.g. eating). The parieto insula cortex is where the physical sensations of pain are registered in the brain. Information from the insula goes to other brain structures involved in decision-making, especially the anterior cingulate and prefrontal cortexes. The insula is also more developed in humans than other mammals, which gives us a much greater sense of what's going on in our bodies.[1] The hippocampus handles short-term memory and spatial navigation.

Finally, on top we have the neocortex, which is divided into three sections: the prefrontal cortex, the middle prefrontal cortex and the posterior cortex. The prefrontal cortex is where higher-level thinking, planning and goal formulation take place. The prefrontal cortex (PFC) gives us the ability to see future consequences and to choose between different courses of action. The PFC is where we find the capacity for attention and mindfulness. Scientists have found that people who are able to recover from negative emotional events have more active PFCs.

The middle prefrontal cortex (mPFC) links the body and the brain, and balances the sympathetic and parasympathetic nervous systems. The sympathetic and parasympathetic nervous systems are like the accelerator and brakes of your nervous system. The sympathetic nervous system reacts to events, and the parasympathetic nervous system calms you down afterwards. The mPFC is also important for self-awareness, intuition, and the ability to have attuned communication with others. Figure 3.1 shows where the basic brain structures are located and their role in information processing.

Figure 3.1   Brain structures and functioning

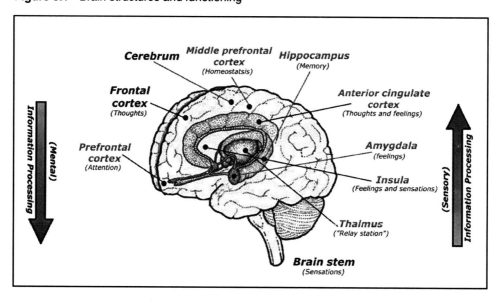

The cerebrum is also divided into left and right, again with each side being responsible for different aspects of information processing. In very simple terms, the right hemisphere is responsible for receiving information about bodily states and emotions. The left hemisphere is responsible for rational abstract thought (e.g. maths and problem-solving) and language. The right hemisphere is responsible for much of the distress you feel when you have physical or emotional pain. Even emotions such as disgust involve physical sensations. Your right hemisphere is where you get your sense of emotional self and emotional now. The right frontal cortex has close connections with parts of your brain responsible for emotions, such as the amygdala and the anterior cingulate cortex. Your right hemisphere is also the side of your brain which receives inputs from your body—it's where your body meets your mind.

The right and left sides of your brain work together to blend different elements of experience into what we perceive as reality. Your right hemisphere sees a forest; your left hemisphere notices how many trees there are. Information processing involves the coordinated action of both hemispheres. For example, when listening to music your right hemisphere notices the melody, but your left hemisphere notices the timing of the music. Normally, the two sides of your brain work together to coordinate sensory information and generate an appropriate behavioral response. The two hemispheres communicate through a structure called the corpus callosum. Figure 3.2 shows the left–right division of the brain and the different tasks that the two hemispheres are responsible for.

In terms of the flow of information, your nervous system generally operates in a "bottom–up" direction; sensory data is received via the brain stem and relayed up to the emotional brain, where it gets an initial raw emotional appraisal, and then sent to the

Figure 3.2   Left and right view of brain functioning

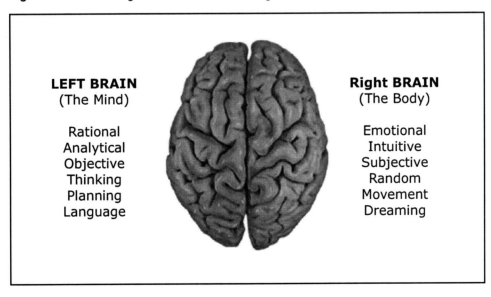

LEFT BRAIN
(The Mind)

Rational
Analytical
Objective
Thinking
Planning
Language

Right BRAIN
(The Body)

Emotional
Intuitive
Subjective
Random
Movement
Dreaming

neocortex where it gets analysed more comprehensively. There are some exceptions: smells go directly to your amygdala, but generally speaking this is the direction in which your brain processes sensory data. The top half of the brain feeds back down to the emotional brain and body, sending signals for action. The top half of the brain also has the power to moderate the impact of sensory-emotional information, by ignoring unpleasant feelings or soothing them with reassuring thoughts. This ability of the neocortex to suppress the emotional part of the brain is unique to humans. It can also be a source of emotional conflict, as when we deny our feelings or accept pain in order to achieve a higher-order goal. For example, we may know that XYZ corporation is an unsafe place to work, but we keep working there because we need the money.

The different parts of the brain communicate via neurotransmitters. Neuro-transmitters are like chemical messengers that turn off and on all the different systems of the brain that regulate physical functioning. There are four important neurotransmitters: GABA, noripeniphrine, serotonin and dopamine. GABA is a kind of regulatory neurotransmitter; it helps keep the other neurotransmitter levels in balance. Norepinephrine helps you remember painful or stressful events, so that you will know to avoid them next time. It is also necessary for maintaining wakefulness, attention and mood. Serotonin helps regulate your body clock, sleep, mood and pain. Dopamine is involved in many aspects of human functioning including thinking, concentration and memory, feeling pleasure, and the regulation of natural pain-killing substances. Neurotransmitters travel across a narrow space (the synaptic cleft) and bind to receptors on the target cell.

Remember:

- *GABA.* Keeps everything in balance.
- *Norepinephrine.* Maintains altertness and attention, guides memory.
- *Serotonin.* Regulates sleep, mood and pain.
- *Dopamine.* Involved in pleasure, concentration and pain.

Another type of chemical messenger in the nervous system is the Glucocorticoid. Glucocorticoids are hormones and part of a feedback mechanism from the immune system which turns immune activity (inflammation) down. Cortisol is the most important glucocorticoid and essential for life. Cortisol maintains heart rate, immune functioning and anti-inflammatory functions. Cortisol is produced by the endocrine system which acts with the nervous system to coordinate the body's activities, especially metabolism, growth and development. Your body also produces proteins which help stimulate cell growth and repair, among other things. One of the most important proteins is BDNF (brain-derived neurotrophic factor). BDNF is like plant-food for your brain and is essential for neurogenesis, neuroplasticity and cell maintenance.

Your brain starts out a bit like a new computer: it comes with a certain amount of predetermined hardware and software. Developmental expert Daniel Siegal estimates that about 30 per cent of intellectual capacity is genetically determined. The brain is programmed to evolve during your developmental years when neurons are produced and connections develop, a process known as neurogenesis; but, as mentioned earlier, your brain is also shaped by experience, a capacity known as neuroplasticity. According to this relatively new theory, thinking, learning and behaving actually change the structure and organization of the brain throughout the lifespan. An often-quoted example is the finding that London taxi drivers have enlarged hippocampi—the part of the brain that is involved in memory and probably navigation. Another example is the finding that some parts of the brain seem smaller than normal in adult survivors of severe abuse.

Ideally, your mind and body develop in an integrated way which enables you to get your needs met as effectively as possible in the environment in which you find yourself. According to Abraham Maslow, human beings have six basic survival needs: food and shelter, safety, love and support, self-esteem, learning, and the ability to be nourished by beauty/nature. Maslow also suggested that we have two higher needs: self-actualization and spirituality, which he described as growth needs. Maslow felt that people attend to these needs in a hierarchical fashion, with basic needs taking priority over higher needs, e.g. food and shelter come before education or career success. The human brain seems to be organized in such a way that it attends to basic survival needs first, and higher needs second.

How stress leads to pain

Stress happens when your survival needs are threatened—the more basic the need, the greater the stress. Stress is an increased state of alertness which prepares you for fight or flight. Stress is thus your nervous system's way of preparing you to cope with threats to your survival. Your nervous system is designed to cope with a certain amount of stress, and certain types of stress, but severe or prolonged stress disrupts your nervous system's ability to maintain homeostasis and cope with pain. Severe stress not only reduces your nervous system's protective abilities, it can also damage the physical organs that make up your nervous system, including your brain. It's these effects which increase your vulnerability to physical and emotional pain.

Severe stress affects your nervous system at all levels. Physically, stress involves increased physiological arousal, biochemical imbalances and energy fluctuations. Emotionally, stress involves anxiety and depression, emotional disconnection, mood swings and feeling numb. Neurologically, stress can disrupt the communication between the left and right hemispheres of the brain and the normal functioning of different areas of the brain. Psychologically, there are five main types and effects of stress, all of which involve stress-related changes in brain structure and functioning:

- lack of safety and support
- increased physiological arousal (including anxiety and depression)
- emotional disconnection
- negative thinking
- traumatic stress.

These five types and effects of stress are what maintain physical and emotional pain beyond what would be expected for the original injury or event. Thanks to recent discoveries in the areas of stress and neuropsychology, we also know a lot more about how these processes coalesce to maintain pain. Understanding these processes and how they affect your physical and emotional well-being is the key to overcoming pain.

Lack of safety and support

The first thing to consider when trying to understand stress is what level of need is being threatened. Safety and having access to social support are the most basic human needs. Feeling safe means knowing who you are and feeling reasonably confident in your ability to obtain whatever you need for your survival. Safety comes from the absence of threat: the knowledge that no one or nothing is threatening your physical safety. Safety is connected to social support; feeling loved gives you self-confidence and security. Despite all the advances of modern civilization, safety and support continue to be problematic for many people. In many urbanized societies, lack of social support has become an urgent social issue as families break down and communities become more fragmented. Poor social support can increase the risk of coronary artery disease, cancer, chronic pain, psychological problems (following trauma) and premature death.[2-4]

Of course, lack of social support is not like breaking your leg, so how might this type of stress lead to pain? There are four main ways in which inadequate social support can lead to pain:

- increased likelihood of unhealthy behaviors
- poor self-care
- increased stress reactivity
- decreased healing capacity.

People with poor or absent social support are more likely to engage in unhealthy behaviors (such as smoking and drinking) as a substitute for the emotional soothing that they would otherwise obtain from close relationships. People with poor social support may even heal less well as a result of reduced immune system functioning. People with poor social support are more vulnerable to illness and pain because of feeling isolated.

> Gemma developed fibromyalgia and chronic fatigue syndrome after falling ill while on a teaching assignment overseas. Gemma was an anxious, insecure 19-year-old who applied for an overseas teaching position when she couldn't find a job in her home state. Gemma was a gifted teacher who could cope with most classroom situations, including foreign students. What she hadn't counted on was how stressful living and working in a foreign land could be. After a few weeks living overseas, Gemma felt quite anxious and unsafe being so far away from loved ones and her hometown. As the weeks turned into months, she developed severe sleeping problems, fatigue and anxiety. Along with the fatigue, she noticed bodily aches which seemed to suck what little energy she had left. One day, about six months into her contract, Gemma collapsed at work. She was diagnosed with "post-viral syndrome" and repatriated to her home country. It would be years before she could work again.

Increased physiological arousal

One of the most common effects of stress is increased physiological arousal. Although as the phrase suggests, increased physiological arousal involves increased physical tension, there's more to it than that. Increased physiological arousal also involves a range of physical and mental symptoms including biochemical imbalances, alterations to brain structure and functioning, sleeping problems, fatigue, anxiety and depression. Cumulatively, these effects can cause, maintain and exacerbate physical and emotional pain.

One of the most important ways in which increased physiological arousal leads to pain: is through its effects on brain chemistry, particularly your neurotransmitter levels. Initially, stress triggers a surge of adrenaline and cortisol, raising energy levels and preparing you for "fight or flight." Heart rate and blood pressure increase, the pupils dilate, appetite is suppressed, even the ability to talk may be affected. In the early stages, stress also stimulates increased levels of neurotransmitters associated with fighting infection and pain. This may be why injured sportsmen sometimes don't feel pain; they are anaesthetized by the high levels of endorphins being produced by their brain. Many victims of severe stress maintain surprisingly good health for many years, only to succumb to chronic pain after some relatively minor illness or injury.

Unfortunately, over time the effects of stress become harmful. Too much cortisol damages the neurons in your brain, especially in the hippocampus. Glucocorticoid receptors (GR), which are receptors for cortisol, may become desensitized, resulting in disruption of your neuroendocrine system. This overactivity of the neuroendocrine system, specifically the hypothalamic-pituitary-adrenal (HPA) axis (your fight-or-flight system), can cause the release of cytokines causing further instability in the neuroendocrine system, leading to fatigue, loss of appetite, hypersensitivity to pain, and reduced libido. Levels of BDNF also appear to be affected by all this upset in the HPA and hippocampus. Reduced BDNF has been linked to depression, schizophrenia, obsessive compulsive disorder and dementia.

Serotonin, dopamine and noripeniphrine are a particular type of neurotransmitter known as monoamines. After they are released into the synaptic cleft, monoamines are quickly broken down by an enzyme called monoamine oxidase A (MAO-A). Then their constituents are taken back up into the neuron and recycled for future use. Thus, monoamines are metabolized more quickly, allowing less of them to reach their receptors on the other side of the synaptic cleft. Low levels of monoamines can negatively affect mood, cognition, motivation, and sensation of pain. Depression is thought to be caused by increased MAO-A levels, resulting from increased cortisol, which increases the rate at which your brain churns through seratonin. Antidepressants such as SSRIs, (selective serotonin re-uptake inhibitors) are thought to work by slowing down the rate at which serotonin is absorbed, as well as stimulating production of BDNF and neurogenesis.

Excessive stress causes a drop in neurotransmitter levels, particularly those associated with fighting pain and stress. The longer the stress continues, the more depleted these neurotransmitters become. Low GABA levels cause a reduction in serotonin absorption, leading to sleep and mood problems. Sleeping problems weaken your immune system, leading to increased susceptibility to inflammation and pain. Low GABA levels also lead to an increase in norepinephrine, making you more emotionally reactive and less able to think slowly. Decreased dopamine triggers a reduction in endorphins (your body's natural painkiller). Decreased dopamine makes it harder to feel happy or derive pleasure from normally enjoyable activities. Decreased dopamine is one of the leading biochemical causes of depression. Victims of severe stress have been found to have increased levels of substance P, a neurotransmitter that actually increases your ability to feel pain.[5] Numerous other hormones are known to be affected by severe stress, with various effects on mental and physical health and functioning.[6]

The longer your nervous system has to cope without the necessary amounts of these vital chemicals, the more out of balance it becomes. Eventually, a self-reinforcing cycle of stress and pain develops: reduced GABA causes reduced norepinephrine, which causes reduced serotonin, dopamine, endorphins and increased substance P, which causes sleeping problems, depressed mood, fatigue and pain, which creates more stress, which leads to less GABA, and so on. This cycle can continue even after the original stressor has ended. Figure 3.3 illustrates the self-perpetuating nature of stress-related biochemical changes.

In addition to its effects on neurotransmitter levels, stress also affects the structure and functioning of your brain. People who were abused or neglected as children have been found to have a smaller hippocampus and corpus callosum than normal.[6,7]

Figure 3.3 The stress cycle: how stress-related biochemical changes create a self-
perpetuating cycle of stress and pain

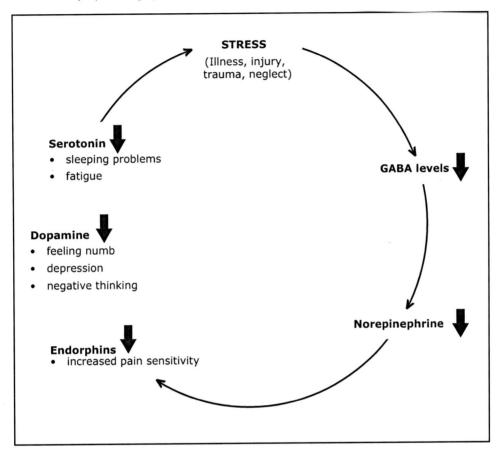

PTSD sufferers" brains tend to be over-active in the right, emotional hemisphere, at
the expense of the left, analytical hemisphere. The frontal cortex is also less active
in people affected by severe stress and pain. Fibromyalgia sufferers have also been
found to have reduced gray matter in brain areas involved in processing stress and
pain. Gray matter decreases with age in everybody, but in fibromyalgia sufferers the
rate of decrease is three times greater than normal.[8] The main effect of stress-related
structural damage is to decrease the brain's ability to process experience, leading to
decreased ability to control pain, decreased ability to regulate emotions, decreased
ability to verbalize experience, and concentration and memory problems.

Sleep, stress and pain

Another important aspect of increased physiological arousal is the effects of stress
on sleep. Since stress affects your neurotransmitter levels, and sleep is regulated
by neurotransmitters, sleeping problems are an almost inevitable consequence of

severe stress and/or pain. For example, abused children are more likely to suffer from sleeping problems, and over 70 per cent of chronic pain sufferers experience sleeping problems.[9]

Lack of sleep causes a range of physical and mental problems including:

- fatigue
- impaired immune system functioning
- decreased growth hormone
- impaired healing
- increased sensitivity to pain
- reduced reaction time
- depressed mood
- concentration and memory problems
- weight gain.

Lack of sleep can even cause brain damage. Animal studies indicate that lack of sleep reduces neurogenesis in the hippocampus.[10] Not surprisingly, the effects of lack of sleep can significantly increase your vulnerability to pain. Poor sleep has been linked to pain and fatigue in sufferers of fibromyalgia, chronic low back pain, and chronic fatigue syndrome (CFS).[11] As the name suggests, CFS is a severe form of fatigue wherein the body's homeostasis and replenishment systems break down completely. Gemma, whom we met earlier, felt so tired that she could not continue working as a teacher. For months she felt like she had no energy and struggled to complete the most basic tasks. Even after she'd slept the whole night through, she woke up feeling tired. It's not hard to understand how fatigue might exacerbate pain. Tired people are less optimistic, less socially outgoing, and more prone to aches and pains than non-tired people. Fatigue is also dangerous: people with sleeping problems are twice as likely to have hypertension, three times more likely to have a heart attack, four times more likely to have a stroke, and five times more likely to be involved in a car crash.[12]

Anxiety and depression

Anxiety and depression are emotional manifestations of increased physiological arousal. Anxiety is an emotional response to perceived threat or danger involving increased physiological arousal (increased heart rate and respiration) and feelings of dread and apprehension. Anxiety is a common emotional reaction to stress and pain; up to 59 per cent of chronic pain sufferers may have an anxiety disorder (compared with around 16 per cent normally).[13] Anxiety can exacerbate pain in various ways including increased physiological arousal, increased sensitivity, decreased tolerance, memory effects and avoidance. An example of how anxiety exacerbates pain comes from anxious mothers who have more pain during childbirth and remember the birth experience more negatively.[14]

Depression is an emotional response to feeling unable to cope. Depression tends to come after anxiety, when a person has reached the point where they feel overwhelmed by what is happening. In contrast to anxiety, depression involves decreased levels of physiological arousal, feelings of resignation or defeat, and negative thinking. Depression is involved in pain as both a response and a predisposing factor. Depressed people are more than twice as likely to have chronic pain than normal people.[15] One researcher found that more than 75 per cent of depressed people also complained of painful symptoms such as neck and back pain, and non-specific generalized pain.[16] Depression is common in injured people with chronic pain; more than 50 per cent of people with disabling occupational spinal disorders are clinically depressed.[17] Depression is also involved in other health problems including coronary artery disease, and changes in bone density.[18] So great is the physical dimension of depression that a recent article in *Psychology Today* described it as a disorder of the body as much as the mind.[19] Depression is thought to add to pain through its effects on mood, energy levels and perception. Depressed people feel numb, tired, and negative about life.

Emotional disconnection

One of the most common and often overlooked effects of stress is emotional disconnection. Severe stress reduces your ability to recognize and respond to your feelings. You might think this sounds great; not noticing how you're feeling means not feeling your pain, right? Wrong. Although not feeling pain can help initially, such as in battle or sports injuries, in the long term not feeling decreases your ability to regulate physical and emotional pain. Emotional disconnection makes you less able to recognize and act on bodily signals regarding survival needs, which can make you more at risk of injury, illness and pain. Emotions also guide your behavior in helping you meet survival needs such as pacing activity levels, rest, social support, etc.

When Gemma started feeling anxious and tired, her initial response was to dismiss her feelings. However, as Gemma learned to listen to her body more, and realized how important family connection was for her, her illness became less mysterious. She had learned to disconnect from her feelings from an early age, after her father left her mother for another woman and her mother became depressed. As a young girl Gemma had sensed her mother's vulnerability and "learned" to be a quiet, unobtrusive person who didn't burden others with her needs. It was only after Gemma collapsed at work and couldn't get any answers from the medical profession that she began to explore psychological factors as a possible cause for her problems. Gemma was initially skeptical when the psychologist suggested she might be suffering from the effects of stress; up until then she felt like she had coped so well with life.

Inability to recognize and/or respond properly to emotions is called alexithymia. Alexithymia literally means having no words for emotions (derived from the Greek: *a* = lack, *lexis* = word, *thymos* = emotions). Alexithymic people are disconnected from their feelings; their emotions are a mystery to them. An alexithymic person will insist that they have no problems, that life is fine even though they may be in the middle of a major crisis. Alexithymia is thought to occur as a result of not being able to learn about feelings normally, as a result of physical abuse or emotional neglect. Alexithymia can also be a defense mechanism against unpleasant feelings. Alexithymia can also be reinforced by cultural factors; many societies reinforce the notion that we can and should be able to separate from our feelings.

Alexithymia is often associated with a strong sense of responsibility and denial of one's needs. Many chronic pain sufferers have an unusually strong work ethic, idealize relationships, have a care-giver role identity, and are overly self-reliant.[20] A researcher named Barsky coined the term counter-dependent to describe these personality characteristics.[21] Barsky's study of chronic pain sufferers found that a large proportion of them had started work at a young age, avoided conflict and had a tendency to deny emotional problems. Barsky concluded that these people were more prone to chronic pain because they worked longer and harder, making them more at risk of suffering injury.

Alexithymia is often associated with chronic pain. Alexithymic people are more prone to anxiety and depression, and more likely to complain of somatic (bodily) symptoms for which there is no obvious physiological cause.[22,23] Alexithymic people also experience pain more intensely and are more prone to emotional distress in response to pain.[24] Alexithymia exacerbates pain in five main ways:

1   *Increased physiological arousal.* Alexithymic people have higher levels of physiological arousal and increased reactivity to stressful events. They spend less time in deep sleep and more time in stage 1 (shallower) sleep.[25,26] Alexithymic people are thus more likely to suffer from fatigue, a major exacerbating factor of pain.

2   *Decreased emotional regulation skills.* Alexithymic people are less confident in their ability to regulate their emotions.[27] Since emotional distress is part of chronic pain, alexithymic people are more vulnerable to pain because they are less able to regulate negative emotions associated with pain.

3   *Catastrophizing.* Alexithymic people are more likely to feel anxious and fear the worst, a thinking style psychologists refer to as catastrophizing. Catastrophizing has long been known to exacerbate pain through increased anxiety and its effects on perception. When you expect the worst, you're more likely to notice bad things and ignore good things, something psychologists refer to as "negative bias". Catastrophizing thus becomes a kind of self-fulfilling prophecy.

4   *Poor pacing/lack of self-care.* Alexithymia makes it harder to recognize and respond to feelings of fatigue, pain or stress, so alexithymics find it harder to pace themselves and are less likely to seek treatment after injury. Because of this lack of attunement with the self, alexithymics are also more likely to engage in unhealthy behaviors such as smoking, excessive drinking and workaholism.[28]

5   *Brain damage.* Alexithymia is often caused by emotional neglect and abuse in childhood. Abused children have been found to have smaller corpus callosums and a tendency to rely on one hemisphere at the expense of the other when processing information. Young adults who were exposed to severe parental verbal abuse were found to have a reduction of 10 per cent in the size of the superior temporal gyrus—an area of the brain responsible for auditory processing and language.[29]

PTSD sufferers are also prone to a severe form of emotional disconnection called dissociation. In dissociation, normally unified physical, mental and emotional aspects of experience are stored in a compartmentalized fashion; dissociated material remains completely outside of conscious awareness. Dissociation is a kind of mental disappearing act where our mind stores painful memories in a hidden file-folder. As trauma expert David Calof describes it, "Dissociation lets us step aside, split off from our own knowledge (ideas), our behavior, emotions and body sensations, our self-control, identity and memory. Dissociation is the splitting of mind and the pigeon-holing of experience." [30]

Dissociation is so powerful at concealing painful memories it can seem like some events from your past never happened, until something happens that reminds you. If you imagine your mind as a doctor's surgery, dissociated material never gets past the "waiting room"—it sits in your mind in a raw, undigested state, ready to spring out whenever something happens that reminds you of the trauma. For example, Kathy had to spend several days in hospital as a result of a lung problem when she was only four. It was a traumatic experience for the young girl, particularly being separated from her parents. Although Kathy eventually "forgot" about her stay in hospital, as an adult she always felt nauseous whenever she smelt disinfectant or went near hospitals, but she never knew why. Kathy's nausea was part of an unconscious memory of her childhood stay in hospital. Because of how it separates feelings from normal sensory-emotional processing, dissociation is one of the most powerful effects of stress when it comes to maintaining pain.

Dissociation tends to occur as a response to severe trauma such as physical or sexual abuse.[31,32] Dissociation is also more likely if the trauma involved physical pain and/or helplessness; however, dissociation can also occur as a response to emotional abuse, family conflict and low family cohesiveness.[33] Abuse and neglect cause a disruption in the emotional bond between the parents and the child, something psychologists refer to as attachment. A healthy emotional attachment between parent and child is necessary for the development of self-esteem, emotional self-regulation and self-care, and the ability to form relationships with others. People who grew up without a healthy attachment are more likely to dissociate, to engage in self-destructive or self-neglectful behaviors, and to have trouble forming relationships. Adults who grew up without secure attachments actually display similar symptoms to those associated with PTSD, including anxiety and depression, alexithymia and dissociation, increased stress response and decreased ability to form close relationships.[34,35]

Dissociation is more than just splitting off from emotions; in people who were severely abused as children, dissociation can involve self-harming behavior such as head-banging, cutting, burning and self-starving. People who were traumatized in this way may swing from one extreme to the other—from feeling emotionally overwhelmed to feeling emotionally numb (dissociated). This process can happen almost spontaneously and the person may not be consciously aware of the process. Self-injurious behavior can help cope with these emotional extremes. The pain from self-injury can provide a circuit-breaker for the emotional overload by replacing it with a strong somatic distraction (the physical pain of the self-inflicted injury overrides the emotional pain of the abuse). Self-injury can also negate the numbness associated with dissociation, thereby helping the sufferer feel more alive and real. It is not that the dissociated person wants to hurt themselves; they just don't want to feel so bad inside.

Given the negative effects of alexithymia and dissociation, why do we ignore our feelings? For one thing, since emotional disconnection is about not feeling or seeing, it's hard to recognize. Secondly, the belief that we can separate what we think from how we feel has undeniable survival value; the injured factory worker wants to believe that his pain is "just a strain"—how can he support his family if he can't work? The grief-stricken widow needs to feel that she is "getting on with life"—how else is she supposed to cope with the loss of her soul-mate? Unfortunately, not paying attention to our feelings is often a short-term solution to a long-term problem, and one that can create a whole new set of problems of its own.

Negative thinking

Negative thinking is an intellectual response to stress and pain which can also exacerbate these problems. Negative thinking tends to be maintained by negative emotional states, such as anxiety and depression. Negative thinking can take the form of self-criticism and self-blame, negative interpretations of events, believing that nothing will ever change, and catastrophizing. One of the most common forms of negative thinking is catastrophizing. Catastrophizing tends to be associated with a pessimistic lifestyle and increased sensitivity to pain.[36] People who catastrophize are also more likely to die from an accident or violence as a result of being "in the wrong place at the wrong time".[37]

Another form of negative thinking is to have a negative schema. A schema is a way of perceiving ourselves and the world. Schemata automatically guide our sense of emotional meaning and determine how we experience ourselves in the world. Negative schemata obviously involve seeing ourselves and the world in a bad light. For example, we might have an other-directed schema wherein we are excessively focused on the desires and needs of others at the expense of our own needs. Or we might have a schema wherein we see ourselves as alone in a dangerous world. Once a schema is established, we tend to filter information through that schema, looking for experience that confirms it and overlooking experiences that contradict it. It not hard to imagine how having a negative schema can exacerbate pain. If we see ourselves as faulty or unlovable, we will find it harder to ask for help or act in our own interest. We'll be more likely to overlook potentially beneficial information which might help us see ourselves and the world in a more adaptive way. Negative schemata can obviously reinforce many of the pain-maintaining physical and psychological effects of stress.

Traumatic stress

Traumatic stress is a kind of memory, involving a blend of powerful physical, mental and emotional symptoms which follow some sort of life-threatening event or circumstances. Unlike normal memories, traumatic memories remain stored in the nervous system in a raw, unprocessed state, a condition known as post-traumatic stress disorder (PTSD). In PTSD physical and emotional pain may overlap in a very direct way—for example, the pelvic pain suffered by many female victims of rape or sexual abuse. Another example is recurring surgery pain in surgical patients who regained consciousness while under general anesthesia. Combat veterans often suffer from chronic pain at specific sites in their bodies, as part of combat-related trauma.

The mechanisms by which traumatic stress leads to pain involve all of the processes mentioned in this chapter, including lack of safety and support, increased physiological arousal, neurological changes, sleeping problems, negative thinking and dissociation.[38] The process by which the effects of traumatic stress can lead to pain is known as kindling. Psychologists have long known that when an event is paired with intense emotional arousal, the memory of the event and the emotional reaction become joined (associated). Afterwards, if you experience a similar event, it can trigger the feelings you felt in response to the original event. With PTSD, our reaction to a current event can be based on neuroplastic changes and emotional triggers rather than a here-and-now appraisal of the situation.

It has been estimated that our emotional reaction to any situation is 10 per cent based on our current emotional reaction and 90 per cent on our emotional reactions to similar situations from the past. Further, similar events are essentially stored together in what could be metaphorically called "file folders". When a new event is occurring, the brain is essentially preparing the event for initial storage, followed by long-term memory storage. At a neurochemical level, the brain is simultaneously "scanning" the existing "file folders", searching for any that have stored events conceptually similar to what is now occurring. If the brain finds a folder that is conceptually similar to the current event, two things will automatically occur beyond our level of conscious awareness. The first is that the stored memory will be "uploaded" into the current situation. As a result, the emotional reaction to the situation will be "fused" with the stored emotional reaction from the prior event that has been uploaded. Over time, with the storage of new situations into the same file folder, a greater build-up of anxiety and stress occurs, making us more and more sensitive to later stressful events.

It's also important to know that because your brain stores emotional memories in an area that is separate from consciousness, you may not consciously realize why you're "over-reacting" to the current event. There are basically two types of memory: conscious (or explicit) memories, and unconscious (or implicit) memories. Unconscious or implicit memories are "bottom–up" in the sense that they originate in the body. Unconscious memories are necessary because experiences such as pain often involve more information than can be processed at a conscious level. Researchers at the University of Florida applied heat stimuli to the hands of healthy controls and fibromyalgia patients. In contrast to normal controls, fibromyalgia sufferers reported a greater amount of cumulative pain. This "pain memory" also appeared to linger for an abnormally long period in the fibromyalgia sufferers, and it was widespread and not limited to a single area of the body. "Because the effect of the first experimental stimulus does not rapidly decay in fibromyalgia patients, the effect of subsequent stimuli adds to the first, and so on, resulting in ever-increasing pain sensations," said lead investigator, Roland Staud, MD.[39]

Conclusion

In this chapter we have reviewed the five main types and effects of stress, and how they cause, maintain and exacerbate pain. We have also seen how stress-induced changes in brain chemistry, structure and functioning create a kind of negative feedback loop which perpetuates physical and emotional pain. Even if you don't remember all the details of this chapter, you can see how stress disrupts normal communication between your body and your brain, and your brain's ability to down-regulate pain. Knowing what those effects are, and how they affect your nervous system functioning, not only makes it easier to understand pain that is greater than the physical or emotional injury that initially caused it, but also makes it easier to know how to overcome such pain.

4

Understanding pain and how to overcome it

To know cause supplies even the layman with a dependable knowledge
of how to avoid building disease and how to cure it.

J.H. Tilden, MD (1935)[*]

Although we are used to thinking of pain as a physical problem, we cannot understand pain without realizing that it is also in the brain, in the form of stress-induced biochemical, functional and structural abnormalities. Pain is also different for each individual, involving a unique blend of stress, physical injury and life circumstances. Pain can come from a seemingly trivial injury in a person who has endured abuse or neglect, or it can come from a life-threatening traumatic event in a person with a seemingly normal background. Increased understanding of the role of the brain in pain has not only changed the way we think about pain, it's also stimulated the development of "brain-smart" self-help strategies designed to target the patterns of brain activity that maintain pain. These strategies require some insight regarding the contribution of mental factors. The more you understand about how your brain works and the nature of the relationship between your body and your mind, the easier it will be to "change your brain, change your pain".

---

[*] *Toxemia Explained*, 1935. www.soilandhealth.org

What is pain?

Pain has been viewed as a physical problem since the 17th century when Descartes started the whole mind–body separation thing. Before Descartes, the mind and the body were viewed as one, and physical and emotional pain were thought of in very similar terms. Descartes' idea wasn't bad—it opened the way for anatomy and the study of the body, and a way of understanding the physical causes of disease. Arguably, modern medicine would never have developed without Descarte's idea. But there are limits to how far you can go with this view of pain, and in recent years it has been questioned. By the 1960s pain had been re-defined as both a physical and an emotional problem. The modern reconceptualization of pain began in the mid-twentieth century when it was noticed that people with similar injuries reported vastly different levels of pain. A researcher named Beecher observed that soldiers and civilians with similar injuries required different amounts of treatment—indicating they were experiencing different levels of pain. Beecher speculated that the reason for this difference was the differing meanings the soldiers and civilians ascribed to their pain. To the soldiers, being injured meant leaving the battlefield—a good thing—but to the civilians being injured meant having to leave their families—not such a good thing.

The first theory of pain to incorporate the mind was Melzack's gate control theory (1962). According to this theory, there is a kind of gate in the dorsal horn which opens or closes depending on what stimulus most attracts our attention. This theory explains how if we pay too much attention to pain, we open the "gateway" to more pain. This very simple theory neatly explained how different people with the same injuries could experience different levels of pain and require different amounts of treatment. GCT also introduced the mind into the equation, opening up a whole new range of treatment possibilities including distraction, relaxation and meditation, and changing your thinking. However, the gate control theory was based on a very limited understanding of the brain processes involved in pain.

Recent discoveries regarding brain structure and functioning have led to more sophisticated theories of pain, involving memory, emotion and brain processes. For example, Melzack's neuromatrix theory (1996) posits that pain is a kind of memory created by a combination of genetic susceptibility and repeated stimulation of the areas of the brain involved in pain.[1] Neuromatrix theory proposes that there is a kind of neural network in the brain which maintains pain. Rome and Rome's limbically augmented pain syndrome (2000), or LAPS, emphasizes the role of the emotional brain in maintaining pain.[2] The limbic system is a term that used to refer to the emotional brain, but it has fallen out of favor with neuroscientists for a variety of reasons, including the fact that the parts of the brain which deal with emotion are so diverse that they don't really consititute a system. According to LAPS theory, every time you experience pain or stress the emotional parts of your brain are activated.

The more often this happens, the more sensitized your brain becomes to future pain. Like the search for the theory of everything in cosmology, these theories are based on the discovery that there are common underlying processes which can be invoked to explain different types of pain.

As outlined in the previous chapter, recent discoveries in neuroscience have uncovered the processes behind these theories. Brain scans of chronic pain sufferers show specific patterns of electrical firing in areas of the brain associated with perception, emotion and motivation including the ACC, the amygdala, the orbito frontal cortex and the insula. The ACC is also one of several areas in the brain which have been found to house "body-maps". A.D. (Bud) Craig, a brain neuroscientist, has isolated the areas of the brain responsible for the physical and emotional components of pain. He found that the physical sensations of pain are represented in the parieto insula cortex, and the "emotional" component is represented in the ACC.[3] These areas of the brain are also involved in emotional stress, including PTSD. These findings confirm that pain is in the brain and that physical and mental pain involve similar brain structures. This is hardly surprising—all emotions start out as sensations. Physical pain inevitably triggers feelings, which must become a part of the pain experience.

How to change your brain, change your pain

Knowing how your brain works and the role it plays in pain makes it possible to know how to change your brain, change your pain. The notion that you can change your brain is a relatively new one. For most of the twentieth century, the accepted wisdom was that we can alter patterns of synaptic firing, but that we are stuck with the amount of neurons and the brain structure we have. This all changed in 1998 when some Italian researchers noticed that a dye they'd injected into cancer patients to track proliferating cancer cells turned up in their hippocampi. The only way that this could have happened was if the patient's neurons were dividing and propagating, something previously only believed to occur during development. Scientists refer to the process of cell repair and reproduction as neurogenesis. Neurogenesis is necessary for neuroplasticity—the brain's capacity to change its structure in response to experience. Although most people are familiar with the concept that biochemical imbalances are involved in problems such as pain and depression, experts now regard neuroplasticity as the key to understanding these problems.[4]

The discovery of neuroplasticity has stimulated a range of new treatments designed to change brain activity associated with physical and emotional pain. Researchers at Stanford University have found that pain sufferers can be taught how to control an area of their brain which is involved in pain perception (the anterior cingulate cortex) by manipulating a live fMRI image of their pain on a computer screen.[5] Another technique being investigated is electromagnetic brain stimulation. This method involves stimulating particular areas of the brain with an electromagnetic pulse. Although the technology still has a long way to go, early research suggests this technique can alter brain activity associated with chronic pain, depression and fatigue in beneficial ways. As exciting as they sound, these methods are obviously expensive and impractical for the average person. Fortunately, there are other, much cheaper ways to change your brain.

There are many, many things you can do to change your brain. Consuming drugs or alcohol, or engaging in highly pleasurable activities such as gambling or illicit sex, are powerful and quick ways of changing brain chemistry. Unfortunately, after the initial rush of enjoyment, these methods also tend to involve negative long-term consequences. They also fail to stimulate the kinds of mental states necessary for emotional processing, let alone neurogenesis. But for some desperate people, ingesting psychoactive substance is a way of stimulating feelings of pleasure in place of pain. Fortunately, there are other, more healthy ways of changing negative brain activity. Relaxation, regular exercise and even just talking to a friend not only make you feel good, they also stimulate reduced stress hormones, increased levels of natural opioids, and improved mood and thinking. Scans of monks' brains during meditation show increased activity in an area of the brain associated with positive emotions (the left prefrontal cortex). Exercise has been found to stimulate increased levels of mood-enhancing neurotransmitters such as dopamine and serotonin. The challenge is to apply these discoveries to the management of pain.

One area of psychology where we already have some experience in changing brain functioning associated with the effects of severe stress is in the treatment of post-traumatic stress disorder (PTSD). Trauma experts have long known that highly stressed people have problems with emotional processing, and that these problems have a neurological basis. They posit that emotional pain can only be overcome through addressing the deficits in emotional processing that maintain post-traumatic stress. They also recognize the complex, multi-layered nature of traumatic pain, and recommend a phase-oriented approach incorporating safety, exposure and emotional regulation skills training, and reintegration (learning to think and behave more adaptively).[5] Each phase of treatment addresses a different element of the problem, with all the phases forming a comprehensive treatment strategy. Drawing on the phase-oriented approach, and what we know about the different types and effects of stress which maintain pain, the following five-stage strategy is recommended:

1   safety and support
2   reconnecting with your feelings
3   learning how to control stressful feelings and pain
4   changing your thinking
5   building resilience.

These five strategies address each of the five types and effects of stress that maintain pain, from basic safety needs through to emotional processing of traumatic stress (where applicable). The strategies are also designed to work with *how* the nervous system processes information, from the sensory ("bottom") aspects of pain to the cognitive ("top") ones. For example, because safety and support are such basic needs, and often problematic in sufferers of severe stress and pain, they must be addressed before attempting to learn strategies that rely on higher intellectual capabilities, such as changing how you feel. It's a lot easier to focus on changing how you feel when you feel supported by family and friends than if you feel alone and unprotected. It's a lot easier to change your thinking if you know how to generate positive feelings which provide a natural basis on which to grow more adaptive attitudes and beliefs. Each strategy thus builds on the one before it, following the order in which the nervous system processes information. Figure 4.1 shows how these strategies match with how the brain processes information (in a simplified way).

Figure 4.1   How sensory-emotional strategies fit with different levels of brain functioning

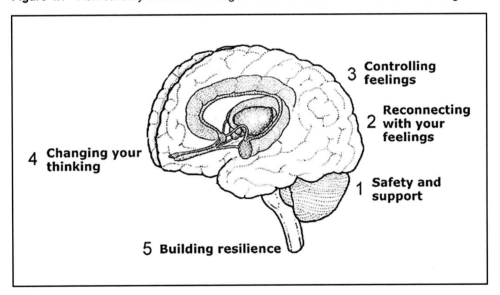

Psychologists have actually already begun applying these insights in the treatment of PTSD where there is a growing trend away from top–down methods such as talk-therapy in favor of experiential ("bottom–up") interventions such as mindfulness training, eye movement desensitization and reprocessing (EMDR) and body-centered psychotherapy.[6–10] EMDR is one method which incorporates the five sensory-emotional steps into a single therapeutic process. At the heart of EMDR is a moment where the client is asked to focus on their pain in a detached way, including how and where they feel it in their body, while simultaneously attending to a bilateral stimulation. The process of attending to two things at once is also referred to as a dual attention stimulus (DAS). The combination of bilateral stimulation and focused attention creates a kind of positive bio-feedback loop wherein the client can learn to re-experience the problem in a less distressing way. Following the bilateral stimulation, the therapist guides the client's attention toward noticing any changes that may have occurred. Clients often report feeling more relaxed and less distressed. This is then reinforced by having the client review their self-concept, defined by a negative self-related cognition, in the light of the changes that have occurred. In the treatment of physical pain, this might also involve the creation of resources such as pain-relieving imagery.

EMDR seems to work, often more efficiently than talk-therapy. Dozens of case studies have been published describing people being "cured" of PTSD, phantom limb pain phobias and addictions. Since its arrival 20 years ago, the method has gained professional recognition as a gold-standard treatment for PTSD.[11] EMDR has also shown promise as a treatment for chronic pain. Chronic pain sufferers who received EMDR treatment report less pain and emotional distress, an increased sense of connection and an increased ability to live with things as they are.[12-13] For example, when George saw an EMDR therapist for help with his chronic low back pain, he discovered that by focusing on his pain while simultaneously concentrating on a bilateral stimulation, he felt less pain. In a process called "resource installation", the EMDR therapist then taught George how to develop pain-relieving imagery out of the changes he had just experienced, by blending them with memories of past pleasant experiences. After the bilateral stimulation, George noticed a feeling of softness where the pain had been before. This feeling reminded him of how watching clouds float by used to make him feel as a child—a feeling of relaxation and carefreeness. George found that the EMDR not only helped reduce his pain, it also helped him learn how to control it and reduce its impact on his life.

EMDR appears to be one of the most neurologically smart methods for the treatment of traumatic pain. In addition to the method's proven efficiency, brain scans of PTSD sufferers who received EMDR treatment show more normal patterns of brain activity in the areas of the brain involved in traumatic pain,[14] e.g.:

- increased activity in the anterior cingulate cortex
- increased activity in the prefrontal cortex
- more evenly balanced electrical activity between left and right hemispheres.

EMDR has also been found to stimulate physiological changes consistent with a reduced stress response including changed respiration, decreased heart rate, decreased skin conductance and improved sleep.[15] It seems likely that the method's efficacy stems from its congruence with how the brain processes information. The unique bilateral stimulation component of EMDR, wherein each lobe of the brain is stimulated in a rhythmic pattern, seems to complement this method's ability to facilitate changes in mental and emotional activity associated with pain.

Understanding *your* pain and stress

Now that you know how the effects of stress can cause pain, and the basic program for reversing the pain-maintaining effects of stress, you are ready to learn how to use these strategies to reverse the patterns of brain activity that are maintaining your pain. But just before you do that, because everyone is different, you first need to assess which types and effects of stress you are affected by. This will guide you regarding which strategies you need to adopt to neutralize your stress and pain. It may also save you from the negative effects of adopting inappropriate self-help strategies. Bernie, an alexithymic chronic pain sufferer, was told that there was nothing wrong with him and that he should just try to keep as physically active as possible. Bernie took this advice literally and joined a gym program where he would try to push through his pain to increase his activity limits. Not surprisingly, because he was unaware of his inability to use his emotions to pace himself, Bernie's well-meaning efforts only aggravated his pain and led to his feeling more frustrated and depressed.

What are your pain risk factors?

As a result of reading the preceding chapters, you may already have some ideas about what types and what effects of stress might be contributing to your pain. The pain risk factors questionnaire (Table 4.1) will help you determine exactly what types and effects of stress, including physical injury, are maintaining your pain. This will help you know which of five self-help strategies you need to adopt. Read each statement carefully and place a tick in the box to indicate whether that statement is true or false ("not true"). Try to answer in terms of how you really *feel* rather than what you think is the right thing to say or how you wish things had been. In other words, be honest—no one else is going to see what you say. After you have completed the questionnaire, you will find a scoring key which will help you match up your results with the relevant treatment elements.

The 20 items are divided into eight sections. Each set of questions assesses a different type or effect of stress. To assess your risk-factor levels, give yourself one point for each "true" response in the scoring key (Table 4.2). Write your total number of true responses for each risk factor in the right hand column of the scoring key. For example, if you answered "true" to two items in questions 3–5, your score for "Emotional neglect" would be "2". If you answered "not true" to all questions 6–8, your score for "Childhood trauma" would be "0", and so on.

Table 4.1   Pain risk factors questionnaire

		True	Not true
1	I have suffered an accident, illness or injury.		
2	I have chronic health problems/pain.		
3	As a child I didn't have anyone to turn to for help, or even if I did I kept my feelings to myself.		
4	I can't remember being shown affection.		
5	I can't remember being hugged or kissed much.		
6	One of my parents had a mental illness/drug or alcohol problem/committed suicide/died.		
7	My family life was very unstable.		
8	I was physically and/or sexually abused.		
9	I have suffered or am facing threatening circumstances over which I feel I have no control.		
10	If I have a problem, the only person I can rely on is myself.		
11	I have trouble sleeping.		
12	I often feel tired and lacking in energy.		
13	I find it hard to relax.		
14	I don't know what's going on inside me.		
15	I have feelings I can't quite identify.		
16	Sometimes I feel like my body is disconnected from my mind.		
17	I fear the worst.		
18	I worry all the time about whether my problems will ever end.		
19	Sometimes I have disturbing memories or dreams about the past.		
20	I often feel "super alert" or watchful or on guard.		

Table 4.2   Scoring key

Question	Risk factor	Total
1–2	Physical injury or illness	
3–5	Emotional neglect	
6–8	Childhood trauma	
9–10	Safety and support	
11–13	Increased physiological arousal	
14–16	Emotional disconnection	
17–18	Negative thinking/"catastrophizing"	
19–20	Post-traumatic stress disorder	
	Total	

Once you have completed scoring the questionnaire, evaluate your pain and stress risk factors as follows:

1   A score of 1 or more for any individual risk factor means you are affected by that type or effect of stress.
2   If your total score was over 3, you have suffered moderate but significant stress.
3   If your total score was over 5, you have suffered severe stress.

> The pain risk factors questionnaire is based on a combination of personal observation and other validated questionnaires known to measure risk factors associated with stress and pain.[16] Remember, just because you have stress does not mean that your pain is not real. Chronic pain can be maintained by many biological factors which are not necessarily related to the effects of stress.

Planning your treatment

The next step is to use your results to develop your own individualized treatment program, using the strategies in the second half of this book. This simply involves matching up your pain risk factors with the relevant self-help strategies.

- *Injury and illness* (Questions 1–2)

  If you scored one or more on this risk factor, you have been exposed to one of the leading medical risk factors for chronic pain. In addition to learning how to control stressful feelings and pain, you should focus on the chapters dealing with:
  - emotional aspects of stress, injury and pain (Chapter 2)
  - safety and support (Chapter 5)
  - exercise (Chapter 8).

- *Emotional neglect/childhood trauma* (Questions 3–8)

  If you scored one or more for either of these risk factors, you have been exposed to one of the leading psychological risk factors for chronic pain. In addition to learning how to control stressful feelings and pain, you should focus on the chapters dealing with:
  - safety and support (Chapter 5)
  - reconnecting with your feelings (Chapter 6)
  - exercise (Chapter 8)
  - resilience (Chapter 11).

- *Safety and support* (Questions 9–10)

  If you scored one or more for this risk factor, you have insufficient safety and support. In addition to learning how to control stressful feelings and pain, you should focus on the chapters dealing with:
  - safety and support (Chapter 5)
  - building resilience (Chapter 11).

- *Increased physiological arousal* (Questions 11–13)

  If you scored one or more for this risk factor, it is likely that you are suffering from the effects of increased physiological arousal and you should focus on the chapters concerning:
  - safety and support (Chapter 5)
  - reconnecting with feelings (Chapter 6)
  - controlling stressful feelings (Chapter 7)
  - exercise (Chapter 8)
  - sleep (Chapter 9).

- *Emotional disconnection* (Questions 14–16)

  If you scored one or more for this risk factor, it is likely that emotional disconnection is contributing to your pain and stress and you should focus on the chapters dealing with:
  - safety and support (Chapter 5)
  - reconnecting with feelings (Chapter 6).

- *Negative thinking/"catastrophizing"* (Questions 17–18)

  If you scored one or more for this risk factor, negative attitudes and thinking patterns are likely to be exacerbating your pain and stress and you should focus on the chapters dealing with:
  - safety and support (Chapter 5)
  - controlling stressful feelings (Chapter 7)
  - changing your thinking (Chapter 10).

- *Post-traumatic stress disorder* (Questions 19–20)

  If you scored one or more for this risk factor, it is likely that symptoms of post-traumatic stress are exacerbating your pain and you should focus on the chapters dealing with:
  - safety and support (Chapter 5)
  - reconnecting with your feelings (Chapter 6)
  - controlling stressful feelings (Chapter 7)
  - exercise (Chapter 8)
  - resolving trauma (Chapters 7 and 12)
  - building resilience (Chapter 11).

Table 4.3 is a treatment planning chart where you can match your risk factors with the treatment strategies you need to concentrate on. Place a tick in the box for each self-help strategy indicated by the results of the pain risk factors questionnaire. Feel free to include any additional elements which feel necessary. For example, sleep management is often an issue for sufferers of severe stress and pain. Use this chart to help you coordinate your overall treatment. There is also a blank column at the end which you can use for any additional elements of treatment not mentioned here. For example, you may feel dissatisfied with the medical treatment you have been receiving, but you have done nothing about it. Finding a good doctor who understands you is a vital pre-requisite to using psychological methods for managing your pain and associated stress. Remember that each step builds on the one before it, so you should learn the steps in the order in which they are presented.

Table 4.3   Planning your treatment

Risk factor	Self-help strategy						Comments
	Safety and support	Reconnecting with your feelings	Controlling stressful emotions	Changing your thinking	Resolving trauma	Building resilience	
Injury or illness							
Emotional neglect							
Childhood trauma							
Safety and support							
Increased physiological arousal							
Emotional disconnection							
Negative thinking							
Post-traumatic stress disorder							
Total							

As you can see, knowing which risk factors are contributing to your pain and stress enables you to know which strategies and skills you need to focus on most to resolve your problems. Gemma, the fibromyalgia/chronic fatigue sufferer we met in Chapter 3, found she needed to apply all of these strategies to overcome her pain.

Gemma's treatment began with her becoming aware of what was missing emotionally from her life as a child and how a lack of safety had led to her problems. When Gemma's therapist asked her who she felt able to trust when she had a problem as a child, she couldn't answer. This made Gemma realize that she had no safety or support in her life. When Gemma thought about it, she realized that she didn't even feel entitled to these basic human needs. Gemma felt that it was wrong to have any sort of needs that might be burdensome to those close to her. Then Gemma made the connection between her feelings of insecurity and her own lack of self-care, including the isolation and overwork associated with her decision to work in a foreign country. For the first time Gemma could see very clearly that just the thought of needing anything from anybody made her feel anxious and somehow bad about herself.

Once Gemma understood the link between her safety issues and her stress and pain, she was ready to start reconnecting with her feelings and learning how to control these problems. Gemma thought about how having to ask others for help made her feel, including how it made her feel about herself as a person ("I'm bad"), while simultaneously concentrating on a dual attention stimulus (her therapist moving his hand bilaterally in front of her eyes). It felt very strange to face a problem without trying to avoid it, but somehow having to concentrate on something else at the same time made it easier. Gemma noticed that when she concentrated on the bilateral stimulation, her attention went off the problem and her body relaxed (it actually felt as though the tension was draining out of her body). For a moment, Gemma felt completely lost in another world, and all she was aware of was the therapist's finger moving backwards and forwards in front of her face. Gemma's spell was interrupted by the sound of the therapist's voice saying, "Take a deep breath and relax." After a brief pause he asked her: "And how do you feel now?" Gemma felt totally relaxed; her mind was completely blank. "And how do you feel about yourself when you think of having to ask others for help now?" Gemma noticed that she no longer felt anxious about having needs or asking others for help. Gemma's negative attitude toward herself had also changed from "I'm bad" to "I'm worthwhile."

Once her emotional block about obtaining support was removed, Gemma felt a new sense of connection with herself, and somehow more able to pace herself and live a day at a time. When she became aware of having needs, it felt natural and Gemma was no longer afraid to have or express her needs. Gemma also learned how to relax, using pre-recorded CDs of guided imagery and bilateral stimulation. Associated with this, she learned how to manipulate her pain, using healing imagery based on positive memories. Although Gemma was never completely cured of her chronic pain, once she resolved her anxiety about having needs, and learned to take care of herself better, she found the pain became a much less troublesome part of her life.

Once Gemma no longer felt anxious or conflicted about having needs and asking for help, it felt natural to live and function in a way that was appropriate to her physical and mental needs, rather than her imagined expectations of others, etc. Gemma's story illustrates how, when used together, the five pain-coping strategies can help reverse the sensory-emotional patterns that maintain pain. Gemma had to:

- learn to trust others with her feelings and needs (safety and support)
- learn how to recognize her physical limitations and pace herself (reconnect with her emotions)
- learn how to soothe feelings of stress and pain through relaxation and mind control techniques (controlling stressful feelings and pain)
- learn how to think more adaptively (changing her thinking)
- resolve the emotional trauma of her childhood emotional neglect (resolving trauma).

Summary and conclusion

In this chapter you have seen how increased understanding of the nervous system and the effects of stress have changed how we think about pain. You've learned about some new theories of pain, based on increased understanding of the involvement of the brain in pain. You have been introduced to a series of sensory-emotional strategies specifically designed to reverse the brain processes that maintain pain. You have also assessed which types and effects of stress might be affecting you, and how to use that knowledge to develop an effective treatment program. You now have a road map for the journey ahead of you, one that is designed for your specific needs.

In the following chapters you will learn how to apply the five sensory-emotional strategies necessary for reversing the pain-maintaining effects of stress. Although the exercise in this chapter will have highlighted certain strategies for you to focus on, you will probably find all these strategies helpful to some degree. You should approach your treatment as though you were going on a journey: pack an open mind and a patient attitude. *Look out* for little differences or changes; *notice* when your responses are different; and be prepared to *learn* from these changes. Your rate of progress will depend upon many factors; the longer you have endured stress or pain, and the more severe the abuse or deprivation you suffered in childhood, the more time you may need. Be patient.

PART TWO

Change your brain, change your pain

5

Safety and support

Shared experience is the greatest of human goods.

John Dewey*

Feeling safe and having support are two of the most basic human needs. You must have safety and support prior to attempting to overcome pain. Without safety, people feel anxious and on edge. Concentration is poor and it's hard to learn new skills. Without support, people feel the full weight of their problems—plus the burden of knowing that if they fail there will be no one to rescue them. Lack of safety and support means different things to different people. Although lack of safety suggests a physical threat, for chronic pain sufferers it might mean inadequate treatment or physical disability due to injury. For victims of emotional neglect or trauma, lack of safety can come from fractured relationships, uncontrollable anxiety associated with PTSD, and/or unstable living circumstances. Having insufficient safety and support creates a state of permanent alertness or hypervigilance, which makes it impossible to focus on building the resources necessary for overcoming pain. Creating more safety and support in your life is thus one of the most basic steps in learning how to reverse the physical and mental processes that maintain pain.

What is safety and why is it important?

Feeling safe means feeling free from threat to your physical or emotional well-being. Feeling safe means knowing who you are and feeling reasonably confident

* *Experience and Nature.* John Dewey, 1925, p. 202.

in your ability to get whatever you need to survive. Feeling safe means having confidence in your ability to move in the world, ward off threats and achieve your goals. Safety also comes from the absence of threat: the knowledge that no one or no thing is threatening your physical safety. Unless you live in a country that is at civil war or under a dictatorship, safety may not at first appear to be an obvious issue. However, even stable, well-developed societies can harbor dangers: illness and disability, isolation, dysfunctional families, domestic violence and unsafe working conditions are ever-present threats in many so-called civilized societies. Feeling supported means knowing that you are not alone and that there are others you can turn to for help and understanding.

Safety and support are linked: lack of safety increases your need for support; lack of support can undermine your ability to feel safe and cope with adversity. For example, after being raised in conditions of physical and emotional abuse, Marie was afraid to trust anybody with her innermost feelings. She developed a very tough-seeming exterior so that she would not ever appear vulnerable or needy, conditions which she associated with being in grave danger; however, when she hurt her back and could not work, she soon found that she was very alone. Even her relationships with those closest to her were all based on her being the supportive one. Marie found this feeling of aloneness made her injury harder to cope with.

Lack of safety and support can weaken your ability to cope with adversity and increase your susceptibility to physical and emotional pain. For example, victims of terrorism with low social support are more likely to develop anxiety.[1] Chronic pain sufferers with low social support suffer more than those with good social support.[2] One study showed that the more dysfunctional a married fibromyalgia sufferer's relationship was with their spouse, the worse their pain was.[3] Lonely people are more likely to suffer from heart disease and early death.[4,5] Safety and support are thus essential for combating stress, trauma and pain. The ancient Greeks understood the importance of safety and support; they built healing temples where sick people could rest and heal. In these places the sick person was cared for by a physician/priest who treated them with a combination of drugs, diet, exercise and prayer. The Greeks seemed to understand the concept of safety, as they built their healing temples outside their cities in the purer air of the countryside and away from the cares and responsibilities of normal life. They also ensured that the sick person was not left alone, but was cared for by another person. In modern times, we are more likely to seek refuge in a rehabilitation clinic or visiting relatives in the countryside, but the principle is the same: unwell people need time out and care.

Safety and your brain

Safety and support are necessary for normal brain functioning. Loving relationships stimulate the development of the parts of the brain involved in safety, self-awareness and identity. Developmental expert Daniel Siegal has suggested that secure attachments are necessary for the development of neural networks responsible for emotional regulation, memory, and information processing. Secure attachments are thought to be necessary for the balanced development of the left and right hemispheres of the brain, which mediates our ability to relate emotionally to our self and others. Secure attachments also allow the balanced development of the sympathetic and parasympathetic nervous systems—our ability to balance arousal with self-soothing.

There is a link between our ability to feel pain and our ability to relate to others. Researchers have found that many of the same areas of the brain involved in pain are also involved in empathy. These include the frontal lobe, the anterior cingulate cortex and the somatosensory cortex. These areas of the brain are also involved in monitoring of bodily states, emotional processing and sensory perception, respectively. Researchers have also discovered certain neurons that fire as a result of just *watching* someone else in pain, so-called mirror-neurons. The discovery of mirror neurons has profound implications for understanding empathy. Our brain doesn't just react because we see someone in pain; it also recreates what's going on in their mind—enabling us to feel their pain. The ability to feel the pain of another involves attunement—our brain's ability to stimulate bodily states that match those of the other. Attunement also requires interoception—the ability to recognize what we are feeling in our own body. So when we experience empathy, we are connecting with both the other person and our self.

Being able to perceive what's going on in our own bodies and notice what others are feeling is important for several reasons. Firstly, if we can feel our pain, we can feel others' pain, and vice-versa. Shared pain is always easier to tolerate than lonely pain. Australian POWs in WWII Japanese concentration camps describe their bond with each other as their greatest defense against the horrors inflicted by their captors. The ability to share pain may even have evolutionary advantages. Neuroscientist and pain expert Sean Mackey believes that without empathy to bind us together, we would never have survived as a species. Mackey has also found a link between the amount of love we experience in childhood and pain: both involve the brain's reward system (dopamine). Dopamine is responsible for the "runner's high" that people get after exercise. If the brain's reward system is deficient, it leaves us more vulnerable to pain. For example, it's been found that fibromyalgia sufferers don't get a runner's high following exercise. Lack of connection thus appears to sensitize our brains to pain in a profound way.

People who were abused or neglected as children seem to have problems in maintaining their own safety, and seeking the support of others.

Roy had grown up in a harsh family environment where his mother lived in fear of his father's drunken rages. Roy learned from an early age that it was best to never show his feelings, particularly feelings of weakness. If you can't stop the violence, at least you can pretend that it's not hurting you. Many years later Roy was working as a butcher and there was an urgent export order that needed to be prepared, but the meat was not properly thawed, making it difficult to cut. In fact, none of the other butchers would work on this meat. But Roy's boss pleaded with him, threatening that the business would go broke if they didn't get this order out. Roy knew he was their best butcher and felt responsible. For eight solid hours he cut those semi-frozen carcasses. By the end of the shift his arms were stinging with pain and he could barely drive home. The next day Roy could barely move and his arms were aching. Roy's doctor told him he had permanently damaged the tendons in his arms and that he would never be able to return to work as a butcher.

Caring relationships help repair the emotional disconnection caused by poor attachments in childhood, through the creation of new neural pathways.

How to tell if you do not have enough safety and support

Lack of safety and support can create a permanent sense of unease and feelings of stress, which can maintain stress and pain as well as inhibiting your ability to unlearn the sensory-emotional patterns that maintain stress and pain. You should already have some idea about whether or not safety and support are issues for you as a result of your responses to the questionnaire in Chapter 4. Other signs and symptoms that indicate insufficient safety and support include:

- feeling anxious a lot of the time
- "overreacting" to things
- feeling "jumpy" or "on edge"
- worrying a lot
- catastrophizing (fearing the worst)
- feeling empty or alone
- feeling unable to cope.

If you are experiencing any of these, you probably have insufficient safety and support and you should address this prior to attempting to overcome your pain.

Before looking at how you can increase your safety and support, it also needs to be remembered that stress can affect our desire to be with others. Some people prefer less contact with others during periods of acute stress. When we're trying to cope with a significant threat or challenge, we don't have the energy or mental space for normal social intercourse. This tendency to withdraw socially is a normal part of the "fight-or-flight" response. When an animal is threatened or wounded, it either fights back or it retreats to its lair and rests until it feels strong again. An animal instinctively knows when it is weak and needs to rest and recharge. It's also not safe to approach a wounded animal; it will probably bite you. Human beings are no different. When we're feeling vulnerable we don't like to be intruded upon. We know we need to conserve energy for our own self-healing. The challenge is often to find the right balance between having our space and being supported. It is important that friends and family are understanding of the changes in the stressed person. Just because stressed persons isolate themselves doesn't mean they don't need help and support; timing and sensitivity are important. People generally need more space in the early stages of a stressful experience, and gradually become more able to re-engage socially as they feel more stable, which may take some time. If people try to force themselves to interact with others before they are ready, their stress levels will be increased.

A word about medication

If you have chronic physical pain, chances are you are taking some type of pain medication. The aim of pain medication is to relieve the pain, but medication is rarely effective with chronic physical pain, and its effectiveness tends to reduce with time. Medication is frequently an issue in the management of pain—most people do not like having to take drugs on a regular basis. Many medications involve unpleasant side-effects, including constipation, nausea, decreased energy, and impaired concentration and memory. Many pain sufferers are afraid of becoming addicted, which can lead to inappropriate use of medication.

> Jan had suffered from chronic low back pain for over five years after too much heavy lifting in the course of her employment as a warehouse worker. Jan's physician had prescribed a range of pain medications to help her manage the pain. Having to take medication like this made Jan feel very uncomfortable; she was terrified of becoming a "pill-popper" like her mother. Jan's mother had been addicted to an over-the-counter pain-killer called "Bexs" and she would excuse herself every afternoon for "a Bex and a lie down". Even though she was a very different person to her mother, Jan was so afraid of becoming addicted that she would avoid taking pain medication until her pain was unbearable. Unfortunately, this seemingly heroic effort only made the problem worse, as it exposed her to more pain than she could really cope with, leading to exhaustion, clinical depression and decreased overall ability to cope.

The reality is that dependency is inevitable with any drug you take regularly, but for most people the risk of addiction is slight. Drugs can be a vital element in the management of any chronic medical or psychological condition, when used appropriately. Different drugs affect different people differently. Some pain medications work for some people and not others. Some antidepressants help some people and not others. Knowing when and how to take drugs is also important. Research shows that people whose pain is well-controlled in the early stages are less likely to develop chronic pain. It's essential that you communicate with your prescribing physician regarding any concerns you may have.

Treatment review

ACTIVITY

Before we go any further, if you are suffering from physical pain due to a physical injury or illness, please check the following:

1   That you are receiving adequate medical care for any injury or illness that is associated with your pain.
2   That your pain is not originating from an undiagnosed medical condition. (If you have a confident, trusting relationship with your medical practitioner, this is unlikely to be an issue.)
3   That you are using medication appropriately. Try to take emotion out of the equation when making decisions regarding medication usage.
4   Communicate with your prescribing physician regarding any concerns you may have.

Five ways of increasing your safety and support

There are many steps you can take to increase your levels of safety and support. One of the most obvious is to simply avoid danger. As obvious as this sounds, many survivors of severe stress have learned to tolerate unsafe conditions or just fail to recognize danger. Some survivors of childhood abuse actively seek out danger in a subconscious attempt to recreate the conditions of their original trauma. Abusive relationships, substance abuse and other forms of risk-taking behavior are some examples. Risky behavior is sometimes rationalized on the grounds that we have no choice; the mortgage needs to be paid or the family needs us. But, unless we live in a war zone, there is something wrong if we have to sacrifice our well-being for a house or for our family. This willingness to accept risk, consciously or unconsciously, suggests that there are maladaptive attitudes at work. It's thus not enough to simply avoid danger; we also have to change any negative attitudes that might be preventing us from ensuring we have adequate levels of safety and support. Increasing your safety and support actually involves a series of strategies, ranging from changing your attitude, to undertaking activities designed to build these important needs. These are:

1   *Attitude.* Get rid of any negative or self-defeating attitudes and replace them with more healthy ones.
2   *Self-protection.* Avoid unsafe places or people.
3   *Safety.* Create a safe place.

4 *Support.* Develop deeper relationships.
5 *Writing.* Support yourself by expressing yourself in writing.

Attitude: getting rid of negative beliefs

The first step for building safety is to identify and get rid of any negative or self-defeating attitudes or beliefs you may have. As we saw in Chapter 3, people who have suffered abuse or neglect often hold subconscious, self-defeating attitudes and beliefs which make them more likely to ignore their own health and safety needs. They may believe that their needs are unimportant and that their welfare does not count. They may have learned to ignore pain. Or they may just lack any awareness of their needs for safety and support. Remember how Gemma (from Chapter 3) developed chronic fatigue after underestimating the importance of family?

Negative attitudes and beliefs are often unconscious, which is what makes them so hard to defeat; however, if you look at your behavior, you will find clues regarding your underlying attitudes and beliefs. For example:

- Do you find it hard to say no?
- Do you find it hard to make time for yourself?
- Do you feel like you are "always on the go"?
- When you are working, do you find it hard to know when to stop?
- Are you willing to risk your health and safety to get the job done?
- Do you often feel overwhelmed by the needs of others?

Answering "yes" to two or more of the above questions is a strong indication that there are some self-defeating negative attitudes and beliefs at work in your subconscious. The exception is if you are facing a normal, transient life stressor, such as having children. Most people are unaware of their subconscious thoughts, unless they have gone through psychotherapy. But you need to identify any negative core attitudes and beliefs you may hold. This will enable you to challenge their influence in your life. This exercise will help you identify and challenge any negative or self-defeating attitudes or beliefs you may have.

ACTIVITY

Identifying negative attitudes or beliefs

1   Using the worksheet in Appendix A, make a note of any situation or memory that makes you feel anxious or unsafe. In the "Feeling" column, record how that situation makes you feel. In the "Negative belief" column, record any self-limiting, negative attitudes or beliefs you have about yourself in relation to that situation. Some examples are provided to help you get started.
    Note: No one likes to admit that they feel weak or helpless, but try to answer honestly rather than how you would like to feel. If you are exposing yourself to unhealthy situations but can't identify any feeling, that too can be an indication of a subconscious negative belief (e.g. "I don't matter"). In general though, try to use your feelings as a guide to your underlying attitudes and beliefs.

2   Once you have identified any negative, self-defeating attitudes or beliefs that you hold, stop and look at them objectively. Ask yourself whether you are really worthless/unlovable/weak, etc. Even if you feel you have made terrible mistakes in your life, the reality is that most people are doing the best they can. No child ever deserved to be neglected or abused.

3   In future, try to be more aware of how your negative attitudes influence the choices you make regarding your self-care.

Being aware of and challenging negative attitudes and beliefs does not mean they will not still arise, but it does give you a means of lessening their power over you and making more healthy choices.

Self-protection: avoiding unsafe places or people

Once you have identified and learned to challenge any negative attitudes, the next step is to improve your self-care by avoiding unhealthy situations and behaviors. We have seen how victims of stress and trauma may have been conditioned to ignore their own safety needs. Modern life also involves a certain acceptance of risk. We drive cars at 120 kilometers per hour, centimeters away from other cars, trusting that they will not cross to the wrong side of the road. We ascend tall buildings inside little metal boxes, trusting that the lift machinery will work. This ability to ignore danger is actually necessary for many activities of modern life. People who can't ignore risk to some degree are unable to drive on freeways, travel in lifts or planes, cross bridges or travel through tunnels.

The trouble with victims of stress, trauma and neglect is that they are less able to weigh the risks of certain activities appropriately. Victims of stress and trauma are more willing to tolerate danger, from abusive relationships to unsafe working conditions. You must learn how to make sound judgments when evaluating risk. This exercise will help you identify and take action to avoid any unreasonably unsafe circumstances which may be threatening your health.

ACTIVITY

Creating safety

Safety is a basic precondition to living well and happily. The following safety review will help you address any safety issues in your life.

1   Are there any threatening circumstances or people in your life that make you feel unsafe or unable to relax?

   _____

   _____

2   Why are you tolerating those circumstances?

   _____

   _____

3   Do a costs/benefits analysis. Whatever benefit you think you're gaining, is it worth the negative effects of those circumstances on your health and happiness?

   _____

4   Remember that for a healthy person, their own health and safety is paramount.
   (The only possible exception would be if there was a threat to the safety of your family, but generally they are better off if you are well.)

5   Decide what action you intend to take—even if it's only to talk to someone.

   _____

   _____

6   Take action. Do whatever you need to do in order to feel safer.

   _____

   _____

Safety: creating a safe place

Another alternative is to create a "safe place", a physical or mental sanctuary where you can feel safe and secure. A safe place can be a real place, such as your bedroom or study, or an imaginary place such as somewhere you remember from your childhood or travels. You can create your own mental safe place by simply lying down and recalling somewhere you have been where you felt really safe and secure. Try the exercise below.

ACTIVITY

Creating your own safe place

1   Think of a time or a place where you felt really safe, secure and calm.
2   Let an image of that place form in your mind . . .
3   Take your time to explore that place and what it is about it that makes you feel good . . . Notice the colors, the sounds, any smells . . .
    Really concentrate on remembering that place.
    Notice any pleasant feelings thinking of that place triggers in your body . . .
    Give yourself a few moments to notice how being in that place makes you feel . . .
4   Try to think of a word or a phrase that summarizes how being in that place makes you feel about yourself, e.g. "peaceful", "safe", "I'm safe", "I'm okay . . . ". The word or phrase should **feel** congruent with how your safe place makes you feel. It is a gut thing.
5   Practice thinking of your safe place together with the word or phrase that summarizes how it makes you feel. The more often you do this, the stronger the association between the memory, feelings and thoughts will become, and the more easily you'll be able to use that mental resource to cope with stressful feelings.
6   Use the word or phrase to mentally summon your safe place. After you've practiced a few times, try thinking of the word or phrase and notice what happens. It should key you straight into your safe place. Then, when you need to feel safe, you can just think of the word or phrase that reminds you of it and you'll be there.
7   If you can't think of a safe place, think of a person, or even an activity, that makes you feel good.

Many recorded relaxation CDs contain safe-place exercises which can evoke soothing and comforting mental imagery. Joseph described the following experience, after listening to the author's *Calm and Confident* CD.

As I finally relaxed with my eyes closed I was taken to a scene where I was traveling in light travel gear (beige cargo shorts, white long-sleeved shirt, brown walking sandals, walking staff, back-pack) in lovely, forested, daylight conditions on a path that led into the mountains. I felt free with the wind blowing through my hair, I was smiling and energetic, and I was moving at a comfortable pace.

A train appeared. I entered the train with me being the sole passenger and was taken on a path up and around alps-like mountains. As I was on my journey, I saw myself glued to the window as a child would be in a car as the car drove past an amusement park with bright, blinking lights and attractions. The scenery was that powerful . . . yet I don't know what I was seeing, just that I was glued to the windows of this small train car.

As the train stopped and I departed, I found myself in a Swiss village overlooking a pristine and calm lake with mountains off in the background and refreshing air surrounding me. I discovered a little patch of grass that had tree shade and I decided this was where I would stop: a safe place in a lovely village overlooking the most beautiful lake known to me and air as fresh as I had ever taken in. I lay down to relax there and take in this marvel—I had no schedule, I had nowhere to be, there was no one to see . . . just to experience the here and now. I noticed that I was without my backpack and walking staff since I had entered the train yet I was OK with this.

It was at this point that a person/entity/guide resembling myself—but more aged with gray, silver hair—came over to my safe patch and we just sat there looking at each other for a moment. Then he raised his hand and a warm, wavy white energy beam slowly came out of his hand toward me and when it did connect with me, it gradually filled me as water would fill a bottle. (I did notice that there was a brilliantly clear, white crystal on his hand or on his fingers.) I saw this energy going in every direction within me . . . from my fingertips, through my arms and shoulders, to my head, through my abdomen, and to my legs and toes. Everywhere! I felt as if I was more complete, having been given this gift and I sensed that there was an encapsulating, opaque presence around me somewhat like a cocoon. I could see out of it and I could be seen from outside of it, but it was nonetheless completely surrounding me. I didn't notice the lake and mountain scenery any more, just really focused on this warm feeling and the protective, opaque shield around me. The energy stopped flowing from his hands, he lowered them, and we started talking of things—nothing really recognizable, but from a third-person perspective I could see myself and him shooting the breeze as two friends would who have not seen each other in a while.

At one point, when I was just taking in the scenery with my new gift, there was something in my mind that resembled a bird that was flying carefree as a bird would.

At first, my mind's eye was trying to manipulate its flying pattern with no success. So I decided to just follow it to see what it was up to. As I did this and let go of trying to control its behavior, I felt a sense of freedom and of enjoying a great ride.

The train appeared, I said my farewell (I was not sad per se, but was hesitant to leave this special place and my new friend), and I boarded the train. I was still without my backpack and walking staff but was not concerned. As I was coming back to the surface, the train had entered a tunnel and my last memory was of the entrance of the tunnel becoming a smaller and smaller white, circular sight as we moved deeper into the tunnel on my way from my special place.

Although Joseph's response is unusually rich and detailed, it is not so surprising given that he once visited a village by a lake in Switzerland where he had very similar feelings to those evoked by the CD. He had never forgotten the sense of peace he felt as he sat by the lake, on a windless summer's day, and marveled at the beauty all around him. Other aspects of Joseph's experience came from his own spiritual beliefs and unconscious resources. As Joseph's story demonstrates, memory is a rich resource for creating a sense of safety, even in the midst of the most unpleasant circumstances. Some unfortunate people really have no happy memories on which to base their safe place. This is where imagination comes in. The human mind is a dreamworks where virtually anything can be dreamed up and used to escape painful realities.

Support: developing deeper relationships

Sharing our fears and concerns with others is also an important aspect of feeling safe and supported. For most people this happens with their family. Boris Cyrulnik, a French psychiatrist, describes what he calls "bastion families". These are families wherein children are given everything they need to overcome adversity. Bastion families are highly structured in terms of gestures of affection, household routines, religious or secular rituals, and parental roles. The family members chat a lot, touch one another with gestures and words, share in the upkeep of the household, pray, and tell stories to give meaning to what is going on. Children are consistently given messages of hope and encouragement, e.g. "anything is possible", "you can do it".[6] If you come from such a family, you should be well-equipped to cope with adversity. If you don't, try to create one for yourself (using the above recipe), or find one — in-laws, neighbors and acquaintances are all potential sources.

Not surprisingly, societies with strong family ties have been found to have much lower levels of depression than modern, urbanized societies. For example, the incidence of depression in rural Spain is only 2.6 per cent, compared with 17 per cent in Manchester, a troubled urban area of the UK.[7] In Spain, as with many Latin cultures, the family unit is the center of life; children tend to stay at home longer, and old people are less likely to be parked in "homes". In Spanish hospitals, doctors have to push through ranks of relatives to get near the patient. Although Spain has its share of problems, including terrorism and unemployment, its inhabitants benefit from strong social support structures, based on *la familia*.

One of the most healing qualities of supportive relationships is receiving empathy and feeling understood. The feeling that comes from sharing and having your feelings understood by another is called *attunement*. Attunement involves the creation of a kind of positive feedback loop between one person's feelings and another's. The simplest example of this is the eye contact between a loving mother and her infant, which occurs in the context of a secure attachment. When the child sees its mother's loving gaze, it feels secure and "knows" it is loved and cared for, even though it might not have the language to put those feelings into words. Human beings need attunement and never stop seeking it, particularly where it is missing or broken. The late Pope John Paul II lost his mother when he was 10. In his autobiography he hardly mentions her, leading one biographer to speculate that he could not remember her. But after John Paul II read a best-selling book about attachment (Daniel Siegel's *The Developing Self),* he summoned the author to the Vatican and begged him to "tell me about the mother's gaze". Everyone, no matter who they are, is seeking this sense of oneness with others.

It is no accident that expressing your feelings about your problems to someone who cares helps. Scientists have discovered that talking in this way activates *both* the left and right sides of the brain, leading to greater integration between mental and emotional aspects of experience.[9] (Remember from Chapter 3 how severe stress disrupts the normal pathways of communication between the left and right hemispheres of the brain?) Expressing your feelings seems to stimulate the whole brain, bringing your nervous system "on line" to process negative sensory-emotional experiences. Feeling connected with others can provide a powerful buffer against stress, trauma and pain. Siegel feels that it is possible to learn how to develop secure attachments in adulthood, despite early childhood and neglect. He recommends sharing your emotions as being the best way to connect with others. Human relationships, Siegel argues, are one of the key ways in which we organize our minds. There is no doubt that human relationships are the key to feeling supported.

Medical anthropologist Arthur Klienmann tells the story of how, as a young intern, he was given the task of comforting a young burns victim as she underwent painful daily de-bridement procedures (removal of dead skin tissue). Klienmann held the young girl's hand, reassuring her and trying to distract her, but nothing he did seemed to have any effect. Klienmann could barely tolerate the "daily horror" of the screams, dead tissue floating in blood-stained water, peeling flesh, oozing wounds, the battles over cleaning, and bandaging. One day, at wit's end, he simply asked the anguished young patient, "How do you tolerate it?" She looked back at him with a surprised expression, but there was a pause in her screaming. Then she tried to answer his question, all the while grasping his hand harder. As she talked, Klienmann noticed that the young patient screamed less. After this rapport was established, the young girl seemed to cope with the painful procedure with less distress.[8]

Siegel also notes that some of the most important emotional communication happens non-verbally, via facial expressions, gestures and tone of voice. Supportive relationships can be found in families, social groups, workplaces, churches and psychotherapy. Jerry was a depressed chronic pain sufferer who had grown up without affection and a strong sense of responsibility for others. Jerry found it almost impossible to express his feelings or show his needs. In therapy Jerry was assisted to connect with and express long-denied feelings about his childhood. It was not easy, but afterwards Jerry felt more "whole" and freer to express his feelings. He made contact with his sister, whom he hadn't seen in many years, and began to have regular talks with her on the telephone. Jerry's story demonstrates another important element of finding support— the need to resolve early attachment issues and/or past trauma.

Opening up

ACTIVITY

1 Take a moment to review your closest relationships.
  Whom do you confide in?
  If no one, then whom do you trust, or whom could you learn to trust?
2 Try "opening up" to that person or persons a little more than you usually do, and sharing how you are feeling with them.
3 Notice their response; notice how your body feels.

Note: Although it can feel strange to reveal your inner feelings if you are not used to it, the feelings of connection and relief you experience will quickly outweigh any feelings of discomfort. For tips on how to talk about pain, see Appendix B.

Writing as a supportive exercise

Another alternative is to express your feelings by writing. In *Opening Up*, an excellent book about the importance of support, James Pennebaker recommends writing as an alternative method of expressing feelings. In a now famous study, Pennebaker found that people who expressed their problems through writing about them were healthier than people who did not.[10] He found that self-disclosure triggers measurable physiological changes, including a decrease in blood pressure and an increase in immune function (as measured by an increase in T-lymphocytes, which stimulate production of antibodies).

Mary suffered anxiety and social problems after being raped by an acquaintance. She found writing about her experience relieved much of her distress.

"I haven't been able to talk about the rape in detail to anyone. In the last three months, it has dominated my being. I've had fears and problems with other people that I've never experienced before. Being in this [writing experiment] has made a difference. Somehow, just writing about what happened has made it all less overwhelming. I won't forget what happened, but I see more clearly that it was an isolated event in my life."[11]

Before he became a famous author, Stephen King suffered from many fears and phobias. King used his fears as a basis for his first horror stories. By writing about his fears in this way, he was eventually able to rid himself of them. Research with surgery patients found that alexithymic individuals derived the greatest benefit from expressing their feelings this way.[10]

Pennebaker believes writing helps because it satisfies our need for completion, understanding and self-expression. Writing forces us to structure and organize our thoughts; it also allows detachment and objective observation. Writing doesn't suit everyone, but if you think this approach might work for you, try the following exercise.

ACTIVITY

Self-support through writing

1   Think about a problem or situation that is bothering you.
2   Write about it.
3   Focus on your feelings about it, rather than just describing what happened.
4   Write continuously.
5   Write whenever you need to.
6   Write where you won't be interrupted.
7   Write only for yourself.

Pennebaker reminds writers not to expect to feel better immediately; in fact, he warns that you may initially feel worse! However, for many people, writing this way eventually leads to a better understanding of their emotions, relief from distressing feelings and increased options for coping.

6

How to reconnect with your feelings

There is deep wisdom within our very flesh;
if only we can come to our senses and feel it.

Elizabeth A. Behnke*

Emotional disconnection is one of the most common, yet overlooked, pain-maintaining effects of severe stress. Many pain sufferers have either never learned how to recognize their feelings (alexithymia), or experience feelings in a way that is disconnected from some parts of their present reality (dissociation). Although it starts out as a defensive reaction, emotional disconnection can also maintain physical and emotional pain through increased physiological arousal, decreased ability to regulate stressful feelings, impaired decision-making and lack of self-care. Learning how to recognize and understand your emotions is vital for regulating the stressful feelings and sensations that maintain pain. Reconnecting with your emotions also restores one of the most important aspects of brain functioning and physical homeostasis.

What are feelings and why are they important?

Feelings are a vital link in the chain of communication between your body and your mind. Feelings act as "messengers" that alert your brain to relevant stimuli and guide you on how to react to them. For example, if a mugger comes at you, your nervous

* Elizabeth A. Behnke, *Bone, Breath and Gesture*.

system generates fear, which stimulates you to "fight or flight". If you feel tired, your brain tells you that you should rest. In addition to their signal value, feelings are also involved in memory and relationships. Any significant memory includes an emotional aspect, either positive or negative depending on what happened. Emotional memories are important repositories of past learning: they help us avoid making the same mistakes; they help us prepare for situations we know might be challenging. Painful memories involve bodily sensations. Emotional expert Anthony Damasio refers to the feelings that we have as a result of memories as "somatic markers". They're our body telling us that something important has happened or is happening. In relationships, feelings such as love and desire are the glue that binds us to others. Without feelings, close relationships would be impossible.

Daniel Siegal describes emotion as a two-step process involving an initial state of heightened activity in the brain that orients the person to whatever is happening.[1] In those first nanoseconds after an event, we sense that something meaningful has occurred, but we are not yet conscious of its significance. In another split second an emotional response is registered in the brain and a cascade of elaborative appraisal-arousal processes occur. As a result of these processes, we make sense of what is going on and we decide how to respond. Damasio also points out that emotions are not actually caused by external stimuli but occur *in response to physiological changes* triggered by external stimuli.[2] Emotions can, of course, also be stimulated by remembering stressful or painful situations, but again it is the bodily response to these memories that gives rise to the emotion. This understanding of emotion, which is based on recent discoveries in neuroscience, differs from the popular notion that emotions are caused by thoughts. As you will learn shortly, this has implications for how we go about changing our emotional reactions.

Reconnecting with feelings and your brain

As discussed earlier, your emotional connection with yourself is normally "learned" in childhood through your attachment with your parents. Every time your mother or father responded positively to your cry, you received a little lesson about your feelings—primarily that they are OK. You also learned that it is OK to have and express your feelings. Positive emotional experiences stimulate the development of brain structures and functions involved in emotion, including the frontal lobe, the anterior cingulate cortex, the corpus callosum, and the level of reactivity of the HPA-axis and the amygdala.

However, if no one responded to your feelings—or worse, if they humiliated or hurt you—the brain structures and processes necessary for emotional integration do not develop properly. As described in Chapter 3, people who were emotionally abused or neglected in childhood have structural and functional impairments to their brains. These include smaller hippocampus, corpus callosum and superior temporal gyrus. You may recall that the hippocampus is responsible for memory. The corpus callosum links the right and left hemispheres of the brain. The superior temporal gyrus is thought to be responsible for speech, language and communication. PTSD sufferers' brains tend to be over-active in the right emotional hemisphere (the amygdala) at the expense of the left, analytical hemisphere. Subjectively, the result is a disconnection between mental and physical aspects of experience, and problems understanding, regulating and expressing feelings. If you were physically or sexually abused, you might also have become dissociated from your emotions.

Adult survivors of abuse, neglect and stress also experience a reduced range of emotions than is normal, like a painter with only a small range of colors on his palette. They also tend to experience more negative emotions, such as anxiety and depression. Feelings of numbness and an inability to feel pleasure are not uncommon. Figure 6.1 shows the difference between a stressed person's emotional range and the emotional range of a healthy person.

Figure 6.1 Difference in the emotional range of a healthy person compared with a stressed person

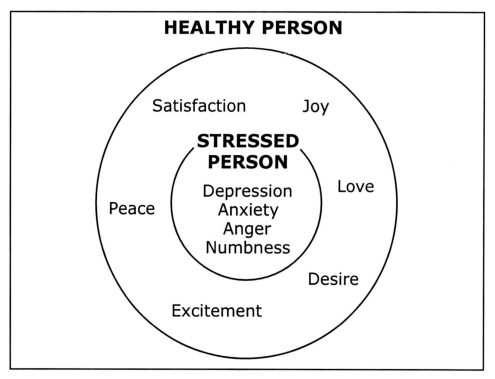

The reduced emotional range and increased propensity to negative emotions following severe stress greatly increases your vulnerability to physical and emotional pain. As you can imagine, being unable to feel pleasure or joy means stressed people have nothing within them to counteract the negative feelings and sensations that maintain pain. Emotionally disconnected people also have trouble regulating their emotions and are prone to mood swings and overreacting to negative stimuli. Stressed people are also more vulnerable to getting stuck in emotional lows which they find it hard to get out of. Collectively, these problems with emotional range and integration deprive sufferers of chronic pain of one of the most important resources for controlling pain.

Reconnecting with your feelings can enhance your ability to overcome pain. People who are able to control their emotions are more able to control physical pain. People with good emotional regulation skills are better able to manage pain.[3] Connelly found that people who are able to recover from negative emotions quickly, and/or regenerate positive emotions, are more able to control chronic pain. Positive emotions such as calmness, confidence, and even joy, involve biochemical reactions and physical sensations which can help alleviate pain and stress. Emotions such as excitement and desire help sustain motivation and goal-oriented behavior. Love and trust maintain relationships, a vital source of safety and support.

> Bridget, a chronic pain sufferer, was disconnected from her emotions as a result of the emotional neglect she endured as a young girl. Bridget learned that it was safer to not feel and to present as neutral a facade as possible. As an adult, Bridget habitually ignored her own physical and emotional needs to maintain her relationship with her partner, her job and her home. Bridget's lack of emotional integration and inadequate self-care eventually led to her being injured and developing chronic pain. Bridget was, of course, initially unaware that there was anything different about her emotional make-up that might be contributing to her pain.
>
> In therapy, Bridget was helped to reflect on her life and the impact that family problems had on her emotional development. Bridget realized that, unlike her daughter, she had no one to turn to when she was a little girl. Bridget came to see how this had made her withdraw into herself and inhibited her capacity for emotional expression. She could also see that although this strategy had enabled her to survive, it had come at a cost in terms of her ability to recognize and attend to her own needs. These insights helped Bridget start to see her injury as less of a catastrophe and more of an opportunity. Bridget realized that if she started listening to her feelings more and learning to balance her needs against the demands of life, this could help her to manage her stress and pain more effectively.
>
> With her therapist's support, Bridget started learning how to reconnect with her feelings. Slowly and steadily she learned how to tune in to her body and identify what she was feeling. Bridget learned how to feel the "no" in her gut when asked to do something that was against her values or needs, and to express that. Bridget learned how to "listen" to her body and rest when she felt tired instead of pushing herself to complete the task. As a result of being more able to "read" her body and express her needs, Bridget became more able to pace herself

physically, and more able to relax. Although her pain was not cured, over time Bridget found that living "in tune" with her feelings was less stressful and she had fewer pain flare-ups.

In addition to increased ability to pace yourself, increased emotional connectedness helps with brain functioning involved in social support and emotional regulation. Studies with animals have found that increased affectionate behavior in infancy stimulates biological changes which shape the central circuitry of emotion and consequently alter the animal's emotional, behavioral and biological responsivity to stress. Siegal and others have suggested that by having positive emotional experiences, we can not only learn how to understand and respond to emotions; we can also mitigate the negative neurological effects of negative attachments. As mentioned earlier, expressing emotions stimulates activity in both the left and right hemispheres in humans. Through the mirror neuron system, expressing emotions facilitates empathy. Expressing emotions also stimulates the release of neurotransmitters which strengthen synaptic connections.[4]

How to reconnect with your feelings

Reconnecting with your feelings begins by reviewing what you know about emotion. Experts have identified over 20 different types of emotion, with eight basic emotions: fear/anxiety; anger; sadness; boredom; shame; disgust; excitement; and joy/happiness. Each emotion signifies a different meaning in terms of the stimuli that triggered it. For example, fear means danger; anger means self-defense; sadness means loss. As noted, although ideally we should know instinctively what our emotions are telling us, neglect, stress and trauma can rob us of this innate capacity. Table 6.1 shows the eight most common emotions and what they mean.

Human beings were designed with the capacity to experience all these emotions and more. Like an orchestra, we need to be able to play and hear all the different notes to experience life fully. In fact, research has shown that emotional connectedness is more important for happiness than any other personality factor.[5] Emotional connectedness is also vital for overcoming stress and pain: the more connected you are with your emotions, the more able you will be to use them to transform stress and pain. One researcher found that the more connected people are with their emotions, the more able they are to control physical pain.[6] If you're not sure about the healing power of emotions, just think how much easier it is to cope when you're in a good mood compared with when you're in a bad mood. Even though you're in pain, when you feel good the "hurt" of pain becomes more bearable. Positive emotions can also fuel motivation and stimulate more active coping. When you feel good, you are more confident to try new activities or responses.

Table 6.1   Eight common emotions and what they mean

Emotion	Meaning
Fear/anxiety	Danger
Anger	Self-defense
Sadness	Grief/loss
Boredom	Lack of stimulation/opportunity
Shame	Self-recrimination
Disgust	Self-loathing
Excitement	Anticipation/desire
Joy/happiness	Fulfilment/satisfaction/connection

How to tell if you are disconnected from your emotions

We tend to not pay much attention to our emotions until there is a crisis. It is only when we feel stressed, anxious and/or depressed that we worry about our emotions. At this point there is an urgent need to understand and resolve our feelings of distress. Reconnecting with and understanding our emotions can help us respond to stressors more effectively, i.e. in ways that are more appropriate to our personal needs. For example, Kelly felt stressed and depressed after hurting her back at work, which affected her ability to perform her duties as a nurse. At first, Kelly felt she was weak for feeling stressed, and she tried to ignore how she was feeling. But this did not make her feel better and it kept her focused on the past (pretending that everything was normal) rather than other possibilities. One day, Kelly met an old friend who had been through a similar ordeal. Kelly was surprised to hear that her friend had experienced very similar emotions to her own. This made Kelly more accepting of her emotions and less upset with herself. After that, she found it easier to accept her limitations, and her pain became more manageable.

The first step is to assess whether you have a problem with emotional connectedness. It's not always easy to discern whether one has a problem with emotional connectedness; the very nature of the problem makes it difficult to recognize. Your results from the questionnaire in Chapter 4 should, however, have given you some indication whether you have a problem in this area. There are many other signs and symptoms of emotional disconnection:

- Do you find it hard to feel happiness or joy?
- Do you feel unmotivated?
- Do you often have negative feelings without being able to identify the cause?
- Do you find it difficult to put into words how you're feeling?
- Do you find it difficult to express your feelings?
- Do you sometimes feel detached from what is going on around you?
- Do you sometimes overreact to things without knowing why?
- Do you have any addictions, e.g. drinking, smoking, drugs, sex, work, or just "keeping busy"?

If you are experiencing more than two of these symptoms, you almost certainly have problems with emotional connectedness.

Reviewing your attitude toward your feelings

Improving your emotional connectedness begins with reviewing your attitude toward your feelings. Many victims of stress and pain hold negative attitudes and beliefs about their emotions, seeing them as a sign of weakness or inadequacy. Some cultures even reinforce the idea that this vital aspect of mental life is shameful, unnecessary or "only for girls". These negative attitudes and beliefs can act as unconscious barriers to reconnecting with your feelings. Thus, a useful preliminary step toward reconnecting with your feelings is to review your emotional history with a view to becoming more conscious of the kinds of "messages" you received about expressing your emotions. The "mapping your emotional history" activity will help you identify any mental blocks to accepting and understanding your emotions.

The emotional history exercise should have helped you identify any unhelpful attitudes or beliefs you may hold about emotions, and where they came from. Believing that some feelings are bad, shameful or weak is rarely helpful; your feelings are your feelings, as natural a part of you as the color of your eyes. Now that you have some understanding of what feelings are and why they're important, you are ready to learn how to reconnect with your feelings.

Three steps for reconnecting with your feelings

Emotional connectedness is part of emotional intelligence, a concept which became popular after the publication of Daniel Goleman's (1995) ground-breaking book

ACTIVITY

Mapping your emotional history

1 When you think back to your childhood what kind of feelings mainly come to mind? Do you remember feeling secure, happy and connected; or numb, scared and alone most of the time?

_____

_____

2 Do you have clear memories of your childhood, or are they fuzzy and fragmented?

_____

_____

3 Looking back on how your parents *expressed* their feelings, and/or *reacted* to your feelings, what do you think you would have learned from them? (Did they make you feel free to express your feelings, or ashamed/afraid/unsure?)

_____

_____

4 Looking at yourself now, how emotionally connected and expressive do you think you are? Do you pay much attention to your feelings or do you tend to ignore them?

_____

_____

5 How comfortable are you with your feelings? Do you make space for your feelings or do you try to keep busy so there is no time for your feelings.

_____

_____

6 Looking at the list in Table 6.1, what sorts of emotions do you mainly feel?

_____

_____

Note: When answering these questions, try to respond according to how you really *feel* rather than what you think. Many people have a sort of sanitized memory of their childhood in which they have erased or forgotten the negative parts. Try to remember how you really felt as you were growing up. Of course, if your childhood was really, really awful, you may wish to do this exercise with the help of a therapist.

of the same name.[7] Emotional intelligence involves being able to recognize and experience emotion in yourself and others. Emotional intelligence is normally acquired during your developmental years, but it can also be learned later in life. For many people who missed out on appropriate love and support in childhood, learning how to recognize and live according to their true feelings can be a life-transforming rite of passage. Not surprisingly, reconnecting with one's true emotional self is a theme of many popular movies and books including *Terms of Endearment, Good Will Hunting* and *Shirley Valentine*.

Increasing your emotional intelligence involves three basic skills or abilities:

- mindfulness—the ability to perceive feelings
- labeling feelings—the ability to identify feelings
- understanding feelings—the ability to interpret feelings

Learning these skills will help reduce the impact of negative emotions on your stress and pain, and also help you learn how to use your emotions to alleviate these problems. Below you will find a mixture of information and activities which will help increase your emotional connectedness. Some of these activities involve bottom–up (sensory-emotional) strategies; some involve top–down (intellectual) strategies. To get the most out of these strategies, you must be prepared to abandon the black and white certainties of your conscious left brain and be open to the more intuitive, sensory-emotional capacities of your right brain. Emotional intelligence involves the whole brain.

Mindfulness

Mindfulness is the ability to be aware of what's happening in the present, without reacting or judging. This non-judgmental awareness promotes acceptance of experience, good or bad, which reduces the stress associated with negative mental reactions. Mindfulness also involves being aware of what's happening in your body, including physical sensations associated with particular emotions. Mindfulness is a core skill of meditation. Mindfulness involves three basic skills:

- observing
- being non-judgmental
- staying in the present moment.

Researchers have found that practicing mindfulness meditation for as little as five minutes per day can lead to decreased stress-related brain activity. You can also practice mindfulness as you are going about your everyday business: just noticing the feeling of the water on your body in the shower, or paying attention to the expression on your child's face at breakfast. When you are mindful like this, it's hard to stay worried. Marsha Linehan, an emotional skills training expert, has created detailed guidelines for how to use mindfulness skills to reconnect with feelings.[8]

1 *Observing*. Observing means just noticing your bodily sensations, feelings and thoughts without reacting to them. One of the biggest obstacles to emotional connection is lack of awareness. Stressed or traumatized people are often so taken up with worries and responsibilities that they lose touch with their own sensory reality. Observing your feelings requires dis-attending to your worries or preoccupations and bringing your attention back to yourself. What does the pain *really* feel like? Is it hard or soft? Dull or throbbing? Constant or changing? What does taking a walk really feel like? Have you ever noticed how your breathing changes? Have you ever noticed what the sun on your face feels like, or your feet hitting the pavement? You are taking a walk, nothing else. That's mindfulness.

2 *Being non-judgmental*. The next step is to adopt a non-judgmental attitude toward what you are feeling. Being non-judgmental means accepting what you are feeling without judging it. Pain hurts, but when we react to it with fear or negative thoughts such as "It's awful, I can't stand it anymore", we only feel more stressed. Conversely, if we accept the pain and believe that it will eventually pass, we feel less stressed. You are not your thoughts, or even your feelings; they are just responses.

Having a judgmental attitude toward your feelings can be fatal. Ernest Hemingway famously believed that real men should be strong and keep their emotions under control. Hemingway could not accept it when he succumbed to depression in his 50s, and he turned to alcohol to cope. Hemingway's inability to cope with his depression eventually led to his committing suicide at the age of 61. The point of this story is to demonstrate the dangers of judging your feelings; it is not meant to imply that depression is not a serious problem or something that can be solved just by being non-judgmental.

3 *Staying in the present*. Staying in the present means maintaining your attention on what you are experiencing in the present moment. Many sufferers of stress and pain live in a state of inner mental turmoil, constantly worrying about their problems and what might or might not happen. This worrying makes it hard for them to connect with their current reality. They may feel as though life is passing them by. When PTSD sufferer Jeff attended the birth of his first child, he realized that he couldn't feel any of the joy people normally feel at such a time. All he could think about was what kind of world he was bringing the child into. Jeff's anxiety prevented him from enjoying what is normally a wonderful, life-transcending event. If Jeff could have been more present emotionally at the birth of his daughter, he might have felt joy and hope, feelings which he

could translate to his own problems. Staying in the present is about noticing the little things and living "one day at a time".

Try the following mindfulness activity, which is based on an exercise by Marsha Linehan:

ACTIVITY

Observing feelings

- Focus your attention on your body and mentally "scan" your body. **Notice any physical sensation.**
- Bring your mind away from all other thoughts.
- Maintain your attention on your body and let your mind rest there. **Nothing else matters but being with your experience of yourself for this time.**
- Whatever you notice, just **feel it**.
- Notice **where you feel it in your body**—your chest, your stomach, your back. Be aware of your body.
- If any **thoughts** come, **just notice** them too, and then **let them go** and return your attention to your body.
- When observing your feelings don't react or judge—**just notice**.
- See but **don't evaluate**. Take a non-judgmental stance. Focus on the "what" not the "good" or "bad", the "terrible" or "wonderful", the "should" or "should not".
- If other actions, thoughts or strong feelings distract you, **let go of distractions** and bring your attention back to what you are doing.
- **Monitor your thoughts.** Check in with yourself and make sure that your mind is on what you are doing/where you are. If you find your mind wandering or doing "two things at once", stop and bring your attention back to the present.

Living mindfully may feel awkward at first and you will need time to get used to paying attention to your feelings in this way. You may not immediately see or feel any benefit from these exercises, but be patient and trust that you will feel differently. There is a scene in the movie *The Karate Kid II* in which the aspiring karate expert is made to wax cars for hours on end by his teacher. The Karate Kid is unable to see the point of this mundane physical work ("wax on, wax off"), but this repetitive, mindless activity is actually teaching him how to "block" without thinking about it. When the Karate Kid finally gets into the ring, he finds he is able to block his opponent's blows instinctively, thanks to his work waxing the cars. So it is with learning mindfulness: practice makes perfect.

Labeling feelings

The second skill for reconnecting with your emotions is knowing *how* to recognize your emotions. Recognizing your emotions involves being able to identify and label what you are feeling. Recognizing your feelings enables you to choose the best course of action to resolve the problem that is causing your distress. All feelings begin in the body, as physical sensations. So the key to recognizing your feelings is to use the sensory awareness skills you've been developing to notice when a feeling is occurring and then try to interpret the feeling. Different physical sensations represent different feelings: tightness in the chest might mean anger; butterflies in the stomach might mean fear. The easiest way to label feelings is to know how to recognize them by how they are felt in the body. If you feel unsure of your ability to label your feelings, a good place to start is to learn what physical sensations denote what emotions. Table 6.2 summarizes some of the physical sensations associated with eight of the most common emotions.

Table 6.2   Physical bases of emotions

Physical sensations	Emotion
Tightness in stomach/chest	Anger
Churning in stomach	Fear/anxiety
Chest pains	Sadness
Heaviness in body	Boredom
Feeling hot in cheeks	Shame
Curling of lower lip	Disgust
Heart racing, elevated respiration	Excitement
Euphoric feeling	Joy/happiness

Of course, it's not as simple as that. Some feelings involve very similar physical sensations; there's a thin line between fear and excitement, and sadness and depression are often intermingled. But at least you now have a rough idea of how to recognize and distinguish between different feelings. Recognizing and labeling feelings is another whole-brain activity that involves moving between non-verbal attention processes (observing feelings) and verbal intellectual processes (labeling feelings). Try the following activity to start learning how to label your feelings.

ACTIVITY

Labeling feelings

1   **Put words on the experience.** When a feeling arises, acknowledge it. For example, if you notice your stomach muscles tightening. Say to yourself (mentally), "I'm noticing [*emotion*]." If you feel tired or unmotivated, say to yourself, "I'm feeling tired."
2   **Put experiences into words.** Describe to yourself what is happening. Put a name on your feelings, e.g.: "When [*event*] happens, I feel [*emotion*]."
3   Practice expressing your feelings (to close friends and family). The experience of sharing your feelings with others will enable you to test and refine your emotional intelligence skills.
4   Be aware of the distinction between thoughts and feelings. Thoughts happen in your head; feelings happen in your body. A memory is not a feeling, although memories can involve feelings. Thoughts don't generally involve bodily sensations, but feelings do.

The more you pay attention to your feelings without judging them, the more able you will be to recognize and understand them. The more you practice labeling your feelings, the easier it will become. Although we are sometimes taught that worrying about our feelings is self-indulgent, it is in fact a matter of survival. If we don't know how to recognize when we need to rest, avoid a potential threat or ask for help, we will fail to care for ourselves and we will continue to be vulnerable to the various pain-maintaining effects of stress. Understanding feelings requires understanding where they stand in relation to the self versus external events.

When Gemma, the fibromyalgia/chronic fatigue suffer we met in Chapter 3, started to examine the causes of her problems, she realized she had discounted her feelings of anxiety about living and working in a foreign country. But in therapy, Gemma learned that her anxiety was really signaling fears about unmet safety and support needs. Once Gemma understood her feelings, she became more able to respond to her needs for security, including choosing living options that were more within her comfort zone.

Understanding feelings

The final step in reconnecting with your feelings is learning to understand them. Imagine a triangle where A refers to the event, B refers to your emotional reaction, and C refers to your thoughts about the event (including self-related cognitions). As we know from our understanding of brain functioning, our thoughts (C) are influenced by our feelings (B). Contrary to popular belief, although thoughts can cause feelings, most of the time they are simply *reflecting* and *reinforcing* what we already feel. Figure 6.2 illustrates the relationship between events, feelings and thoughts.

Figure 6.2 The ABC model of emotions

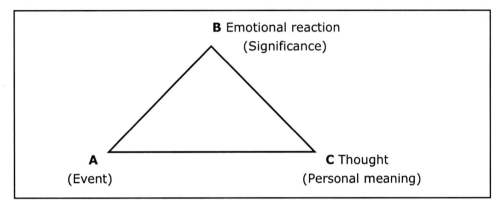

Thoughts are thus a kind of top–down interpretation of feelings. A good way to think about your feelings is to imagine your emotional response as an unopened piece of mail. On the inside you have the content (your feelings), and on the outside you have the address (your thoughts). Different emotions tend to trigger different thoughts. Many people are not conscious of the cognitive meaning of their emotions. Table 6.3 summarizes the sorts of negative thoughts that are often associated with each of the eight primary emotions.

Table 6.3 Emotional bases of unconscious thoughts and attitudes

Emotion	Thought
Anger	"I'm helpless."
Fear/anxiety	"I'm vulnerable."
Sadness	"I'm alone."
Boredom	"I'm useless."
Shame	"I'm bad."
Disgust	"I'm ugly/disgusting."
Excitement	"I'm OK." "I can do it."
Joy/happiness	"I'm lovable." "I'm worthwhile."

If there are situations in your life which make you feel fearful, angry or ashamed, chances are they also involve negative attitudes or beliefs similar to those outlined above. Learning how to interpret negative emotions and bring them into consciousness is an invaluable skill for changing them. Once you know how to interpret your emotions, you will find it easier to know what to do to discharge unhealthy emotions and satisfy physical and emotional survival needs. The following activity integrates everything you've learned in this chapter to understand your feelings.

ACTIVITY

Understanding feelings

Understanding your feelings is the key to using them to reduce physical and emotional pain. This exercise will help you learn some of the skills necessary for understanding your feelings.

1   **Bring to mind** a situation or problem (a physical or emotional pain) which is causing you stress.
2   **Notice** how that problem makes you feel. Notice what physical sensations that problem stimulates in your body. Don't react or judge—just notice.
3   Try to **stay in the moment**.
4   **Label the feelings**. What emotion do those body sensations signify? (If necessary, refer back to Table 6.2 for a summary of the different physical sensations associated with particular emotions.)
5   Going from a sensing mode to a more analytical mode, try to interpret what your feelings signify about your self and your ability to cope.
6   Try to **make an "I-statement"** out of that realization, such as "I feel . . . like a failure/weak/stupid." (If necessary, refer to Table 6.3 and/or Appendix A for some examples of typical "I-statements".)
7   Try to **maintain a neutral, detached observer stance** in relation to your thoughts (don't judge your judging). **Accept your feelings and thoughts** as though they were just neutral pieces of information.
8   Decide on an appropriate course of action.

The Understanding feelings exercise should help you "unpack" any negative self-related thoughts and beliefs incorporated in your emotional responses to your stress and/or pain. Another way to increase your emotional intelligence is to read fiction. Researchers at the University of Toronto found that people who read fiction regularly are more insightful about feelings and more empathic.[9] This is not surprising, as most fiction involves stories about people wrestling with negative emotions to overcome adversity. When we become involved in a story, from *Great Expectations* to the *Harry Potter* series, it stimulates patterns of neural firing in the areas of the brain similar to those that would be activated if we were actually seeing or experiencing the events in the story. Through our emotional engagement with the characters in stories, we acquire emotional experience which we can apply to our own real-life problems. Reading therefore provides a sort of virtual reality where we can explore and learn about how to use our emotions to overcome adversity. Reading fiction may also help compensate for the emotional deficits associated with childhood abuse and neglect.

Summary

Like the Karate Kid who learned how to fight by polishing cars, reconnecting with your emotions requires learning skills that may not seem immediately useful. But mindfulness, labeling and understanding feelings are parts of a larger skill-set which enables you to manage negative emotions and feelings. For example, instead of feeling overwhelmed by feelings of anxiety about a past trauma, you might accept them and give yourself permission to seek professional help. Instead of ignoring feelings of pain or fatigue, you might give yourself permission to rest and finish that important task another day. Emotional connection is also important for relationships and social support, a vital prerequisite for relieving stress and pain. The more connected you are with your feelings, the more able you will be to use them to alleviate negative feelings and sensations. Although a full understanding of the effects of emotional intelligence on brain functioning is not yet possible, understanding and expressing emotions undoubtedly benefits brain functioning through increased coherence between cognitive and emotional aspects of experience, and increased ability to self-regulate. As with any new skill, the more you work at reconnecting with your emotions, the more natural it will feel, and the easier it will be to change.

7

How to change your pain

If my heart could do my thinking, would my brain begin to feel?

Van Morrison

Every pain sufferer wants to feel less pain. Changing your pain requires knowing how to stimulate your brain in ways that change the brain activity that maintains pain. It also involves being able to change the physical and emotional sensations involved in pain. Although we may feel overwhelmed by pain, we all know something about controlling pain—it's part of surviving. We might have learned to keep busy as a way of avoiding pain, or we might have discovered that we could avoid pain by numbing ourselves with drugs. If we are an emotionally integrated person, we might have learned how to soothe the pain by managing its emotional dimension. People who have suffered severe stress before, during or after a physical injury, tend to have poor "pain-management" skills and are less able to regulate painful feelings and sensations. Fortunately, it is possible to learn how to feel differently. In this chapter you will learn how to stimulate your mind and body in ways that will change the brain activity that is maintaining your pain.

Emotions and your brain

As we have seen, pain changes the way your brain processes information. Chronic physical pain causes your brain to react with more anxiety and depression than normal. The more anxious and depressed you feel, the more sensitive to pain you become. Your memories of past pain color your perceptions of present reality, making it difficult to perceive and integrate positive developments. This is not to suggest that pain associated with injury or illness is not real, or that feeling anxious about a life-threatening event is not normal; it is merely that knowing how to change the emotional dimension of these problems can reduce your pain.

Chronic emotional pain also decreases the ability of the different parts of your brain to communicate with each other, particularly the parts of the brain that connect the body with the mind, and thoughts with feelings. The result is concentration and memory problems, unhealthy choices, indecisiveness, impulsivity and uncontrollable pain. Over time, your brain's ability to maintain homeostasis is decreased due to stress-induced structural, chemical and functional changes. The ability to generate pleasurable emotions is lost; it becomes harder and harder to feel happiness and joy, vital emotional antidotes to pain. As a result of unregulated negative feelings, negative thinking arises, which unfortunately reinforces feelings of hopelessness and helplessness.

How can you break out of this spiral? One way is to learn how to change the brain activity that is maintaining your pain. As described in Chapter 4, scientists are experimenting with fMRI machines to help chronic pain sufferers learn to change brain activity associated with pain by observing brain activity associated with pain on a computer screen and learning to manipulate the visual image of their pain. One of the most helpful aspects of this treatment is that the patient is able to really see their pain, and see it changing. Even traditional bio-feedback, which is based on tracing physiological reactions, does not offer this quality of feedback. But unless you have access to an fMRI machine, this technique is a little expensive. Fortunately, there are other ways of employing the strategies inherent in this approach, without the need for an FMRI. The first thing is that you have to be able to connect with your pain. Yes, as strange as it sounds, you have to be able to feel your pain before you can not feel it. Once you can feel your pain, you can develop a mental representation of it, say as a cloud, or a red ball, or anything else you can remember that felt a bit like your pain. Of course, your pain isn't really a cloud or a red ball, but if you can remember seeing those things, and how you felt when you saw those things, then for a moment your pain might just as easily be a cloud or a red ball. Once you can "see" your pain, you can manipulate it. Clouds can be blown away; red balls can be deflated.

The second aspect of controlling pain involves being able to connect with the sensory-emotional dimens ion of pain and having an experience that stimulates different feelings to those associated with the pain. Emotional regulation involves two sets of skills. Managing negative emotions associated with pain involves more than just overcoming negative feelings; you also have to be able to generate positive feelings.[1] It is common to talk of feeling moved by something we have seen or experienced. The idea that you can use your emotions to change how you feel is reflected in the Latin origin of the word—*ex movere*, which literally means "to move". Chronic pain sufferers who learn emotional regulation skills are found to be more able to control the intensity of their pain.[2] Rheumatoid arthritis sufferers who practice emotional regulation strategies are more able to regulate the intensity of their pain. PTSD sufferers who learn how to regulate their anxiety cope better. Although emotions can be controlled in a purely top–down way, e.g. by overriding your feelings, a better approach is to create an experience that changes how you feel.

There are many, many ways of changing the sensory-emotional reactions that maintain pain. Three of the most well-known strategies are relaxation, meditation and self-hypnosis. Relaxation, meditation and self-hypnosis all involve learning how to concentrate your mind in ways that stimulate feelings of calmness and peace. The key to these methods is their use of attention. Attention is where your mind meets with the world. Attention channels information into energy. Attention can be controlled by external stimuli, such as loud noises, or internal processes such as deliberately focusing on a particular stimulus. This is how attention is used in hypnosis, where the mind is directed toward a particular goal such as feeling confident or less pain. Attention can also be detached from external reality, as when we focus on our awareness without attending to anything in particular. Enhancing this receptive awareness in the present moment is sometimes called "mindful awareness". This type of attention tends to be associated with meditation. Relaxation, meditation and self-hypnosis also stimulate changes in physiological arousal associated with pain.

Another strategy involves simultaneously concentrating on your pain and bilateral stimulation. As explained earlier, dual attention stimulus (DAS) is a treatment element of EMDR. DAS works a little differently to relaxation, meditation and hypnosis. DAS combines mindful awareness with soothing bilateral stimulation. The result is a cessation of mental activity (because your attention is on the bilateral stimulation) and a reduction in physical and emotional distress (because of the impact of the bilateral stimulation on your nervous system).

> June sought help from an EMDR-trained psychologist to cope with chronic low back pain. June's pain was coming from a ruptured disk and involved a significant degree of physical pathology; however, after three years, June's pain had also come to involve a great deal of stress, anxiety and depression. June noticed that her pain was worse when she felt stressed or depressed. June felt that if she could learn to control the emotional distress caused by her pain, it might help relieve her pain. In EMDR, June learned how to lower her pain by focusing on it in a detached way, while simultaneously focusing on a bilateral stimulation.
>
> The EMDR therapist began by asking June to describe her pain. At first June didn't understand what he meant; her pain was in her body and it hurt—what else was there to say? The therapist explained to June that even though her pain was physical, it was also in her brain to some degree, and that she needed to pay attention to her pain in terms of its separate sensory-emotional elements. Did the pain feel hot

or cold? How big was it? June had never thought about her pain like this before, but she put aside her preconceptions and just kind of focused her attention on the hurt. June noticed a hot sensation, and that her pain felt hard. It seemed to have a round shape. In her mind she saw the pain as a big red ball.

The therapist then instructed June to hold her attention on the pain in terms of how she'd just described it, while simultaneously attending to bilateral auditory tones, and to notice what happened next. Click . . . click . . . click . . . click. As soon as she started listening to the tones, June couldn't hold the image of the pain in her mind anymore and her mind went blank. After about 30 seconds of this, the therapist discontinued the tones and instructed June to "take a break" and notice what she saw and felt now. June noticed that the pain felt different, smaller and less hot. The image too seemed like it had faded. "Good work," said her therapist. "Just notice that now." Click . . . click . . . click . . . click for another 30 seconds. June's therapist again instructed her to "take a break" and bring her attention back to the pain again. This time the pain felt even smaller, like a 5 cent piece. After a couple more "sets" of bilateral stimulation during which June's pain stopped changing, the therapist asked her to think of a word or phrase that summarized how she felt about what she'd experienced. "Control," June said. "I can control my pain." "Great," said June's therapist. "Just think of that, and your pain the way it feels now, and see what comes next." Click . . . click . . . click . . . click . . . . "Take a break," said June's therapist, "and when you're ready, tell me what you noticed that time." With a smile, June replied, "I don't know how it's possible, but it actually feels true." The session finished with June being instructed to practice thinking of her healing imagery and her positive thought, while listening to a CD of bilateral auditory tones.

Because of the bilateral stimulation element, DAS seems to offer a more direct way of stimulating physiological changes than relaxation, meditation and self-hypnosis. It's also easier to pay attention to an externally generated stimulus than to try to empty your mind and concentrate on your breathing. The practice of mentally reviewing one's attitudes and beliefs in the light of the changes stimulated by DAS helps integrate the changes into new learning.

DAS was "discovered" by Dr Francine Shapiro as she walking in a park one day, feeling distressed about a cancer diagnosis. Suddenly the negative feelings she was experiencing disappeared. Shapiro was curious and reviewed what happened in the seconds leading up to her feelings of relief. She recalled that she had experienced spontaneous saccadic eye-movements. (Saccadic eye-movements are involuntary twitching of the eye muscles which normally occur during REM sleep.) It was after these eye-movements that Shapiro's feelings of distress had evaporated. When she tried to recall the distressing memory of the cancer diagnosis, it no longer felt so painful. Shapiro realized that her spontaneous eye-movements had somehow caused a change in how she was feeling. She started experimenting with friends, and they all reported experiencing a similar reduction in distress when asked to think of something upsetting while attending to her bilateral hand-movements. It's since been discovered that the bilateral stimulation can consist of visual, auditory or tactile stimuli. Shapiro formalized the process into a treatment called eye movement desensitization and reprocessing (EMDR) and tested it on traumatized Vietnam veterans, again with positive results. Some veterans even reported feeling better after a single 90-minute session, an unheard-of result for this kind of problem.[3]

Four strategies for changing pain

Relaxation, meditation and self-hypnosis all involve some combination of focused attention and receptiveness to new experience. But it's also useful to understand the differences between these methods. Meditation expressly attempts to de-activate the thinking process, whereas relaxation may involve thought, such as focusing on an imaginary safe place. Relaxation generally occurs as a result of meditation, and the type of relaxation that occurs during meditation can be deep and transformative. Jon Kabat-Zinn, a leading proponent of meditation, tells the story of a woman with multiple health problems (inoperable heart problems, high blood pressure, arthritis, lupus, insomnia, etc.) who lowered her blood pressure by learning meditation. As a result of learning to meditate, the woman also remembered a previously repressed incident of childhood sexual abuse, which she was then able to resolve. Consequently, the woman not only felt more able to cope, she also felt happier and more at peace with herself. Kabat-Zinn feels that increased emotional connectedness is one of the main benefits of meditation.[4] Relaxation and meditation are core elements of many pain and stress-management programs, and have been found to reduce both physical and emotional pain.[5]

Meditation seems to have a positive effect on brain structure and functioning. Meditation is known to boost brain activity, coherency of brain waves, neural connections, and gray matter. Researchers have also discovered that meditation boosts thickness of brain structure dealing with attention, sensory input, and memory functions.[6] The thickening was found to be more noticeable in adults than younger individuals. The section of our cortex that is thickened by meditation is a part of the cortex that tends to get thinner as we age, indicating that meditation may also ward off the effects of ageing. The scientific study of meditation is another area of cutting-edge research in neuroscience. Although modern neuroscientists have only recently discovered meditation, it is one of the oldest techniques for changing pain. The ancient Greeks believed that meditation could alleviate suffering through learning how to detach from negative feelings. There is a long history of the use of meditation in contemplative prayer as a means of alleviating suffering.

Meditation is thought to work because of the way it makes use of attention. As mentioned, meditation employs executive attention, a flexible form of awareness which enables us to focus our attention in ways that are not controlled by external events. Mindful awareness is defined as paying attention, in the present moment, without judgment. When we learn to focus our attention in a controlled way, we harness the power of neuroplasticity to create new synaptic connections. As neuropsychologist Daniel Siegal puts it, "Where attention goes, neural firing occurs, and where neural firing occurs, new connections can be made."[7] Because meditation involves focusing on events in a non-stressful way, it stimulates new neural connections and new emotional responses.

Hypnosis involves using focused attention to induce a state of relaxation and altered consciousness, also known as trance. Being in trance means being so absorbed in what you are experiencing that you don't notice anything else. When a person is in trance, their mind is more receptive to new information and ideas, including suggestions about how to cope better with their problems. Although the term can conjure up images of hapless people doing ridiculous things on stage, hypnosis is not mind-control and it is not an abnormal or artificial mental state. We have all experienced "highway hypnosis" where we got lost in our thoughts and lost track of where we were. Other naturally occurring hypnotic phenomena include relaxing after experiencing natural sights and sounds such as watching a river, or waves lapping on a beach, or grass waving in the wind. If setting out to experience hypnosis for a specific purpose, you should couple the trance state with suggestions to help you cope with whatever problem you want to work on. The suggestions can be direct ("I will feel better") or indirect ("I wonder what could make me feel better?"). You might imagine a beam of healing light spreading through your body. Or you might get an image of something that you have previously experienced, which triggers feelings of relief. Your conscious mind knows that nothing is really happening, but your unconscious mind, which controls your bodily processes, doesn't care—its reality is inside you.

Hypnosis has been used to control pain for more than 100 years and it was one of the primary means of managing pain until the discovery of ether in the mid-nineteenth century. Documented cases of the use of hypnosis in medical procedures include amputations, removal of tumors, tooth extractions and recurring headaches. Despite the development of ever more effective pain-killers, hypnosis still has an important role in the management of conditions such as chronic pain, where traditional medical methods tend to be ineffective. Milton Erickson, one of the most famous clinical hypnotherapists of the 20th century, used self-hypnosis for most of his life to control chronic pain associated with his post-polio syndrome. Erickson would simply ask his unconscious if it could take his pain away. Because Erickson really believed in hypnosis and the power of the unconscious, and because he was able to focus his attention in this way, he could free himself from the pain of his post-polio syndrome. Relaxation, meditation and self-hypnosis harness both top–down and bottom–up elements of information processing, including focused attention, detached awareness, cessation of normal physical and mental processes, and memory effects.

Dual Attention Stimulus (DAS) involves a combination of attentional processes, bilateral stimulation and cognitive monitoring. Bilateral stimulation has been found to stimulate physiological changes consistent with relaxation, including decreased respiration rate, decreased systolic blood pressure and a decrease in galvanic skin response.[8] Brain scans of PTSD sufferers who have experienced dual attention stimulus suggest that this process actually changes physical and neurological activity associated with the painful memories.[9,10] There is no specific research regarding the effects of bilateral stimulation (Bls) on the brain, but it does appear essential to producing treatment effects of EMDR, which appear to include changes in brain activity associated with severe stress, namely:

- increased bilateral activity in the anterior cingulate cortex
- increased activity in the left prefrontal cortex (the left prefrontal cortex regulates the amygdala)
- more normal brain wave activity between the left and right hemispheres of the brain.[10,11]

The mechanisms by which Bls changes brain activity are yet to be fully understood. Some experts believe that Bls works by promoting a sense of detachment from the problem, similar to that produced by meditation. Of course, unlike meditation, Bls involves paying attention to an external stimulus, which seems to have a soothing effect. Others believe that Bls works by activating the orienting reflex. The orienting reflex (OR) is an innate response to new or novel stimuli from the environment (exogenous attention). But with its use of sustained, flexible attention, Bls also appears to involve endogenous and executive attention. The OR is thought to have an evolutionary basis in that it seems to facilitate scanning for danger. If danger is detected, the OR is triggered, stimulating an increase in physiological arousal. But if no danger is detected, as with Bls, the OR is followed by a decrease in physiological arousal. This would facilitate the processing of physical and emotional pain. Bilateral stimulation probably arouses the OR because:

1 It's different to the pain.
2 It's unusual.

Perhaps the easiest way to understand Bls is to think of it as a kind of positive bio-feedback loop wherein the bilateral stimulates feelings of relaxation, which get noticed and integrated mentally.

Regardless of the mechanisms underlying Bls, the power of naturally occurring rhythmical stimuli to stimulate relaxation is well known. Just think of how listening to rainfall, gentle surf and running water makes you feel. Researchers have found that listening to a recording of ocean sounds can reduce systolic blood pressure significantly, more so than listening to Mozart. Some man-made stimuli can also have the same effect, including visual, auditory and kinesthetic. Many people find the motion associated with train travel soothing. The most popular room on the *QE2* is a small viewing chamber set low on the stern where it's possible to observe the wash of the propellers. Passengers reportedly sit there for hours, mesmerized by nothing more than the sight of the ship's wake ebbing into the distance.

To benefit from meditation, hypnosis or Bls, you must be able to concentrate. If you have suffered severe stress or trauma, the chances are that your ability to pay attention has been impaired. This is a normal side-effect of stress and can be overcome. The solution is to simply practice paying attention to a stimulus such as your breathing, a mantra or a spot on the wall. Don't get frustrated with yourself if you find your mind wandering. When you notice that your mind has strayed from focusing on your chosen stimuli, just notice that and gently bring your mind back to awareness. If you do get frustrated by a wandering mind, just notice and accept that. Tell yourself it's only a feeling; it's okay to be distracted. Be patient with yourself— with practice you will find it easier to concentrate for longer and longer periods of time, which will facilitate the development of those new neural connections.

Below are instructions and exercises about how to use meditation, relaxation, hypnosis and Bls for the alleviation of physical and mental pain. Read through the information about the various methods and decide which one feels most appropriate for you. Each method is accompanied by an exercise to help you learn that particular strategy. For the Bls exercises, you will need the CD that comes with this book.

Relaxation/meditation

The core elements of relaxation and meditation are mindfulness, staying in the present, and having a non-judgmental attitude. Each element helps alleviate stress in a different way. For example, accepting things as they are—even negative things—makes them less distressing. Meditation involves accepting things as they are, thereby removing the layers of judgment, expectation and emotional distress that so often exacerbate stress and pain.

> Favio suffered from sleeping problems and fatigue associated with his chronic low back pain. Before learning meditation, Favio would react negatively to his fatigue with feelings of frustration and thoughts like, "I can't cope." This reaction only increased his feelings of distress. But after learning to meditate, Favio became more accepting of his pain and sleeping problems. Instead of getting anxious about not being able to fall asleep, he just found things to do to keep himself busy until he felt ready to fall asleep. This approach made Favio's sleeping problems much less stressful.

There are two basic types of meditation for people with health problems. One type, known as focused attention meditation (FA), involves focusing on a chosen stimulus such as your breathing, a mantra, a candle, etc. If you find your mind wandering, you simply notice that and then return your attention to the chosen stimulus. This approach helps develop attention by allowing distractions without losing focus on the chosen stimulus. FA also stimulates mental flexibility and detachment through learning to shift your attention back to the chosen stimulus and not getting upset when you notice yourself getting distracted. Open monitoring (OM) meditation involves paying attention moment by moment to anything that occurs in your experience without judging or getting stuck on any particular thing. OM stimulates increased awareness and acceptance, and thereby increased ability to change. All meditation aims to achieve stillness of the mind, where the mind can rest from everyday thoughts and distractions. By decreasing mental anxiety, you can stimulate a decrease in stressful feelings and pain. Relaxation is different to meditation. Relaxation can be achieved by taking a hot bath or sitting under a tree listening to the birds. Relaxation tends to be a by-product of meditation. Formal relaxation practices range from progressive muscle relaxation (progressively tensing and relaxing all the muscle groups in your body) to guided visualizations and breath-awareness exercises. Guided visualization involves visualizing healing symbols and images. For example, you might imagine a pure white light flowing through your body, restoring and healing as it flows. Or you might imagine being in a healing place such as a mountain retreat or even just your garden. When you summon mental imagery that is meaningful to you, it triggers positive emotional associations that counteract stress and pain. Relaxation and meditation are not hard to learn: all you have to do is set aside some time, allow your mind to be still, and focus on a soothing stimulus such as your breathing or a peaceful place that's vivid in your memory.

> Brad suffered recurring headaches ever since returning from combat service in Iraq. One of the most traumatic aspects of his time there had been the feeling of loss of control over his environment. Brad had grown up in a rural setting where survival depended upon being able to overcome harsh realities – he had never felt as vulnerable as he did patrolling the streets of Baghdad. Since returning from Iraq, whenever he felt out of control Brad would get a headache. His headaches could be triggered by an argument with his teenage son, or a tradesman not turning up on time . . . anything. Even strong pain-killers had little effect. Brad's idea of relaxation was a cold beer and a cigarette at sundown. So when Brad's therapist suggested learning how to relax might help, Brad was skeptical. However, nothing else had worked so he agreed to give it a try. Brad was surprised to notice that within a few minutes of focusing on his breathing, and not thinking, he started to feel different. At first he felt the changes in his body, but then the knot behind his forehead seemed to soften ever so gradually, and the intensity of the pain lessened. Relaxation taught Brad that there were other ways to cope with situations that you can't control.

Try the following exercise. Read the instructions slowly, one line at a time, and let the meaning of the words sink in so that you can feel your nervous system reacting to the suggestions.

ACTIVITY

Basic relaxation/meditation script

1 Assume a comfortable position.
2 Begin by attending to whatever physical sensations you notice in your body.
3 Try to "just notice" whatever is happening in your body in a detached way without thinking about it or analyzing it too much.
4 **Just notice** whatever you're feeling . . .
5 Avoid analyzing, thinking or problem-solving. If you catch yourself doing this, bring your attention back to just noticing whatever is going on.
6 Notice your breathing—the gradual rise and fall of your chest with each breath.
   Notice how your chest expands with each in-breath and deflates with each out-breath. You may notice that there is a slight feeling of tension with each in-breath, and a feeling of relief with each out-breath.
7 As you focus on your breathing, you might like to think about how **natural** breathing is, how **connected** breathing makes you feel with your body and the rhythm of life. You might also enjoy the realization that breathing happens **automatically**, without your having to make any special effort.
8 As you continue to focus on your breathing, you may also notice the rate of your breathing slowing down, as your mind becomes more detached from your everyday consciousness.
9 If any other thoughts or feelings intrude into your awareness of yourself, just notice them and let them go by.
10 Notice if anything changes about how you are feeling, including your awareness of what you are feeling. If nothing seems different, that's fine too.
11 Just keep breathing and keep noticing. Whatever you feel or notice, just observe it and let it go.
12 Continue doing this for 15 to 20 minutes.
13 At the end of that time, give yourself a few moments to gradually reorient yourself.
14 If you have been able to maintain your attention on your breath reasonably consistently, you should notice mild feelings of detachment and lightness (some people notice other sensations, such as tingling or numbness). Whether you do or not, regular practice of this technique will help you learn how to experience your pain differently, in ways you might never have imagined.

Notice any differences in how you experience yourself after this exercise. You may notice feelings of calmness or detachment. You may have a feeling that things have slowed down, which is a sign that you have slowed down. With practice, you can become more mindful, more detached and more relaxed in your approach to everyday living. This will reduce your underlying levels of stress and tension, and your vulnerability to stress and pain. If you do nothing else but practice this simple meditative relaxation exercise every day for a month, you will almost certainly experience increased feelings of calmness and a reduction in your overall levels of pain and stress.

If you are unaccustomed to being with your self this way, meditation can take a little getting used to. Like a child learning how to swim, you need to enter the waters of awareness slowly and patiently. An insightful and amusing account of one woman's struggle to learn meditation can be found in Elizabeth Gilbert's best-selling *Eat, Pray, Love* (Bloomsbury, 2007). Remember, the benefits of relaxation and meditation cannot come from conscious effort or deliberate intention. In the unlikely event that meditation causes you distress, don't dismiss it; talk to a friend or seek professional help.

Self-hypnosis

Hypnosis can be thought of as an extension of relaxation and meditation. While the aim of relaxation is to achieve a state of calmness, hypnosis goes one step further and introduces information or suggestions designed to alleviate the problem we are seeking relief from. Hypnosis is an altered state of consciousness which many people are able to access spontaneously, without special instruction; however, harnessing the power of hypnosis to overcome pain is another matter. Below, you will find some information about how to practice self-hypnosis. This information may or may not be sufficient for you to learn how to use hypnosis for your problems. If not, there are many other options: you can always purchase a pre-recorded CD or consult with a trained professional. Without professional guidance, self-hypnosis is not recommended for persons suffering from psychiatric conditions such as psychosis or dissociative identity disorder.

Using hypnosis to control pain means letting your unconscious go to work; it's not about sitting there telling the pain to go away, or trying to make anything in particular happen. It's about focusing on something that arouses different sensations, feelings and thoughts to those associated with your pain, and letting yourself respond to those feelings. A very simple approach might be to sit in a comfortable chair in your favorite place, acknowledging your surroundings and any discomfort you may be feeling, and then letting whatever happens happen. If your attention is drawn to the pain, you can notice that . . . just noticing your pain without judging it . . . and as you're noticing your pain, you might notice something else . . . something you hadn't noticed before . . . which reminds you of something you've experienced elsewhere, something that resembles how your pain feels, and yet is slightly different; and as you think about that, you might notice that your experience of your pain *can* change, as you learn to think differently about it. Just let whatever happens happen, have an open mind and be curious about what you *can* experience. Let your mind wander; like a stray horse it will eventually find its way home.

> When Bill practiced attending to his pain in a non-judgmental way, he became aware of a burning quality that he had not noticed before. As he maintained his attention on that, he got a mental image of a hot coal. Although this was very unpleasant to imagine, he just accepted it. After a while he noticed that the pain seemed to subside a little bit; that burning coal did what all hot coals eventually do; it started to burn out.

Try the following self-hypnosis exercise.

ACTIVITY

A basic trance induction

1   Assume a comfortable position.
2   Allow your eyes to wander around your surroundings until they come to rest on a particular spot. It should be a spot that your eyes feel "drawn to". This may take a few minutes, but eventually your eyes can come to rest on a particular spot or detail of your surroundings. It should be a distinct, definable spot. For example, if it is a painting, you should be concentrating on a particular feature of the painting, rather than the whole painting.
3   Check again that your body is in as comfortable a position as possible physically.
4   Maintain your attention on that spot. Monitor your attention and keep bringing it back to that spot if it drifts off.
5   As you continue focusing on that spot, you might notice that everything else around that spot has become blurry. This is normal, and you should try to keep your attention fixated on that spot.
6   You might notice the spot becoming blurry after a while. Again, just keep noticing. You might notice your eyelids start to feel heavy and want to close, but try to keep them open . . . and the more you try to keep them open, the more they want to close. You might notice your eyes start blinking; just notice that too. Whatever happens as you are focusing on that spot, just keep noticing.

ACTIVITY

7   At some point your eyes may want to close. That's fine.

8   Whether your eyes remain open or closed, you should notice your attention being drawn inwards toward your body. You might then notice some changes in how you feel: your breathing will almost certainly slow down, and your body might start to feel heavy.

9   Since you are feeling more relaxed, you might as well enjoy that feeling of relaxation and allow it to deepen. You could help deepen it by slowly counting backwards from 20, breath by breath, imagining yourself going deeper into trance with each number.

10   When you get to 1, you can remain where you are and enjoy whatever you are experiencing.

11   Let your awareness of whatever you are feeling guide your experience. If you notice your body feeling rigid and straight, you might get an image of something that represents strength and support, such as a bridge. Imagine if your body was a bridge . . . Or you might notice your body feels light and airy, like it was a cloud. Imagine if your body was a cloud . . . Whatever you notice, you can let it stimulate your imagination.

12   Don't try too hard to make anything happen; just focus on what you are feeling and then let whatever happens happen.

13   Just let your body guide you as to how long you want to enjoy that moment. Take as much time as you want—you'll know when it is time to return to normal consciousness.

14   When you are ready, you can return to normal wakeful consciousness.

15   Even if you've only spent a few minutes in trance, you will almost certainly notice a variety of physical and emotional changes, including a feeling of calmness, a feeling of heaviness or lightness, and a narrowing of your attention.

16   Imagine that you can keep those feelings with you for the rest of the day.

17   The more often you practice this exercise, the more you will learn about the capacity of your mind to change how you feel.*

* Adapted from *Ericksonian Approaches*, Rubin Battino & Thomas L. South (1999). Crown House. pp. 201–202. With permission.

When you begin to practice hypnosis, you may wonder how to tell whether or not you are really in trance. Being in trance generally involves a feeling of detachment from your everyday surroundings, sensations of lightness or heaviness, and an altered sense of time (it seems to pass more slowly). Being in trance means feeling totally absorbed in that experience, to the exclusion of all else. There are also different levels of trance, but even a light trance can still result in increased feelings of relaxation and comfort.

Remember, relaxation, meditation or self-hypnosis should always begin by getting yourself into a comfortable, quiet position, free of distractions or interruptions. Just making this space and time for yourself is one of the most important elements of these techniques. You must be able to quiet your mind and dis-attend to your normal preoccupations. Relaxation, meditation and self-hypnosis are also best practiced on an empty stomach. Although the goal of practicing these techniques is obviously to feel and cope better, you cannot force yourself to feel these things; you just have to practice the skills and let it happen. Like any learned skill, the more you practice, the easier it will come. Some experts feel that these techniques need to be practiced for at least six months before significant benefits can occur.

Dual attention stimulus

Dual attention stimulus (DAS) is another way of stimulating your nervous system to reduce physical and emotional pain. DAS involves focused attention, bilateral stimulation and cognitive monitoring. The first element of DAS is being able to focus on the problem in a felt sense (e.g. bodily sensations associated with physical or emotional pain). This means being able to notice how the problem makes you feel in your body—not what you remember or think, but what you physically feel in the now. Following this, you focus on the bilateral stimulation for 30 to 60 seconds. Once you start attending to the bilateral stimulation, you do not have to make any effort to try to make anything happen; just pay attention to the bilateral stimulation and how you feel in your body, and let whatever happens happen. After 30 to 60 seconds, bring your attention back to your body. In a neutral, detached way, observe the pain and notice whether it feels any different. Pay particular attention to the bodily sensations associated with the pain. Don't confuse a memory or an expectation with the present felt sense of the pain. Don't *try* to make the pain change; it will either happen or it won't happen. The more able you are to attend to the bilateral stimulation mindfully, the more likely it is that change will happen.

There is nothing special or strange about the idea that focusing on a bilateral stimulation can stimulate changes in your nervous system—any sensory experience does that. The difference with DAS is its bilateral nature, the effects of that on the brain, and the fact that you experience those effects while simultaneously concentrating on your pain. In order to benefit from DAS you must be able to focus on your pain both in terms of how you feel it in your body and how you perceive it mentally. DAS involves the following elements:

1   Being able to "see" the problem in your mind, based on how it feels, without judging it (mindful awareness).
2   Being able to hold the problem in your mind while concentrating on the bilateral stimulation while simultaneously focusing on the problem as you see and feel it.
3   Maintaining a non-judgmental attitude while attending to the Bls: "Let whatever happens happen." You don't have to DO anything!
4   Being able to notice any differences in how you feel in your body following the Bls.
5   Integrating those changes into your self-concept.

The bilateral stimuli in DAS can take the form of visual, auditory or tactile stimuli. In EMDR the therapist generates the bilateral stimuli through hand movements, clicking their fingers, or tapping. Outside of EMDR, the safest and easiest way to re-create bilateral stimuli is through listening to pre-recorded bilateral auditory tones.

The CD at the back of this book contains four recordings of guided bilateral stimulation exercises, which you can use to soothe physical and emotional pain. The first track is designed to stimulate pain relief. The second track is designed to help you discover your own personal healing resources, based on the changes generated by bilateral stimulation. The third track blends bilateral stimulation with soothing music to provide a healing emotional journey which will take you from pain to pleasure, or at least relief. The fourth track is just bilateral tones, which you can use in conjunction with the activities on the following pages and/or as an aid to relaxation. Remember when you are listening to the bilateral stimulation that you can control how much or how little attention you want to pay to it, depending on what feels right for you. If you are feeling a lot of pain, you might want to pay a lot of attention to the bilateral stimulation to take your mind off the pain. But if you are not feeling too bad, you might only need to attend to the bilateral stimulation as a secondary, background stimulus. There is no "supposed-to"—just listen to the bilateral stimulation and let whatever happens happen. Because of the unique qualities and intent of this CD, you may need to adjust the volume on your audio equipment when listening to the recordings.

If you have a dissociative disorder or epilepsy, you should proceed with caution as the Bls can trigger physiological changes associated with these states. If in doubt, you should consult an EMDR-trained therapist who specializes in the treatment of these disorders (see Appendix D). You can also use physical tapping as a form of Bls. If you prefer this sensory modality, all you need to do is to tap chosen areas of your body in a rhythmic, alternating pattern. Popular areas are knees, shoulders and elbows. So instead of listening to bilateral tones, you concentrate on the tapping, while simultaneously focusing on your pain. Most people find it easier to benefit from Bls that is externally generated for the simple reason that it's one less thing to have to think about; however, if you would like to learn more about tapping, a good resource is Laurel Parnell's book *Tapping In: A Step-by-step Guide to Activating Your Healing Resources Through Bilateral Stimulation*. Although Bls is a central element of EMDR, it is not a substitute for EMDR and its use here represents a sub-component of this multifaceted treatment approach.

To introduce you to the idea of using Bls to stimulate relief from physical and emotional pain, try the following exercise. Use Track 4 of the CD for the bilateral stimulation element of your DAS.

ACTIVITY

Controlling pain with DAS

1 Find a quiet place where you can sit or lie for a few minutes without being disturbed. Close your eyes. Tune in to yourself.

2 Think of a physical or emotional pain you'd like relief from. This is a *mental* activity.

3 Once you have identified the problem you want to work on, notice how and where you feel that situation in your body.

4 Notice whatever physical sensations you feel in your body that go with that problem. This is a *physical* activity.

5 Now, back to your mind. Once you have identified the physical sensations that go with the problem, see if there is an image or memory that goes with those feelings. What do the feelings feel like? What do they remind you of?

6 Think of a word or brief phrase that summarizes the situation. For example, if you're seeking relief from low back pain, it could be "back pain". If you're seeking relief from emotional distress following an argument with your partner, it could be "argument".

7 Holding the image, feelings and thought in your mind, concentrate on a DAS in the form of bilateral tapping or audio tones. In this activity you go from focusing on the mental to focusing on the physical.

8 Do this for 30 to 60 seconds. Maintain an open mind, and just let whatever happens happen.

9 Take a break from the DAS, bring your attention back to your body, and notice any changes in how you feel physically.

10 Hold your attention on whatever you noticed, even if it's "nothing", and do another round of DAS as above.

11 Repeat steps 9 and 10 until you feel completely free of pain, or no further change occurs.

Note: This activity is not recommended for individual use with severe or multiple trauma.

Remember, the aim of this exercise is not to *try to make* yourself feel differently, but to create the conditions where calmness and relief can occur naturally. Creating an effective dual attention stimulus requires planning and the right combination of detached awareness and bilateral stimulation. It's also important to adopt an open mind and pay attention to how you feel after exercises like this. Let the bilateral stimulation enter your brain freely, without judgment. If you judge the bilateral stimulation, perhaps as an irritating thing, your nervous system won't respond in a beneficial way. Pay attention to how you are feeling in your body. Look out for changes, no matter how small or seemingly insignificant. When you can notice a change in how you feel, you have taken the first step toward learning how to change the negative feelings that maintain stress and pain. All you have to do then is to allow that feeling to continue, and keep building on this ability. If you find it too hard to concentrate on the steps of this process, listen to Track 1 of the CD, where you will find verbal instructions and bilateral stimulation to guide your Bls experience.

Building resources with bilateral stimulation

The most effective self-help strategies involve developing or discovering your own inner resources. A resource is any skill or ability that enables you to cope with pain. A resource can be based on memory, or it can be something you imagine. Generally, for a resource to be effective it should involve positive emotion. For example, you might imagine a healing light or an anesthetic mist as a means of alleviating your pain; however, these images would not necessarily have much effect unless they also trigger strong positive emotions in you. Maybe you have had previous experience of healing lights at meditation classes, or you can remember the pleasant feeling of going under with anesthetic. Or you might remember an experience of feeling pain fading away, which almost everyone has had at some time. You might attach a visual image to that feeling, maybe seeing the pain as a shrinking red ball or a fading color. Voila! You have created antidote imagery.

Stress, trauma and pain can make you feel resourceless. When this happens, you need some means of reconnecting with your resources. Resources are often located in the unconscious mind, where memories, connections and pre-verbal skills reside. While your conscious mind can think of logical strategies, they are often just that: logical-sounding strategies that lack any emotional power. But when your unconscious mind connects with an idea or memory, it is more likely to be backed up with previous embodied knowledge and experience. This gives it much greater power to influence how you are feeling in the present.

A good way of reconnecting with your resources is to invite your unconscious mind to give you a solution to the problem and see what emerges. This involves learning how to access that creative right hemisphere of yours. It is what Milton

Erickson used to do when he needed to overcome his post-polio pain. Unless you were brought up in a closet, there will be memories, experiences and learning which can be brought to bear on the present problem. One difficulty that many people have is getting the conscious mind to be quiet long enough for the unconscious mind to do its work. Meditation and mindfulness can help develop concentration and the suspension of conscious thought necessary for accessing inner resources. Hypnosis is another method,

Yet another method is reinterpretation of sensory changes stimulated by Bls. For example, when June analysed the changes in how she felt after Bls, she noticed how much smaller her pain felt, and she got an image of her pain as a 5 cent piece. After this she started to believe that she could control her pain. Try the following exercise to create your own pain antidote imagery. Again, use Track 4 of the CD for the bilateral stimulation element. If you find it too difficult to work this way, listen to Track 2 of the CD, which contains guided instructions for relieving pain and building a resource.

ACTIVITY

Resource installation with DAS

1 Find a quiet place where you can sit or lie for a few minutes without being disturbed. Close your eyes. Tune in to yourself.
2 Remember the problem you worked on earlier, and the thoughts, feelings and images that went with it.
3 Think of something that could take it away or make it better, but don't do this consciously; just have that idea in your mind.
4 Holding your mind on that thought, commence DAS.
5 After 30 to 60 seconds, take a break. Notice any differences in how you feel in your body.
6 See if there is an image or memory that goes with those new feelings. What do those feelings feel like? What do they remind you of? For example, if you notice a feeling of softness where before there was hardness, you might get an image of a sponge. If you get a feeling of coolness where before there was heat, you might get an image of a cold compress.
7 If you can, think of a word or brief phrase that summarizes that image. For example, if you got softness while seeking relief from low back pain, it could be "comfort". If you got a reduction in tension while seeking relief from emotional distress associated with an argument with your partner, it could be "peace".
8 Holding the image, feelings and thought in your mind, resume DAS for another 30 to 60 seconds and focus on that.

ACTIVITY

9 Take a break and notice again what and how you feel in your body. The image and the feelings associated with it should have strengthened.

10 Repeat steps 8 and 9 until the antidote imagery feels strong inside you, or no further change occurs.

11 As you go about your daily life, remember what you discovered and how it made you feel.

With practice, the above exercise should help you learn how to create pain-relieving imagery which you can use to combat future episodes of pain. It's not uncommon for antidote imagery to change and evolve, so keep an open mind and "let whatever happens happen". Repeated practice of the above two exercises will increase your ability to generate different sensations to those associated with pain and, eventually, less painful feelings. You can use the written instructions and Track 4, or you can listen to Tracks 1 and 2; whatever is easiest for you is just fine. You can also use Track 4 as a distraction and a relaxation aid. Just focusing on a bilateral stimulus when you have pain can close the gate on your pain. Focusing on a bilateral stimulus can also help alleviate anxiety and stress.

Music is well known for its capacity to evoke emotion and memories. The third track on the CD incorporates bilateral stimulation and music. "Clare de Lune" is a very beautiful piece of classical music which evokes emotions of drama (the first movement) followed by resolution (the second movement). The combination of this music and bilateral stimulation is designed to evoke a healing emotional journey which may or may not be accompanied by conscious thought. You can play this track as an aid to emotional processing without needing to get too caught up in the content of the problem. For example, before listening to this track, think of some situation or feeling that is troubling you; hold that problem in your conscious mind or at the back of your mind, listen to the clicking, and let your attention move between your thoughts and feelings. Enjoy the music. Just let your mind wander freely between the bilateral stimulation and the music, and your thoughts and feelings. Let your mind be stimulated by the sounds in whatever way it wants to be. Then notice how you feel afterwards. Where is the problem now? Do you notice anything different about how it feels? This track is also good to play at night if you have trouble sleeping because of an over-active mind.

If you like the way Bls makes you feel, and you would like to hear other recordings for the purposes of relaxation or pain management, you may also enjoy *Calm and Confident based on EMDR* and *Pain Control based on EMDR* which blend Bls with hypnotic suggestions for relaxation and pain control (see Appendix B). Thousands of people have found these CDs helpful for overcoming physical and emotional pain.

Summary

In this chapter you've been introduced to a veritable smorgasbord of strategies for changing the brain activity that maintains physical and emotional pain. From relaxation and meditation to Bls, all of these strategies are designed to stimulate your nervous system in ways that change the sensory-emotional patterns that maintain your pain. Each of these strategies involves some degree of focused attention, bodily awareness, and openness to change. The main difference between these methods is that while meditation and relaxation involve a certain amount of mental effort to enter the desired state, Bls does it for you. The CD that comes with this book will enable you to harness this simple but powerful strategy. In addition to the uses suggested in this chapter, the CD can assist in managing short-term pain and stress such as performance anxiety, worry, pain associated with minor medical procedures, dental pain, etc. Feel free to experiment. EMDR therapists should also find the pure bilateral stimulation track (Track 4) useful as a dual attention stimulus when using EMDR. Whether you use the bilateral brain stimulation CD or some of the other strategies described in the chapter, the main thing is to practice regularly. The more you practice, the more the pain in your brain will change and the better you will feel.

8

Exercise

Exercise supports the spirit and keeps the mind in vigor.

Marcus Cicero (65 BC)

Human beings need to move. It is through movement that we accomplish the basic tasks of life—working, loving and playing—which make life meaningful. Stress, injury and pain can all cause us to stop moving. We might avoid moving to avoid aggravating physical pain, or because we have lost hope in our ability to change things. Unfortunately, despite its protective intent, not moving only reinforces the sense of helplessness associated with these problems. Inactivity leads to lost muscle tone, increased disability, depression, and a decreased sense of well-being. Not moving also inhibits neurogenesis and leads to decreased levels of serotonin and dopamine, the neurochemicals necessary for energy and feeling good. For these reasons, exercise has long been recognized as a vital antidote to the physical and emotional effects of stress and pain. Regular physical activity is known to provide health and fitness benefits (increased muscular strength, cardiorespiratory functioning, muscular endurance, and flexibility), and decrease the risk of chronic conditions (coronary heart disease, diabetes, obesity, hypertension, stroke, colorectal cancer, breast cancer, osteoporosis, and anxiety and depression). Regular physical activity is also known to help reverse brain activity associated with stress, illness and pain.[1,2]

Exercise and your brain

Exercise has beneficial effects on your body and your brain. For starters, exercise relieves the physical tension in your muscles, which breaks the stress-feedback loop to the brain. When your body feels relaxed, your brain realizes it can relax too. Because exercise represents a physical activity you are in control of, it also stimulates feelings of self-mastery. When you move in a purposeful way, you generate feelings of efficacy and confidence. It's not hard to imagine how important moving your body is for your self-esteem: from infancy, when you learned to crawl, walk and then run, your survival depended upon developing and maintaining your physical capacities. The more your physical capacities developed, the more confident you became. Exercise thus provides a natural, on-going conduit from the body to the brain for feeling good in yourself.

Exercise also builds stress resistance. In the 2008 best-selling book about exercise and the brain, *Spark*, Harvard psychiatrist John Ratey describes how physical exercise can supercharge (provide a "spark" to) mental circuits to neutralize stress, sharpen thinking, lift mood, and so on.[3] Physical activity increases levels of tryptophan in the bloodstream and, thus, serotonin in the brain. It also balances dopamine, norepeniphrine, and synaptic mediators such as BDNF (brain-derived neurotrophic factor). Whereas neurotransmitters such as seratonin and dopamine enhance mood and energy levels, BDNF actually helps build and maintain the infrastructure of cell circuitry. Not surprisingly, many treatments for depression, including antidepressants and ECT, act to boost BDNF levels in the hippocampus. Ratey cites research showing that exercise stimulates the growth of stem cells that can, in turn, become brain cells. MRI studies of people undergoing exercise regimes found that the capillary volume in the memory area of the hippocampus (an area of the brain which is susceptible to damage by stress) increased by 30 per cent. Exercise also turns on the genes that produce GABA, which puts the brakes on excessive cellular activity associated with stress. Regular exercise also stimulates the production of IGF-1 (insulin growth factor), which increases neuroplasticity and neurogenesis in the hippocampus. The astounding conclusion is that exercise can stimulate the replacement of brain cells lost or damaged as a result of severe stress.

Over time, regular exercise increases the efficiency of the cardiovascular system, lowering blood pressure. In the brain, the mild stress of exercise fortifies the infrastructure of your nerve cells by stimulating the production of proteins that protect the cells against damage and disease. Exercise stimulates production of insulin receptors, which means your body makes better use of glucose (sugar) and stronger cells. Increased blood flow assists in the circulation of glucose, as well as stimulating the recovery process in your muscles and neurons. Regular exercise also increases your capacity to maintain energy, even when there is a drop in glucose levels. Biochemically and neurologically, exercise keeps the stress hormone cortisol in check and increases levels of regulatory neurotransmitters serotonin, norepeniphrine and dopamine. Exercise gives your neurons everything they need to connect.

Exercise, stress and pain

Exercise has also been found to reduce stress and pain. In one famous study in 1999, researchers at Duke University found that exercise was just as effective as Zoloft in alleviating depression The exercise group was assigned to supervised walking or jogging, at 70–85 per cent of aerobic capacity for 30 minutes (not including a 10-minute warm-up, and a 5-minute cool-down), three times a week. Around half of the people who exercised overcame their depression completely, a similar proportion to those taking medication. The researchers concluded that exercise is just as effective as antidepressants for treating depression. Numerous other studies have found that people who exercise regularly over their lifespan are less anxious, less depressed, less neurotic and more socially outgoing.

Although not a pain-control strategy per se, appropriate exercise can lead to improved coping and mild pain relief in some cases. A survey of 1800 women who suffer from PMS pain found that that at least half of them use exercise to alleviate the symptoms of PMS. In addition to decreased pain, the women who exercised regularly also had better concentration and mood. Another study found that exercise in waist-high warm water decreased pain and improved health-related quality of life and strength in the lower extremities in women with fibromyalgia. The benefits of exercise vary according to what type of pain you have. Exercise therapy seems to be slightly effective at decreasing pain and improving function in adults with chronic low back pain, particularly in health care patients. With acute low back pain, exercise therapy is as effective as either no treatment or other conservative treatments.[4] Patients with complex medical conditions who exercised needed fewer medical consultations.[5]

How does exercise reduce stress and pain?

Exercise helps reduce stress and pain through its effects on biochemistry, neurobiology, mood and physiology. In the brain, exercise stimulates the production of neurotransmitters that augment mood, reduce pain and improve well-being. Exercise gets us moving naturally, which stimulates the brain stem, which stimulates energy, motivation and well-being. Exercise also makes use of the brain's capacity to process information in both a top–down and a bottom–up manner. In this sense, exercise may have some advantages over antidepressants; unlike antidepressants, exercise doesn't specifically target any particular neurotransmitter—exercise adjusts the chemistry of the entire brain in a more normal direction.

Exercise also has a number of psychological benefits. At the every least, exercise takes your mind off your problems (distraction). Just this brief interruption from everyday cares and concerns can have a therapeutic effect. But exercise also leads to a shift in your thinking, through its effects on neurotransmitters associated with thinking and information processing. Exercise builds self-esteem. When you exercise, you create a different outcome for yourself—accomplishing physical tasks generates feelings of efficacy and achievement—as opposed to feeling weak and helpless. Exercise is the most powerful means of overcoming the immobility associated with stress and pain. Exercise can also lead to increased social support. Inactive people tend to be less socially outgoing, but exercising forces you out onto the street, gym or tennis court, where you are more likely to meet other people.

Physically, exercise stimulates increased blood flow, which is necessary for transporting nutrients and waste products to and from various organs of the body, as well as brain functioning. Exercise has long been known for its ability to reduce muscle tension. In 1982, a researcher named Herbert deVries found that exercise reduces excessive electrical activity in the muscles of anxious people, which leads to feelings of relaxation. deVries called this the "tranquilizing effects of exercise". Most people have experienced the feeling of well-being that follows exercise, even if they haven't exercised for many years. Exercise also stimulates greater physical capacity through increased muscle strength, flexibility and endurance.

There are thus many ways in which exercise facilitates reduced stress and pain, including physical, mental and emotional effects. These can be summarized as follows:

Biochemical:
- increased dopamine, serotonin, BDNF and GABA.

Neurological:
- increased brain resources
- re-routing of brain circuits.

Psychological:
- distraction
- learning different outcomes
- increased self-confidence
- increased social support.

Physiological:
- increased blood flow
- reduced muscle tension
- increased strength, flexibility, range of movement.

How much exercise do you need, and what kind?

Regular exercise is undoubtedly the cheapest, most effective weapon in your battle against stress and pain. How much exercise should you do? Everyone is different, but health experts recommend that adults engage in at least 30 minutes of moderate physical activity, five days a week. There are different levels of exercise, from low intensity (walking), to moderate intensity (jogging), to high intensity (running). Walking is an easy, effective way to start exercising. If you walk, your heart rate should be operating at 55 to 65 per cent of maximum. To calculate your maximum heart rate, subtract your age from 220. To measure your heart rate, you will need a heart rate monitor. You can buy a wristwatch heart-rate monitor from eBay for around $50.00.

Aerobic exercise, which involves a heart rate of 60–65 per cent capacity, ideally requires 4 × 30–60 minute sessions per week. Aerobic exercise of this intensity will burn fat and stimulate the structural changes in the brain discussed above. If possible, you should also consider weights or strengthening exercises such as tennis, dancing or running. Exercise that involves complex motor movements, such as dance or martial arts, seems to benefit both body and brain. Yoga, Pilates, Tai-Chi and martial arts are all good for balance and flexibility; however, just walking for half an hour per day, five days per week, can be beneficial.

Obviously, whatever exercise you do must be appropriate to your age and physical condition. If you have a bad back, you may find it easier to walk than doing Tai Chi or Yoga. If your pain is in your legs, walking may not be suitable, but swimming or hydrotherapy could be. If you have a medical condition, you should consult with your physician or physical therapist about what sort of exercise regime is best. An exercise physiologist can develop a program that will develop specific muscles and physical capacities. It is not recommended that you engage in exercise that aggravates your pain to any significant degree. Whatever physical benefits this might confer are cancelled out by the increased pain memories you are creating — better to start slow and small, and work within your comfort zone. It's also important to choose exercise that suits your personality. Engaging in exercise that you like is going to be more rewarding and beneficial than forcing yourself to do something that you don't enjoy.

> Lisa was a working wife and mother who simply never had time to exercise. From 6 a.m. when she woke up until 10 p.m. when she went to bed, Lisa's life was a whirlwind of domestic responsibilities, punctuated by a full-time job as a foreman at a processing plant. Lisa had to work so that she and her husband could pay off their mortgage and the costs of educating and raising three children. Lisa's job involved some walking, but not of sufficient intensity or regularity to have any significant effect. Not exercising was not a problem until Lisa developed chronic pain after she hurt her back in a fall at work. When her back didn't get better in the expected

time-frame, Lisa became increasingly stressed and depressed because the doctors couldn't tell her when she would feel better, and she couldn't complete all the tasks she needed to. She also started suffering from fatigue and mood swings as a result of not getting enough sleep. Lisa's physician referred her to a psychologist after she refused to take antidepressants.

Lisa's psychologist gave her a lot of helpful information and advice about how to cope with her injury and pain. Lisa found it helpful just to be able to share how she was feeling with someone outside the family, i.e. someone she didn't have to worry about being upset at hearing how she was really feeling. He also advised her to start exercising, and told her that she needed to walk at least 30 minutes per day, five days per week. Lisa laughed—the psychologist obviously had no idea how busy her life was. She also couldn't see any need to exercise; apart from her injury she was perfectly healthy. "I know you're busy," said the psychologist, "but you're also hurt, and when you're hurt it's more important than ever that you take better care of your health." With this he also outlined the physical and mental benefits of exercise. Lisa grudgingly accepted that perhaps exercise could help, but who was going to take care of the housework? Lisa's husband worked long hours and he depended on Lisa to maintain the family home.

The psychologist explained that Lisa was going to have to make some changes in her life, and in her expectations of herself and others. Lisa felt a little hurt by this: she hadn't chosen this way of life—it just seemed that whenever something needed fixing, the responsibility fell on her. Lisa's sense of responsibility dated back to her childhood when, as an eldest child, she assumed the role of mother while her real mother underwent frequent hospitalizations for severe depression. Lisa didn't have much of a childhood, and she wanted to protect her children from a similar fate. But something had to give, and Lisa could agree that it wouldn't hurt the children to help with some of the housework. It would also make the family more of a family, helping each other rather than everybody relying on one person.

After discussing things with her husband, Lisa called for a family conference where she told her children that there would have to be some changes because of how she was feeling. Lisa felt very anxious—she had never asked anything of her family before. To her surprise, the children seemed to accept what she was saying and were more than willing to make up a list of tasks that they could help out with. Lisa also set aside 30 minutes per night, three week-nights plus weekends, to walk. After about the third day of walking, Lisa started to notice a difference in her energy levels and mood. Whereas she felt sore after the first walk, she soon felt relaxed and energized. She also seemed to fall asleep more easily. On weekends her husband joined her and they enjoyed some private time together. Lisa's back pain was still a problem, but she seemed to be able to tolerate it more, and it seemed to be having less impact physically. As the weeks turned into months, the evening walks became a part of Lisa's life and she looked forward to the time-out as much as the walking.

She also noticed a change in her thinking: her concentration and memory seemed to improve and she definitely felt sharper mentally.

ACTIVITY

Developing an exercise regime

You are made to move. You need to move. Regular exercise is good for your body and your brain, so start exercising and make regular exercise a part of your life.

1   Choose a form of exercise or exercises you feel you can cope with and that you will enjoy. If necessary, consult with your physician or physical therapist about what kind of exercise might be most appropriate for you.

_____

_____

2   Decide when, how often and how long you want to do that exercise.

_____

_____

3   Decide whether you want to exercise on your own or with a friend.

_____

_____

4   To help with motivation, make a list of reasons why you need or want to exercise.

_____

_____

_____

_____

5   Create a chart of how, when and how much exercise you do, and your progress. Stick your progress chart on your fridge door or some place where you can easily see it.
6   Start exercising on a regular basis, and record your progress on your progress chart.
7   Keep exercising. Even if you miss a day or a week, keep exercising.

Note: **Be patient. Start slowly**, and build up as your fitness increases. If you have been inactive for a while, your body will need time to develop the strength necessary for regular exercise.

Motivational tips

Mark Twain used to say, "Giving up smoking is easy—I've given it up hundreds of times." Developing a regular exercise program can be a bit like that: you start with all the best intentions, but it's not always easy to keep going. Exercise is that crucial missing piece that we all think is something we have no time for in our schedule today, as if it were a luxury. It's estimated that less than 3 per cent of adults over the age of 24 stay in shape through playing team sports. Of course, it depends who you are and where you live; rickshaw drivers in India have no need to exercise. But for most urban dwellers, exercise and strenuous movement are not part of their daily routine. Exercise is something that many of us did naturally as children, but forgot about once we left school, started working, got married, etc. There may be an evolutionary reason we don't exercise. Our hunter-gatherer ancestors spent most of their day moving—hunting and foraging. They only rested after they had enough food. We only have to walk from the couch to the fridge to find food, so there is no immediate need to exercise. Even work, which is part of most people's lives, may not necessarily involve any great physical effort, depending on the type of work you do. So for most of us, it takes a health scare to get us exercising—but, if you think about the long-term effects of stress and lack of fitness, your survival really still depends on maintaining a certain amount of physical activity.

No matter how busy you are, exercise is essential for maintaining physical and mental health, and negating the effects of stress, injury and pain. There are several things you can do to make it easier for exercise to become part of your life.

Set clear goals

Make a list (mentally or on paper) of the reasons *why* you need to exercise. What are you aiming to achieve by exercising? Is it to feel better, lose weight, improve your mood, or some other specific objective? The clearer you are about why you are exercising, the easier it will be to maintain your motivation to keep going. Remember too that because exercise immediately increases dopamine, you should start experiencing a biochemical reward fairly soon after you start.

Develop a routine

You must exercise regularly, and ideally at the same time each day. If you only go for a walk one or two times a week, the benefits will be less, but if you walk every day the benefits accumulate because your starting point each day is higher. Try to set aside a particular time to exercise every day—it just makes it easier. Like brushing your teeth, once you develop the habit of exercise, it becomes automatic. If other priorities intrude, remind yourself about why you are exercising and how important it is to your overall health.

Pace yourself

Experts recommend exercising a little, but often. Don't be in too much of a hurry and don't overdo it—developing an exercise regime is an incremental process. If you push yourself too hard, you will experience discomfort or injury and become discouraged. Remember the story of the Tortoise and the Hare: "Slow and steady wins the race." If you don't like exercise, perhaps as a result of bad experiences as a child, it's especially important to develop an exercise routine that suits your personality; go at your own pace, and give it time.

Get support

Exercise with a friend or group. It's a lot easier to exercise with others than on your own. Having an exercise-buddy adds a social element to your exercise that makes it more enjoyable and increases motivation. Animal studies indicate that exercising with a group stimulates greater neurogenesis than exercising alone. If all else fails, take the family dog!

Don't give up

Once you have developed an exercise regime, don't give up because of temporary interruptions or setbacks. It's easy to not exercise, particularly after a holiday or other demands have eaten into your exercise routine. Remember why you are exercising and don't despair if you feel unfit. Researchers have found that even after a hiatus, the benefits of exercise are quickly recovered once the regime is resumed. Some people avoid exercise because they find it boring—that's why iPods were invented! If you must be constantly mentally stimulated, make your daily walk a chance to catch up with your favourite music or podcast. Exercise is not a luxury or an optional extra—it's an essential part of your self-care and building resistance to stress and pain. When you exercise you are building resistance to stress and pain: physically and mentally.

9

Sleep

Sleeping problems are another effect of severe stress which can exacerbate physical and emotional pain. Disturbed sleep is a symptom of increased physiological arousal. The main effects of lack of sleep are fatigue, depression, and concentration and memory problems. Fatigue and depressed mood lead to increased susceptibility to pain and stress, and decreased ability to cope. Good sleep enhances your ability to resist pain through the increased energy and functioning it brings. Good sleep is not a luxury; it is necessary for physical rejuvenation, immune functioning, mood and thinking. Learning how to sleep better is thus a vital strategy for reversing the vicious cycle of stress and pain.

What is sleep and why do you need it?

Human sleep is a complex, multi-staged process involving two basic types: rapid eye-movement sleep (REM) and non-REM sleep (NREM). Sleep begins with a gradual descent though drowsiness, light sleep, and eventually deep sleep. These first four stages (NREM) are the most restful and involve decreased heart rate, body temperature and brain activity. NREM occurs during the first third to half of the

---

* Shakespeare, William. *Macbeth*, 2.2., 46–51.

night and is the most restorative type of sleep. The amount of NREM sleep you need increases when you are sleep-deprived. REM sleep involves increased brain activity and increased physiological activity, including rapid eye-movements. REM sleep is when dreaming occurs. REM sleep is also thought to be necessary for memory consolidation. REM sleep occurs cyclically throughout the night, alternating with NREM sleep about every 80–100 minutes. Most people sleep about seven hours, two of which will be in REM sleep.

The sleep cycle is determined by an innate 24-hour body "clock" known as a circadian rhythm. The term comes from the Latin *circa* or "about" and *dia* which means "day"; circadian literally means "about a day". Circadian rhythms are affected by the amount of light your body receives. At night your body produces certain hormones, in response to darkness, which trigger sleep. In the morning, sunlight stimulates wakefulness. Circadian rhythms can be disrupted by stress, jetlag, shift work and even being woken up by an alarm clock. Your sleep cycle is also partly determined by your body's own in-built homeostasis mechanisms. For example, the more time that has elapsed since you last slept, the sleepier you will feel. Figure 9.1 shows the 24-hour circadian rhythm, including the proportion of time spent sleeping each day.

Figure 9.1 The circadian sleep cycle

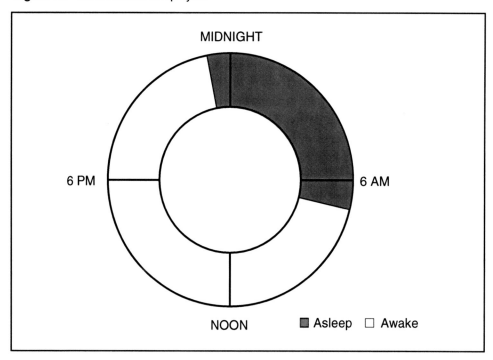

Your sleep cycle is also determined by your chronotype—whether you are a morning or a night person. Morning people (or "Larks") function best in the morning and prefer to go to bed early and rise early. Larks represent about 20 per cent of the population. Another 20 per cent of people are night people ("Owls") who function best at night and prefer to go to bed late and wake later. The other 60 per cent of people fall somewhere in between those two extremes. Knowing your chronotype is important; if you are an Owl, but have to get up early for work every morning, you are going to need to schedule a nap in the afternoon and perhaps a couple of sleep-ins come the weekend. Night people seem to be more sensitive to disruptions in their sleep rhythms. If you are a Lark, working night shift is probably not such a good idea.

The exact purpose of sleep is still not fully understood, but it certainly has a restorative role in recharging our physical and emotional selves. Restful sleep is known to be necessary for:

- the production of serotonin and other mood-enhancing chemicals
- the production of growth hormones and other substances necessary for maintenance of the physical self
- immune functioning (through the production of Interleukin-1)
- memory consolidation and learning.

The importance of sleep for health has long been recognized. The Talmud (an ancient Jewish text) lists sleep as one of the most important activities for healing a sick person.[1] Good sleep can help reduce physical pain.[2]

Sleep can also be a time for mental rejuvenation and inspiration. Many people find solutions to life problems during dreams, or after "sleeping on it"—remember Aron Ralston's story from Chapter 2? When Stephen Hawking, the famous mathematician and astrophysicist, was first diagnosed with the muscle-wasting disease ALS[*], he was told he had two years to live. At the time Hawking was a bored, directionless 21-year-old. Devastated by the prospect of a slow physical decline followed by an early death, Hawking fell into a deep depression. Then one night he had a dream he was about to be executed. When Hawking awoke and reflected on this dream, he realized that even though he might not have a choice about how he died, he did have a choice about how he lived. Although Hawking still felt there was a cloud hanging over his future, he began to live life more fully. He became engaged and put more effort into his research. He devoted himself to his work about the origins of the universe and went on to write a best-selling book, *A Brief History of Time*. Hawking's dream helped him to see his situation differently and find a way through his feelings of depression. It probably saved his life.

[*] Amyotrophic lateral sclerosis or motor neurone disease.

How stress affects your sleep

Severe stress and pain can all disrupt your ability to sleep normally. The most common forms of stress-related sleep disturbance include trouble falling asleep, night-waking, non-restful sleep and irregular sleeping patterns. Many sufferers of chronic physical or emotional pain find it difficult to fall asleep, and when they eventually do, it may only be for two or three hours. There is also no routine; every night is different, including when you fall asleep, how long you sleep, and when you awaken. The quality of sleep is also poor. Even after a supposedly normal night's sleep, you may awaken feeling tired and as though you have not slept at all. Physiological studies of chronic back pain sufferers show they have an arousal disturbance in their brain waves so that they awaken feeling unrefreshed.[3] Your chronotype can also change; early morning people suddenly find themselves unable to sleep at night and needing to sleep in.

Insufficient sleep disrupts the body's natural "rest and repair" cycle. Lack of sleep is known to be associated with decreased immune functioning, decreased ability to metabolise glucose (blood sugar), decreased cognitive abilities, and even decreased emotional intelligence.[4,5] One group of researchers found that sleep-deprived people exhibited decreased self-regard, independence, capacity for empathy, and impulse control; and found it harder to relate to others. Sleeping problems, particularly with stage 4 NREM sleep, have also been found to induce musculoskeletal pain.[6] The fact that stress should have an impact on sleep is not surprising; sleep and wakefulness are part of a continuum. What happens while you're awake affects how you sleep, and what happens while you're asleep affects how you function while you're awake.

The negative effects of stress on sleep may be magnified by early childhood abuse and neglect. Lack of secure emotional attachment or safety in childhood can inhibit the development of a normal sleep pattern. Adults who suffered stress in childhood are more likely to have sleeping problems. Even a temporary separation from the mother, such as with a hospitalization, can have a disruptive effect on sleeping patterns in children.[7] People who are already poor sleepers can be expected to have more disturbed sleep in response to stress, and to find it harder to establish a healthy sleeping routine.

The mechanisms by which stress affects sleep include increased physiological arousal, biochemical imbalances, and desynchronisation of circadian rhythms. As described in Chapter 2, stress causes a reduction in your levels of serotonin. Serotonin is necessary for the production of melatonin, the neurotransmitter responsible for inducing sleep. The result is that sufferers of stress and pain feel sleepy when they should normally feel awake, and awake when they should be asleep—rather like jet-lag. It's not uncommon to feel tired during the day, but unable to sleep at night.

Six strategies for improving your sleep

Learning how to sleep well again can greatly reduce the impact of stress and pain. Improving your sleep requires retraining your body to fall asleep and stay asleep longer. One of the best-known methods of doing this is sleep hygiene. Sleep hygiene simply means making sure that you are going to sleep under the optimum conditions (e.g. in a quiet, darkened room with a comfortable mattress, etc.). The aim is to make it as easy as possible for sleep to occur naturally. Stress management is also an important strategy for restoring sleep. If your sleeping problems are caused by inadequately managed pain, simply improving your sleep hygiene isn't going to be enough. How can you sleep soundly knowing that something terrible might be about to happen any moment, or feeling that your life is out of control? You must neutralize any present stressors which may be interfering with your sleep. This could mean deciding on a course of action to resolve a stressful situation, practicing relaxation before going to sleep, or just writing out your thoughts and feelings before going to bed. Trying to fall asleep while faced with an unresolved stressor is like trying to take refuge in a bear's cave: it's pretty hard to relax.

If your sleeping problems are being caused by severe stress or pain, sleep hygiene is unlikely to have much effect (because it's not addressing the causes of your insomnia). In this case, you may need to develop a new sleeping routine, based on letting your body dictate when and where you sleep, as opposed to trying too hard to sleep normally. Have you noticed how stressful it is when you try to go to sleep and sleep doesn't come? "Free-sleeping" means giving up on the idea of normal sleep and accepting that your body is incapable of sleeping for long, regular periods. Instead, you sleep where and when you can. Last but not least, medication can be helpful in addressing sleeping problems. To summarize, there are six strategies for improving sleep:

1   sleep hygiene
2   stress management
3   relaxation and self-hypnosis
4   naps
5   "free-sleeping"
6   medication/natural remedies.

Below you will find detailed instructions on how to implement these strategies. These strategies are designed to remove any obstacles to sleep, and maximize your ability to sleep. The ultimate goal is to facilitate restful if not normal sleep, but the main thing is to try to create the conditions where you can get as much sleep as you can, regardless of how much pain you may be experiencing. As with changing any stress-related disturbances to normal functioning, it may take time for your body to return to normal, so you will need to be patient.

Sleep hygiene

Sleep hygiene involves creating the right conditions for sleep to happen naturally. Sometimes, sleeping problems can be exacerbated by your surroundings or routine. Noise, light, timing, even the type of mattress you have, can all affect your ability to fall asleep and stay asleep. The following sleep hygiene tips represent generally accepted wisdom for how to get a good night's sleep. These are guidelines and may not be practical for everybody. Review this list and see if there is anything you can do to make it easier for your body to fall asleep.

- *Make sure you feel safe and secure.* As stated, you cannot relax and fall asleep if you are worried about your safety or that something bad is going to happen. Beyond obvious considerations of physical security, try to make your bedroom into a place where you can shut the door on your worries and cares. Create a mental boundary between your place of sleep and the rest of your life. Know that you cannot sleep and think about your problems at the same time. In fact, some research suggests that if you stop thinking and get some sleep, you are more likely to find solutions to your problems.
- *Get to bed as early as possible.* Our systems, particularly the adrenal glands, do most of their recharging between 11 p.m. and 1 a.m. In addition, your gall bladder dumps toxins during this same period. If you are awake, the toxins back up into the liver, which then backs up into your entire system and causes further disruption to your health. Before the widespread use of electricity, people would go to bed soon after sundown, as most animals do, and which nature intended for humans as well.
- *Sleep late.* Try to avoid setting your alarm for earlier than 6 a.m. Prepare the night before if getting up at 6 a.m. will be a rush for you. If you must get up before 6 a.m., reset your body clock by ensuring darkness and quiet for an early-to-bed schedule and waking up to bright lights. Remember, sunrise is the trigger for your body clock.
- *Develop a sleep routine.* Try to go to bed at roughly the same time every night. Try to have a bedtime routine, wherein you give your mind and body time to wind down in preparation for sleep and you create a pattern of going to sleep at roughly the same time every night.
- *Create an environment conducive to sleep.* A cool, dark environment is best. Keep your bedroom at a comfortable temperature and minimize noise or distractions. It is better to read something relaxing than watch TV before going to bed. A comfortable mattress is also important.
- *Avoid caffeine and alcohol.* A recent study showed that in some people caffeine is not metabolised efficiently and therefore they can feel the effects long after consuming it. So an afternoon cup of coffee (or even tea) will keep some people from falling asleep. Know that the "nightcap" has a price. Alcohol may help you to get to sleep, but it will cause you to wake up throughout the night.

- *Take a bath.* Warm baths (not showers) before bedtime can help. When body temperature is raised in the late evening, it will fall at bedtime, facilitating sleep.
- *Listen to white noise or relaxation CDs.* Some people find the sound of white noise or nature sounds, such as the ocean or forest, to be soothing for sleep (as is the author's *Calm and Confident CD*—see Appendix C).
- *Exercise.* Exercise is thought to be conducive to sleep, but preferably not too close to bedtime, i.e. at least four hours before bedtime.
- *Do not lie awake in bed.* If you cannot get to sleep after more than 30 minutes, get out of bed and do something boring in dim light until you are sleepy. Do not lie awake worrying. If your mind is overactive in this way, try setting aside a "worry-time" before you go to bed, perhaps writing out your worries in a journal.

Stress management

Stress management means dealing with any current stressors that are keeping you awake at night. The kinds of stressful situations that can inhibit sleep include unresolved trauma, chronic pain, illness, relationship problems and any situation that poses a threat to your goals and security. As mentioned, it's simply unrealistic to expect yourself to sleep normally while facing a major unresolved stressor. Dealing with stressful situations is not easy; that's why they are stressful situations. But you *can* acquire the knowledge, confidence and support to help you overcome whatever threats or challenges are facing you. You should have found the activities from the safety and support chapter helpful in this regard.

It can be helpful to review the stressful situation from a problem-solving point of view. Is the stressful situation something you have any control over? Do you have all the information you might need to know how to resolve that situation? Are you holding on to any self-limiting attitudes or beliefs that might be holding you prisoner to this situation? Is there any reasonable action that you can take to ameliorate the threat or improve your situation? If the situation is not one that you can control, and assuming you have done everything you possibly can to resolve it, what is the point of continuing to worry? If none of that works, you may just have to accept that you are in a stressful period and adopt a different sleep routine (see "free sleeping" on page 137).

Stress management also involves knowing how to manage the stressful feelings associated with the stressful situation. This could mean talking to a friend, practicing meditation or relaxation, changing your self-talk, exercising or taking up a hobby, or some combination of the above. Sometimes stress can be caused by our expectations; if we can learn to look at the stressful situation differently, this can change how it makes us feel. Louise felt stressed and depressed because she couldn't work and provide for her family financially after hurting her back at work. Louise could not accept that her role within the family had changed. After talking with her counsellor, Louise remembered why she got hurt at work in the first place: because she was trying to support her family. The realization that all along she had been doing her best for her family helped Louise to feel less bad about what had happened. Although she missed working, she found other ways to support her family, such as spending more time with her children, helping out at her children's school, etc.

Relaxation and self-hypnosis

As we have seen, one of the main effects of stress and pain is increased physiological arousal. Practicing relaxation or self-hypnosis at bedtime can reduce tension and facilitate sleep. Relaxation helps create a buffer between the stress of the day and the letting go that is necessary for restful sleep at night. We looked at relaxation in an earlier chapter, and you should already have considered adopting regular relaxation or meditation. Another specific technique for sleep is to use creative visualization and self-hypnosis.

> Bob used to prepare himself for sleep by imagining he was on a luxury cruise ship voyaging across the Pacific. He imagined he could feel the throb of the ship's powerful engines and how he didn't have to make any effort to get to where he wanted to. He thought of the ship's bow cutting through the water, and the gentle rolling caused by the ocean swell. He imagined the feeling of protection that came from being on such a large vessel and how the massive walls of the hull kept him safe from the elements. From night to night, Bob added different elements to his fantasy. Some nights he imagined himself being lulled to sleep by the sound of the ocean outside; other nights he imagined visiting a tiny, blue-ringed island and falling asleep on a deserted beach.

Of course, Bob never left his bedroom in suburbia, but by exercising his imagination he was able to lull himself into a relaxed state of mind and body, and ultimately fall asleep more easily. The human mind has the capacity to be a kind of virtual reality tool if you're willing to use your imagination in this way. Try remembering or imagining an experience that stimulates feelings of security and relaxation. Ships, trains and even planes derive their efficacy from the fact that they involve being transported to some place else, but you can just as easily build a fantasy around your favourite holiday spot or travel destination.

Self-hypnosis can also be helpful. It involves focusing your mind on something neutral or relaxing, to the exclusion of all other thoughts or concerns, and using that as a stimulus for entering a more relaxed state. A simple but powerful self-hypnotic technique for sleep is "Mrs Erickson's induction" (Mrs Erickson was the wife of Milton Erickson, the famous hypnotherapist). The beauty of Mrs Erickson's induction is that it uses your senses (sight, hearing and touch) to lull you into a relaxed sleep.

ACTIVITY

Mrs Erickson's induction

1 Begin by making yourself comfortable and finding something to focus on, e.g. one corner of a door frame, a light switch, etc. Then, maintaining your focus on that spot, try to notice four things that you can **see** about the object or spot; and mentally feed them back to yourself. For example:
"Right now I notice the light switch is white; right now I notice the shadow at the edge of the switch; right now I notice the switch is a square shape; right now I notice the switch is in the off position . . ."

2 Try to notice all the things you can **hear**, and make four statements to yourself about them. For example:
"Right now I notice . . . the sound of the air-conditioner; right now I notice . . . the sound of the clock ticking; right now I notice . . . voices in the next room; right now I notice . . . cars passing by outside." You must use the phrase "right now I notice . . ." before each item. These words help create the mental separation from experience, which is one of the essential elements of the hypnotic state.

3 Next try to notice all the things you can **feel** physically. One at a time, repeat mentally to yourself, "Right now I notice [*details*]" (for example, the feeling of your hand on your lap, etc.). Repeat this process four times.

4 Go back to the start and repeat the process, starting with the visual stimuli you focused on originally, but this time you only have to find three things, e.g. "right now I notice . . . [× *3 things you notice about the spot you are focusing on*]"; "right now I can hear . . . [× *3 things you can hear*]"; and "right now I notice . . . [× *3 things you can feel*]".

5 Repeat the process again, but this time you only have to find two things. Then repeat the process again, looking for one thing. *Note*: You will probably run out of different things to see, hear or feel, in which case you are allowed to repeat something you used earlier. But *try* to find something different; you may be surprised at how much more you can notice than at first seems obvious.

ACTIVITY

6 At some point, your eyes will feel tired. Close them and continue making statements about your on-going experience, although the visual representations you may be most aware of with your eyes closed will probably be from your imagination. You can carry on with these internal descriptions just as effectively, finding increasingly finer descriptions within your sensory experience. What you are creating is a biofeedback loop.

Another simple technique is to count backwards from 20 to 1 and keep repeating this until you fall asleep. Since your mind can really concentrate on only one thing at a time, this simple activity will block any worrying thoughts that might be keeping you awake and make it easier for your body to relax.

Taking a nap

Sleeping in the daytime is generally discouraged because it is thought to interfere with night-time sleeping; however, sleep experts have now realized that naps are normal and can help make up for lost sleep. Napping has been found to improve mood in sleep-deprived people.[8] Even a nap as short as 10 minutes can reduce the effects of sleep loss.[9] A 10-minute afternoon nap can stimulate significantly increased energy, alertness and performance. Cancer patients who took naps found they slept longer at night and had less pain.[10] Researchers found that subjects in a nap study felt that it was easiest to fall asleep at night and in the afternoon.[11]

The body is on a roughly 24-hour clock, which makes you wind down twice (peaking in periods separated by about 12 hours): in the night and in the afternoon. So the best time for a nap is 12 hours after the mid-point of the previous night's sleep. For normal sleepers this is around 3 p.m. Many famous people enjoyed naps, including Albert Einstein, John F. Kennedy, Bill Clinton and Winston Churchill. Winston Churchill used to say of his naps, "This gets me two days in one."

There are two kinds of nap: brief ones taken to revive the brain, and long ones taken to compensate for significant sleep loss. Long naps can help when you have accumulated a considerable sleep debt: for example, when you have been sleeping poorly for a long time. The only disadvantage of long naps is that they cause what researchers call sleep inertia, a groggy feeling that can last about half an hour after waking. You should therefore experiment with what length of time works best for you. Generally speaking, the ideal length of a nap is 10 to 45 minutes.

"Free sleeping"

If your sleeping problems are associated with chronic illness, pain or severe stress, you may find it impossible to achieve a normal sleep routine. In that case, it may be best to accept that you are just not going to get a solid eight hours' sleep per night, and allow your body to dictate when and how long you sleep. Although this is not the ideal for most people, it is not so terrible, particularly if you are able to be flexible about the hours you sleep. Free sleeping means letting your body dictate when you fall asleep, and just sleeping whenever you can. Thus, instead of one 8-hour block of sleep every 24 hours, you might have three 2–3 hour blocks of sleep at, say, midnight, dawn and noon. With this method there is no routine or structure; you just let your body decide when it wants to sleep. This method potentially enables you to have your normal eight hours of sleep over a 24-hour period, just not at the usual times. Figure 9.2 illustrates what a "free sleeping" cycle might look like. Of course, everybody is different, and this cycle may not exactly describe your

Figure 9.2 Free sleeping

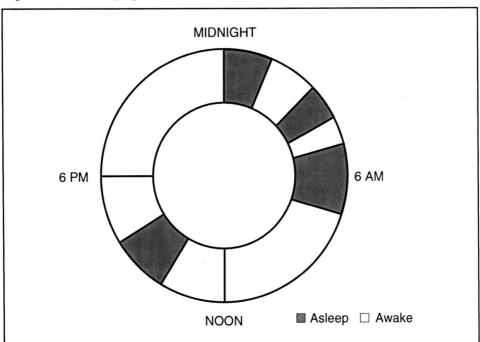

sleeping routine; however, this pattern (or some variation thereof) is common in sufferers of severe stress and pain.

Many sufferers of stress-related insomnia find it difficult to fall asleep in bed. The very act of going to bed with the intention of falling asleep seems to stimulate a state of alertness that prohibits sleep. Sleep should happen naturally, without your having to think about it. Many insomniacs find it easiest to fall asleep while they are doing something else, such as reading a book, listening to a podcast about their favourite subject, or even watching TV. The act of engaging in a mildly interesting, but not too interesting, mental activity seems to distract their conscious mind enough for their body to relax and the conditions for sleep to occur.

Make it easy for your self to sleep. Many chronic pain sufferers dread their beds; they are so accustomed to NOT sleeping in bed. There is no law that says you have to sleep in bed. You should sleep wherever and whenever you can—as long as it's not while driving a car! You might fall asleep while reading a book in your favourite chair; that's fine.

> Jeanine had not slept for more than two hours straight for weeks because of her chronic pain. One night she was watching sport on late-night TV. It was a hot night and she could feel a gentle breeze coming through the open door. Something about the images and sounds from the TV, the gentle breeze and the lack of other concerns made her feel very relaxed, and she just fell asleep in the chair. Four hours later she was awoken by the sun peeking in through the open door. It was the best sleep she had had in weeks.

Listen to your body. As far as practical, build your life around your sleep, not your sleep around your life. The quality of sleep will vary according to the time of day and the circumstances. Many people find that they sleep the deepest in the early morning, because they are exhausted. Because of how the normal sleep cycle works, free sleeping will not give you the same quality of restful sleep you would expect from sleeping a straight eight hours; however, it should at least enable you to get more sleep than you would otherwise. Later, when the crisis is over, you can worry about getting back to a more normal pattern of sleep.

Medication/natural remedies

Mankind has been using drugs to alleviate sleeping problems since before Christ when the ancient Egyptians used opium to treat insomnia, and nowadays there are many prescription and non-prescription drugs available for the alleviation of sleeping problems. Prescription medication can certainly be an important element in the treatment of sleeping problems; however, long-term use of drugs to facilitate sleep is problematic because of the development of tolerance and side-effects. The beneficial effects of prescription medication for sleep are also often only short term. Medication must therefore be used under medical supervision and in consultation with your physician.

Given the problems associated with drugs, many people prefer natural remedies. These can range from teas such as valerian and chamomile, to a hormone supplement called melatonin. As previously mentioned, melatonin is a naturally occurring hormone that promotes sleep. Your body's ability to produce melatonin can be affected by stress. Melatonin supplements have been found to help with insomnia and possibly some of the effects of stress on the immune system.[12] It is recommended to start with as low a dose as possible (0.5 milligrams) and increase by increments of that amount. Melatonin is restricted in some countries. Other natural remedies include St John's wort, vitamin B-6, and even kava (a kind of mild narcotic made out of roots found in Pacific islands such as Fiji). In general, there is not much research regarding the use of natural remedies for sleep. There is, however, some research to indicate that eating carbohydrates (sweets, bread, pasta and rice) can raise serotonin levels, which may be why some people binge on carbohydrates when they feel anxious or depressed.

Using natural remedies, even prescription drugs, can be a matter of experimentation; if the drug is not attacking the right chemical imbalance, it is not going to help. **You should not take more than one drug at a time, and you should not mix natural remedies with prescription medications.** You should consult your physician regarding use of natural remedies or any other drug because of the risk of unexpected effects. Some doctors never ask about sleep, so don't be surprised if you have to initiate the discussion.

Conclusion

In conclusion, there are many things you can do to manage sleeping problems associated with stress and pain. Many sleep strategies are designed to maximize the ideal conditions for sleep to occur. Others, such as medication, are designed to knock you out with brain-altering chemicals. It's important to remember that sleep is part of a natural cycle and that if sleep is not happening it's probably for good reason. It may be unrealistic to expect yourself to sleep normally while you are affected by severe emotional distress and/or physical pain. A less stressful path may be to adopt a more free-flowing approach to sleep while you work on neutralizing the causes of your sleeping problems. Once your pain is under control, your sleep will probably revert to normal naturally.

10

How to change your thinking

The greatest discovery of my generation is that a human being can alter his life by altering his attitudes of mind.

William James

Thoughts are part of our response to pain, but they can also become part of the problem. Chronic physical or emotional pain can lead to negative thinking in the form of worrying, catastrophizing and poor decision-making. Negative thinking is also often accompanied by negative attitudes such as self-loathing and self-doubt. Although negative thinking is driven by negative emotions, it also reinforces physical and emotional pain through increased emotional distress and reduced ability to cope. Because of how negative thinking can maintain pain, changing your thinking is an essential aspect of overcoming pain.

Although changing your thinking is a defining element of some self-help approaches, you will notice that it is only one of a number of strategies in this approach, and also that it is one of the last strategies to be considered. This isn't because thoughts aren't important—merely that they are easier to manipulate after you have addressed the sensory-emotional bases of your pain. Trying to change your thinking without first knowing how to manage the sensory-emotional reactions that are driving your negative thinking is difficult and ineffectual. As you are about to learn, although changing your thinking is a top-down process, you can also utilize both top–down and bottom–up strategies to achieve this.

What are thoughts and why are they important?

Thoughts are electrical impulses generated by the brain in response to sensory information. At the level of consciousness, thoughts are a mental representation of reality, like the images generated by the software in a computer. Thoughts enable us to interpret and manipulate experience, regulate emotions and decide on an appropriate course of action. Thoughts are also inseparable from feelings and are almost always part of our emotional response to events. Even as intellectual an activity as solving a maths problem involves feelings such as anticipation, frustration, satisfaction, etc. The emotional component of thoughts tends to be less accessible to consciousness, and most people go through life with scant awareness of the emotional bases of their underlying thought processes.

The capacity to think begins to develop from around age 3, when children start to have a separate mental representation of the external world. Our ability to think continues to develop for most of our life, in response to familial, educational and cultural influences. Over time, we develop our own unique style of perceiving ourselves and the world. These enduring patterns of feeling and thinking are called schemata. Schemata automatically guide our sense of emotional meaning and determine our holistic experience of being in the world.[1] Ideally we see ourselves as lovable, worthwhile human beings living in an interesting and challenging world. Unfortunately, as we have seen, stress, trauma and neglect cause us to see ourselves and the world in negative terms.[2,3] We may blame ourselves for negative situations that we have no control over, always expect the worst to happen (catastrophizing), indulge in "all or nothing" thinking, or just believe that "things will never change".

Psychologist Jeffrey Young has identified four types of maladaptive schemata:

1 *Disconnection and rejection.* Doubting that needs for security, safety, acceptance and respect can be met.
2 *Impaired autonomy and performance.* Doubting the ability to function independently and/or successfully in the world.
3 *Other-directedness.* Being excessively focused on the desires and needs of others at the expense of personal needs.
4 *Over-vigilance and inhibition.* An approach to life based on excessive worry about things going wrong and suppressing feelings or impulses. This schema also often involves living according to rigid rules and expectations—often at the expense of personal happiness, health and well-being.[1]

Jeffery Young developed schema therapy after realizing that just changing your thinking doesn't have much effect on complex problems such as post-traumatic stress, deep-seated anxiety, poor self-concept, etc. Young felt that overcoming these sorts of problems needed deeper change, at the level of self-concept. He also recognized that changing schemata through rational thinking alone was difficult because schemata tend to be stored in the emotional, unconscious part of the mind, which is less amenable to change from the frontal cortex (thinking brain). Young expanded cognitive therapy to focus more on the influence of maladaptive childhood experiences and more effective ways of challenging the negative schemata that underlie negative thinking. The other advantage of schema therapy is that by knowing your underlying schema, it's easier to identify the types of negative thoughts you are most prone to, and challenge them. Schema therapy uses a combination of cognitive-behavioral strategies, experiential techniques and EMDR to change negative attitudes and beliefs associated with negative self-concept.

Like most aspects of personal development, schemata are largely determined by the quality of attachment in childhood. Maladaptive schemata mostly occur in people who experienced abuse or neglect in their developmental years. If your emotional attachment with your parents was weak or missing, you might have developed a schema wherein you view the world as a cold, unloving place where love has to be earned. If you grew up with overbearing, critical parents, you might have developed a view of yourself as inadequate and unable to cope with life. Maladaptive schemata can also develop as a result of being overindulged, such as when a child is given too much freedom.

As we saw earlier, maladaptive schemata and negative thinking can exacerbate pain in various ways. Negative attitudes lead to negative thought-patterns and poor problem-solving. Negative attitudes toward the self reinforce negative feelings and helplessness associated with stress, injury and pain. Negative attitudes also influence decision-making, increasing the likelihood of placing other priorities ahead of personal well-being and safety. Negative attitudes promote social isolation and lack of access to support; if you believe you are worthless/bad/inadequate, you will find if harder to bond with others. Learning how to change your thinking and any underlying negative schema is therefore an important skill for overcoming pain and stress.

Change your thinking, change your brain

Because thoughts are the most visible aspect of mental processing, and to some degree the most accessible, changing your thinking presents as an obvious and effective strategy for changing the sensory-emotional patterns that maintain pain. There are many approaches to changing your thoughts, including cognitive therapy, rational emotional therapy, schema therapy, and dialectical behavior therapy. Two of the most well-known methods for changing negative thinking are cognitive therapy and schema therapy. Cognitive therapy involves learning how to identify and change the negative thoughts associated with problems such as stress and pain. For example, when you are feeling down or overwhelmed by pain, you might think, "It's hopeless, I can't cope." This negative thought only reinforces the feelings of helplessness that led you to have it in the first place. Cognitive therapy teaches us that no matter how bad things seem, we can change our thoughts about what is happening, and thereby lessen the negative impact of problems. Cognitive therapy aims to teach people how to think differently in general, rather than just in relation to a single problem. Cognitive therapy has been very popular in the management of anxiety and depression.

Changing your thinking can change brain activity associated with physical and emotional pain. For example, in the context of cognitive behavior therapy, (CBT), changing your thinking has been found to stimulate changes in the right anterior cortex, an area of the brain known to be involved in PTSD. CBT has also been found to stimulate changes in brain functioning associated with phobias and obsessive compulsive disorder. Chronic pain sufferers who received cognitive therapy had decreased neural activity in brain areas associated with hypervigilance and emotional regulation. In one of the first studies to investigate the use of brain-scanning technology for controlling pain, irritable bowel sufferers were hooked up to an fMRI and trained in how to change brain activity in areas involved in pain perception. An fMRI provides live moving pictures as opposed to the static photo-like images of an MRI. When subjects deliberately induced increases or decreases in activity in their anterior cingulate cortex (ACC) as imaged on the fMRI, their pain changed. Remember the ACC is involved in attention and pain perception. Chronic pain patients who were trained to control their pain this way had less overall pain after this training.[4] Changing your thinking seems to work by assisting the prefrontal cortex to down-regulate the parts of the brain involved in emotion.[5]

How to change your thinking

The first step in changing your thinking is to identify your negative attitudes and beliefs, challenge them, and then replace them with more adaptive thoughts. If, say, you identified a negative belief that you were worthless, and you wanted to change that, you would look for examples of situations where you functioned competently and then create a more adaptive thought to counter the negative one. For example, if you make a mistake at work and think, "I'm stupid," you could remind yourself of the times you did a good job and tell yourself, "I'm OK, I'm competent." Repeated use of this strategy would make it hard to maintain the belief that that you are stupid.

Changing your thinking this way is not as easy as it sounds. Identifying negative thoughts requires being able to recognize and interpret your feelings, something many victims of severe pain find difficult. Stress, abuse and neglect can all create a split between mental and emotional elements of consciousness, making it difficult to identify and label feelings. There is also a tendency to misinterpret feelings such as anxiety and depression as evidence of failure, rather than meaningful emotional responses. The information in Chapter 2 and the emotional reconnection exercises in Chapter 6 are designed to help you redress this deficit. The idea is to learn to *interpret* what your feelings seem to be saying *about you* in relation to the problem. Do your feelings signify that you are competent or incompetent in this situation? In control or out of control? Useful or useless?

Once you have identified the negative thought, the next step is to replace it with a more adaptive one. An adaptive thought is one that leads to increased coping options and greater feelings of control. An adaptive thought is a helpful, forward-moving thought. To be effective, the adaptive thought must have some truth to it—your subconscious will not accept a thought that is false, no matter how well-intended. Table 10.1 gives some examples of negative attitudes and beliefs, and their more adaptive alternatives.

Table 10.1 Negative thoughts and positive alternatives

Event	Negative attitude/belief	More adaptive attitude/belief
Being injured and/or in pain/disabled	"I'm weak/vulnerable/ useless."	"I can learn how to cope." "I'm doing the best I can."
Being abused	"I'm bad."	"I'm okay—it wasn't my fault."
Being rejected or neglected	"I'm unlovable."	"I'm okay—it's them."
Feeling anxious due to stress or trauma	"I'm weak/vulnerable/ helpless."	"I survived." "I can protect myself."
Avoiding situations or people because of anxiety or fear	"I'm weak."	"I have a right to protect myself."
Being criticised	"I'm stupid."	"I did the best I could."
Feeling like there is no one to talk to	"I'm alone."	"I can find someone to confide in."

As we have seen, severe stress can trigger negative attitudes about ourselves. These attitudes are often unconscious and continue to invisibly influence our self-esteem and coping; however, these negative attitudes also often represent an unfair, faulty and partial view of the self, based on the times we failed to measure up or get the love we needed. We need to replace those negative attitudes with more adaptive, self-affirming ones. One way to do this is to identify your negative attitudes and re-evaluate them in the light of a more objective examination of yourself. Try the Changing Your Thinking activity (opposite).

Changing your thinking (top–down)

Negative thinking is something we do automatically, often without even realizing what we are doing. This exercise will help you recognize negative thinking, and change it.

1   Think of a challenging situation or event from your life which triggers negative attitudes and beliefs.

_____

_____

_____

2   When you think of that event or situation, notice *what it makes you think about yourself.*

_____

_____

Note: We are not looking for an emotion here; we already know that situation makes you feel negative. We need to know what that feeling suggests or implies about you and your ability to cope. Is the feeling saying that you feel able to overcome the challenge before you, or unable? Does it say that you are in control or out of control? Strong or weak? Good or bad?

3   Once you have identified the negative attitude or self-belief, you need to replace it with something less negative. At this point it can help to challenge the negative belief. Ask yourself:
    • Did you ask for this problem?
    • Do you like having this problem?
    • Do you really deserve to suffer?
    • Are you not doing everything you can to cope with this problem/overcome it?

_____

_____

4   Based on your responses to the above questions, try to formulate a more balanced, adaptive self-belief. Look at the examples in Figure 10.1 if you are not sure how to do this.

_____

_____

As noted, changing your thinking this way can be helpful for moderate anxiety and depression, but it is less useful when it comes to changing severe physical or emotional pain. Fortunately, there are other ways of changing your thinking. Some new research suggests that the way we process past life events is important. A series of experiments by Professor Sonja Lyubomirsky and colleagues at the University of California indicates it may be better to analyse negative experiences, and just experience positive ones.[6] In the first experiment, it was found that thinking privately about negative events didn't help, but people who talked or wrote about negative events felt better and coped better. For positive events it's the reverse: people who just thought about positive events they had experienced were happier than people who talked (or wrote) about them. It was also found that analysing positive events has a negative effect on health and well-being; it's best to just remember those happy moments. So if you are the sort of person who likes to analyse everything, you need to be become more selective about what types of events you analyse. You should also express your thoughts and feelings about negative events, either by writing about them or sharing them with others.

Another general rule for changing your thinking is to avoid "black-and-white thinking". Black-and-white thinking means seeing things in all-or-nothing terms. Black-and-white thinking means seeing things as either good or bad. Black-and-white thinking has the advantage of simplifying things—it eliminates doubt, but it also locks you into a very fixed way of seeing the world. If something is not the way you would like it and you can't change it, you're stuck with it. The alternative to black-and-white thinking is to be able to look at things from a broader perspective and accept a range of alternatives. Being able to look at things from different angles enables you to reframe problems and make them less stressful. Jenny, the teenage daughter of a famous family therapist, had a habit of getting very frustrated because no matter how she tried she couldn't organize the items on her desktop perfectly. Noticing his daughter's frustration one day, her father gently advised, "Darling, your problem is that you've got too many ways for it to be wrong and not enough ways for it to be right." Carl Whittaker's wise advice to his daughter contains a simple but profound insight: the more ways we have of viewing a problem, the easier it is to find a way through. If you do nothing more than learn how to identify and challenge your negative thought patterns, you will have acquired a valuable skill for coping with pain; however, if you want deeper and more lasting change, you need to change the schema associated with your negative thoughts.

How to change your schema

Schema therapy is about changing the underlying identity structures that maintain negative patterns of thinking. Schema therapy uses a range of top–down and bottom–up techniques to change negative schemata, including cognitive methods, experiential techniques and interpersonal methods (relationships). Schema therapy is also often used alongside EMDR, when there are early painful memories which need to be processed. As we have seen, unresolved childhood trauma and/or neglect is one of the main causes of negative attitudes and beliefs.

Young recommends people start by becoming aware of their negative schemata, and then challenge them through more adaptive thoughts and actions. You can probably make a fairly educated guess what sort of schema you have by reviewing the list at the beginning of this chapter. Challenging a schema involves doing something that dilutes the strength of the schema. One popular exercise is to rewrite negative formative experiences using your imagination. For a person with an emotional deprivation schema, this might involve remembering a time in their life when they felt lonely or abandoned, and then imagining their parents being present and communicating their needs to the parent in the image. Young believes that facing the painful image of a depriving parent can lead to increased understanding and self-acceptance.

Another technique is to challenge your negative schema by learning to pay more attention to the healthy part of yourself. For example, if you have a defective schema (impaired autonomy and performance), you can be aware of that but also realize that there must still be some part of you that is good and healthy. In practical terms, this might mean consciously remembering your achievements and giving yourself some positive feedback. Young recommends making a list of your talents, skills and accomplishments. Stressed or depressed people are often fixated on their failures and pay little attention to their successes or achievements. Some people even think it's somehow wrong to feel proud of their achievements. Remembering your achievements creates positive feelings which make it easier to integrate more self-loving attitudes. Being able to remember your achievements fills up your inner self-esteem bucket. There is nothing wrong with a little self-pride. As discussed earlier, positive feelings also act as an emotional buffer against negative thoughts and feelings triggered by stress.

When reviewing your achievements, remember that the most meaningful achievements are not necessarily those that attract the most glory or attention. You might be the best worker at your place of employment and rightfully proud of that; but you probably derive more pride from your achievements as a parent, spouse or member of your community. Real success is defined by what's important to you personally, not what others define as success. So think about what's important to you when considering your achievements. Try the following exercise.

ACTIVITY

Remembering past successes

Your memory is the basis of your thinking style and your schema. Your memory is also your greatest resource for changing your thinking. Your memory holds your failures, but it also holds your successes. Many victims of severe stress tend to focus too much on their failures, which reinforces negative thought-patterns. This exercise will help develop and strengthen the neural connections between your successes, which will help create more adaptive thought-patterns.

1   Make a list of your greatest achievements in life. Base the list on the achievements or accomplishments you personally feel most proud of, not what others think. For example, you might have come top of the class in school, but feel more proud about being a parent. Or you might not have done well academically at all, but nevertheless managed to attain a successful career of some kind.

_____

_____

_____

_____

_____

2   Don't overlook the obvious; not giving up or surviving a dysfunctional family without developing a drug or alcohol addiction can be regarded as an achievement.

3   What do those achievements say about you?

_____

_____

_____

4   What would it mean if you were to utilize the qualities you used in those achievements more in your future?

_____

_____

5   What would it mean if you were to pay more attention to your successes in future? What effect do you think that would have?

ACTIVITY *Note*: Making this list and answering these questions will force you to become more conscious of your achievements and their implications for your self-esteem. If you are used to having a low opinion of yourself, this may make you uncomfortable. Don't argue with the part of yourself that feels uncomfortable about acknowledging your achievements; just accept it and let it go. That part of yourself is from the past; it has no place in your future.

Because of the way emotional memories are encoded and the effects of depression, recalling your achievements may not come naturally; but regardless of your mistakes or shortfalls, you have no doubt tried your best to cope with the hand life has dealt you. Once you have accepted that there is a healthy part, even if that part seems very small, you can continue to build on it. For more information about schema therapy, see Young's *Reinventing Your Life: The Breakthrough Program to End Negative Behavior and Feel Great Again* (Plume Books, 1994).

How to use experience to change your thinking

Because of the way the brain is organized, changing your thinking may be of limited use where the problem involves intense emotional distress. Remember how the brain processes sensory information in a bottom–up direction? In this case, a bottom–up approach to changing your thinking may be more effective. One bottom–up technique for changing your thinking is to simply pay more attention to events that contradict your negative attitudes and beliefs.

> Janet had chronic pain and PTSD after a pallet of groceries fell on her at the warehouse where she worked. Because of her injuries Janet couldn't work and she became depressed and withdrawn. Then one day her two sons started taking swimming lessons and she had to take them to the local pools complex. Although she dreaded having to be in a noisy, public place, she forced herself to do it because of her love for her children. But something unexpected happened to Janet once she got there. Seeing the pools brought back memories of how she'd felt as a child when she was learning to swim. She found a smile crossing her face as she watched her sons' enthusiastic efforts to stay afloat. As Janet stood there absorbed in her memories, a stranger approached her and asked if she was all right. Janet snapped herself back to reality and assured the passer-by that she was fine. But she felt touched by this unexpected encounter, and thought, "Wow, people do care!" Janet's reaction to this totally unplanned event, and her realization that she could feel connected to a complete stranger, shook her out of her self-absorption and became the beginning of a gradual re-connection with life. Taking her sons to the pool turned out to be a healing experience for Janet in ways she could never have imagined.

It would have been easy for Janet to dismiss the stranger's comments and return to her usual way of thinking and feeling. But because she paid attention to this relatively small incident, new information entered Janet's brain and a new pathway was opened up in her mind. After this, Janet would feel more motivated to take her sons swimming, and one day she would decide to go swimming herself, and that would lead to her joining classes, and so on. Changing your thinking can also happen spontaneously, if you pay attention to unusual events or outcomes which often represent change.

> Faith encountered her abusive ex-husband in the street a few months after she'd finally summoned up the courage to leave him. It was the first time they had seen each other since her escape, and he launched into a verbal tirade against her, even accusing her of disloyalty. Faith endured her ex-husband's verbal tirade for a few minutes, as was her custom, until she felt a rage well up inside her. Suddenly, she couldn't take the abuse anymore and she punched him in the mouth, so hard that his lower teeth protruded through his lip. Whether out of shock or cowardice he did not immediately retaliate, but he did call the police and have her charged with assault.
>
> When Faith appeared in court to face the charges, the prosecutor came over to her, ready to offer help as she had so many times in the past. Without thinking, Faith waved her away and said, "It's OK, I'm not the victim this time." It was only *after* she'd uttered those words that Faith realized what she'd said, and what that meant for how she felt about herself. She *wasn't* a victim any more. The magistrate knew of the history and threw out the charges, but it was those few words that Faith spoke to the prosecutor that were the most important "verdict" of that day.

Sometimes events can overtake us and we can find ourselves in places or situations that force us to re-evaluate our view of ourselves—if only we pay attention. Faith's story also demonstrates how changing your thinking can involve re-interpreting your self-concept in the light of behavioral changes. In Faith's case, these changes were driven by desperation, and perhaps her own maturation as a person. Faith's decision to leave her abusive partner came after 15 years of enduring his abuse. During that time, Faith evolved from a confused teenager to a young woman. The "wrongness" of her abusive spouse's behavior was more obvious and more intolerable to the older Faith than the younger Faith. As we grow older, our thinking changes, we learn to separate how we feel from what we think, and to (hopefully) analyse our experience more maturely. As we grow older, we have less energy to worry about what others think or worry about pleasing others. As we grow older, we become more conscious of the passage of time, and we realize that we should not waste our precious life worrying about things that may never happen, or tolerating negative circumstances or people. Although the effects of stress, abuse and neglect can delay these developmental changes, most of us do get wiser as we get older.

Another bottom–up technique for changing your thinking is to deliberately generate experiences that stimulate more positive emotions. Feeling good makes it easier to think positively about yourself and your ability to cope. Deliberately generating experiences that stimulate positive feelings puts you in charge of the process, and speeds things up.

> Jeremy, an ambulance officer, felt guilty because he hadn't been able to save the life of an accident victim. Heavy traffic at peak hour had delayed their arrival at the scene, and the victim had died. Jeremy felt that if only they could have got there earlier, they could have saved him. Even though he knew it wasn't his fault, Jeremy felt guilty and responsible, feelings he couldn't shake. He felt so bad he took a week off work and, desperate to escape the bad feelings, decided to go camping with his wife. The peaceful sounds of the nearby stream and the wind in the trees did their work, and within hours of setting up camp he began to feel more relaxed. That night as he sat in front of the campfire mesmerized by the sight of the flickering flames, a thought came to him: "I'm not in the world and things are still happening." This was followed by another thought: "Not everything's my fault." Although Jeremy had always known consciously that the patient's death wasn't his fault, in that moment he felt it in his heart. When Jeremy returned home a few days later, he felt like a weight had been lifted and the memory of the deceased accident victim seemed like it was just that, a memory.

Regularly engaging in activities that stimulate positive emotions is one of the most powerful ways to change how you feel and, thus, how you think about yourself. As we saw in Chapter 8, regular exercise can be just as effective as antidepressants in relieving depression. Other activities that you might consider include:

- taking up relaxation, meditation or yoga
- sharing your feelings with someone you trust
- helping someone in need
- doing something different to your normal routine
- getting a hobby
- taking a course.

It might seem patronizing to recommend you engage in such obvious everyday activities, but the chances are that if you're stressed or depressed you're not practicing many of these simple yet vital, self-nourishing activities. It's also important to remember that the point of the activity is not simply to distract you from thinking about your problems; it's also to allow the generation of positive feelings, and self-reappraisal in the light of those feelings. Regularly engaging in activities that stimulate positive emotions is also one of the foundations of building resilience, as you will see in the next chapter.

ACTIVITY

Changing your thinking (bottom–up)

Although thinking is an intellectual activity, it is also driven by behaviour, experience and feelings. One of the most powerful ways of changing your thinking is to harness the power of experience and emotion to stimulate your brain.

1 Introduce activities into your routine that have the potential to generate positive feelings. Make yourself do something new or different occasionally.
2 Notice how you feel when you are in those new places or situations.
3 Even if you don't notice any difference initially, sooner or later the fact that you are in a different set of surroundings will impact upon your nervous system—that's how you are designed.
4 Take a moment to reflect upon what those feelings say about you. Interest, excitement and enjoyment all stimulate feelings of self-worth and efficacy.
5 Try to pay more attention to your feelings when you are engaged in interesting and enjoyable activities, and use those positive emotions as a basis for feeling and thinking differently about yourself.

Changing your thinking is thus a much deeper activity than just changing your thoughts—it's about changing *how* you think as much as changing *what* you think. Changing your thinking involves paying attention to experiences that generate feelings of efficacy and/or different outcomes to those associated with your usual negative self-concept. Changing your thinking means not interpreting emotions such as anxiety and depression as evidence of inadequacy. Changing your thinking also involves learning to make space for positive emotional responses and re-interpreting your self-concept in the light of those emotions. Changing your thinking requires flexibility: being able to step outside your usual way of looking at the world and yourself. Neurologically, it means being able to balance the emotional parts of the brain with the more rational analytical parts, and being able to move freely between the two.

11

How to build resilience

Every time you fall, get up again.
Hope rises.
Alecia Keyes

Some people seem to be much more able to cope with pain than others. The ability to "bounce back" from adversity is known as resilience. Being resilient does not mean that we don't suffer, but that we are better able to tolerate adversity and move on. Resilient people feel pain, but in the midst of their pain they can also feel hope and even find something positive. Resilient people are also more able to let go of their pain. Resilience is an emotional skill involving the ability to maintain positive emotions in the face of negative circumstances, and the ability to shift from one emotion (e.g. sadness) to another (e.g. hope). Resilience is important when having to deal with long-term stressors such as chronic pain, emotional neglect and chronic PTSD. Although resilience is mainly thought to come from circumstantial factors such as cultural background and good early childhood attachments, it can also be learned. Building resilience creates an emotional buffer against stress, pain and depression.

What is resilience and why is it important?

We tend to think of resilience as a mental thing—the ability to will ourselves through stress or pain; however, being driven or pushing yourself through life is not resilience. The attitude of "I'll succeed even if it kills me" is not resilience.

Resilience is more subtle than that. Resilience is the ability to respond flexibly to negative circumstances and move smoothly between different demands on your nervous system. Resilience is a body-based state that involves a healthy nervous system which can manage energy effectively. People who cope by getting highly stressed are not resilient. Neither are people who cope by switching off. Dr Richard Davidson, a leading authority on resilience, defines resilience as:

> ... *the maintenance of high levels of positive affect and well-being in the face of adversity. It is not that resilient individuals never experience negative affect, but rather that the negative affect does not persist* ...[1]

The term resilience actually comes from physics: a resilient object bends but does not break when under stress. Resilience thus involves flexibility; a resilient person is able to move relatively freely between high energy states (stress) and low energy states (relaxation). A resilient person is also self-regulated. That means they are able to manage their levels of emotional arousal by relying on their own internal resources as opposed to external devices such as drugs or alcohol, workaholism or "keeping busy". Why aren't paraplegic people more depressed? Because they are not paraplegic full time; they do other things. Resilient people are also able to experience both negative and positive emotions during periods of stress. The ability to experience positive emotions is one of the most important qualities of resilience. Positive emotions help people connect with their inner psychological resources. It's easier to "laugh at death" if you have an optimistic attitude to begin with.

Resilience is a kind of energy that fuels endurance, persistence, creative problem-solving, and the ability to learn from almost any experience. Instead of feeling overwhelmed by events, resilience enables you imagine that you can manage. Instead of feeling trapped, resilience enables you to imagine that there is a solution. Instead of feeling that you deserve to be punished, resilience helps you believe that life can be better. You are probably more resilient than you think—since most people have coped with adversity of some kind, it's impossible not to have developed some degree of resilience.

How to increase your resilience

There are many ways of increasing your resilience. One of the most important ways of building resilience is through having supportive relationships. As we saw earlier, loving relationships help develop internal emotional connection and self-regulation. Remember Cyrulnik's concept of "bastion families" from Chapter 5? Resilience also has to do with the allocation of attention. Do you focus on all your mistakes, or are you able to notice your successes too? Are you engaged with life or have you withdrawn into yourself? Engaging in meaningful, interesting activities is one of the best ways to keep your brain healthy. Living an active, meaningful life usually involves having goals. Goal-directed behavior builds purpose and mastery. Setting goals is a top–down strategy involving increased activation of the left prefrontal cortex.[2] Having goals also stimulates the areas of the brain involved in recovery from negative emotions and the generation of positive emotions.

Other resilience-building activities include:

1 having a good attitude toward yourself
2 cultural factors
3 having goals
4 community
5 play/humor
6 having faith
7 knowing how to turn a problem into a strength.

All of these activities will stimulate your brain in positive ways and increase your emotional well-being. For example, religious attendance has been found to add two to three years to a person's life.[3] As you can see, there are many different things that you can do to increase your resilience. Building your resilience will not cure your pain, but it will make you feel stronger and less overwhelmed by your problems. On the following pages, you will find more details of the seven strategies and how to use them to increase your resilience. Everyone is different and not all of these strategies may suit you. But if you adopt just a few of these strategies you will feel more in control, more secure, and more resistant to physical and emotional pain.

Having a good attitude toward yourself

As we have seen, pain and stress can make you feel bad about yourself. Feeling bad about yourself can foster unhealthy behaviors and an uncaring attitude toward your person. Having a negative attitude toward yourself can undermine attempts to get better, through cognitive dissonance and unconscious self-sabotaging. Cognitive dissonance refers to a mismatch between what a person says and what they feel. The idea that having a negative attitude toward oneself can foster self-defeating behavior is nothing new. As the nineteenth-century French author Alexandre Dumas wrote:

> *A person who doubts himself is like a man who would enlist in the ranks of his enemies and bear arms against himself. He makes his failure certain by himself being the first person to be convinced of it.*

If you suffer from self-loathing, self-blame and self-punishment, you probably have an underlying negative attitude toward yourself. As we saw in Chapter 10, having a negative attitude toward yourself can be a manifestation of a negative schema. Most people have never consciously thought about what their attitude toward themselves is. Some "sit on the fence", allowing their attitude to be determined by external events; others seem determined to maintain a negative stance, regardless of events ("nothing I do ever turns out right"). Not liking yourself makes no logical sense, but negative attitudes are often acquired before the age of reason.

Having a positive attitude toward yourself can be a challenge that forces you to have a bigger view of yourself. One of the most powerful injunctions to like ourselves comes from Nelson Mandela's Inaugural Speech:

> *Our deepest fear is not that we are inadequate.*
> *Our deepest fear is that we are powerful beyond measure.*
> *It is our light, not our darkness, that most frightens us.*
>
> *We ask ourselves, who am I to be brilliant, gorgeous—talented and fabulous?*
> *Actually, who are you NOT to be?*
> *You are a child of God. Your playing small doesn't serve the world.*
>
> *There's nothing enlightened about shrinking so that*
> *other people won't feel insecure around you.*
>
> *You were born to make manifest the glory that is within us.*
> *It's not just in some of us; it's in everyone.*
> *And as we let our own light shine,*
> *we unconsciously give other people permission to do the same.*
>
> *As we are liberated from our own fear,*
> *our presence automatically liberates others.**

Mandela's words may seem challenging, particularly if we hold negative views about ourselves, or come from a culture that discourages having pride in oneself. But there is surely nothing wrong with his encouragement to "let your light shine". Look where it got Mandela; and after 30 years in prison, no one could have blamed him if he'd felt bitter. Actions speak louder than words. Why don't you photocopy the above excerpt of Mandela's speech, stick it up somewhere you will see it often, and take the challenge? There are many books about positive thinking where you can learn how to think differently. Maxwell Maltz's classic book *Psychocybernetics* is a good place to start. Deciding to have a positive attitude toward yourself won't make you start feeling good about yourself immediately, but it will lead to better self-care and less self-destructive patterns of behavior. Try the following activity.

---

* Words by Marianne Williamson.

ACTIVITY

Developing a positive attitude toward yourself

Having a good attitude begins with making a conscious decision to like yourself. Deciding to like yourself is an adult decision—it's you taking responsibility for yourself rather than letting it be dictated by the past.

1   Begin by making a conscious decision regarding where you stand in relation to yourself. Imagine its World War II: there are Nazi Germany, the allies and Switzerland. You have to decide whose side you are on: are you going to side with the enemy; sit on the fence with Switzerland; or join the allies and fight evil? Where do you stand?

2   Start treating yourself with kindness and respect—even if you don't feel deserving. Rest when you feel tired. Eat when you feel hungry. Say no when you need to.

3   Don't allow others to dictate how you feel about yourself—even if they are people you should supposedly trust. Just as you are selective about what food you eat, you can be selective about what kinds of feedback you take in.

4   Avoid negative people; ignore unfair criticism.

5   Seek out positive people.

6   Accept compliments (when someone pays you a compliment, breathe inward and imagine the compliment is entering your body with your breath).

7   Learn to use failure as a learning experience, and mistakes as opportunities. Mistakes are only mistakes if you don't learn from them.

8   Introduce activities into your routine that have the potential to generate positive feelings. Make yourself do something new or different occasionally.

Having a goal

Goals give life meaning. A goal is something external to yourself; it's something that you care about more than the present circumstances. Having a goal reminds you that there are things beyond the present circumstances. Having a goal keeps you forward-focused and generates motivation to keep going. Having a goal takes focus off your pain, and projects you into a more active coping mode.

As a child, Milton Erickson was diagnosed with poliomyelitis. Soon after being diagnosed, the family doctor came to the house and Erickson overheard him telling his mother, "The boy will be dead by morning." Erickson recalls, "Being a normal kid, I resented that." When his mother came back into the bedroom, Erickson said nothing about what he'd overheard, but instead asked her to move a large chest of drawers away from where they were blocking the window. Then he asked her to move it back. He kept this up for some time, asking his mother to move the chest back and forth, until he was finally satisfied. Erickson's exasperated mother thought he was delirious, but wanted to humor what she thought was her dying son's last wishes. Erickson, however, had decided that he was "damned if I wasn't going to see the sunset" before he died. Erickson's strategy of keeping his mother busy until *after* sunset kept his mind off his condition and helped him survive. Three days later Erickson emerged from a coma and went on to live a long and very productive life.

Erickson believed that one of the best prescriptions for enjoying life was having a real goal—in the near future.[5] Studies of survivors of the Nazi concentration camps found that the people who survived best were those who set short-term goals, such as looking forward to extra rations, or a cup of coffee. Having something to look forward to, no matter how seemingly trivial, made the difference between life and death. In order to be helpful, goals must be personal, based on what you want or care about, rather than what's expected of you by others. Whether it's getting your children though high school, or world peace, having a goal gives you something to make you want to keep going during difficult times. Having a goal gives you something positive to focus on, and builds motivation and efficacy. Interestingly, caring about something else that matters, in a healthy way, also increases your self-care. When you invest energy in a meaningful goal, you are saying that you matter.

Some experts recommend writing down your goals. This is certainly a good start—it makes them more real. Goals should be specific: wanting to be happy is not a viable goal, but wanting to play the guitar or own your own home is. Big goals may need to be broken down into smaller sub-goals in order to feel a continuous sense of achievement. The most important goals are not those we write down on a piece of paper; the most important goals are written on the heart, when we wake up at 3 a.m. and *know* that we want to be the best father, electrician, piano-player or whatever. These sorts of goals come from deep within. In this way, goals are an expression of our innermost self and serve to reaffirm our identity. Most people live with a combination of short- and long-term goals. Short-term goals can keep you going through more intense crises, while long-term goals can sustain you through more chronic situations.

ACTIVITY

Setting goals

Set yourself a goal. It could be a short-term goal such as starting an exercise program, or a long-term goal such as learning a new skill. Whatever you decide to do, it must be something meaningful to you, something that you care about. If it's not meaningful to you, it won't be meaningful to your brain.

1   Write your goal down and/or commit it to memory.

_____

_____

_____

2   Make a plan: what do you have to do in order to achieve that goal?

_____

_____

_____

_____

_____

3   Make a start: do something practical toward achieving your goal.

4   Keep a record of your progress.

_____

_____

_____

_____

5   Be patient. Remember that "Rome wasn't built in a day".

6   *Don't give up.*

Cultural factors

Culture refers to the values, knowledge and attitudes held by the society or social group you live in. Culture refers to how the tribe or group you live in define themselves and what they do. Culture is society's way of teaching us how to cope with stress and adversity. Myths, stories and ways of coping are all part of culture.

Culture is maintained through the kinds of stories we tell about ourselves, our rituals and ceremonies, art, music and so on. Culture is invisible, but it shapes how we react to and cope with stress and suffering. Latin cultures are more expressive of their feelings, and suffer less depression. Anglo cultures are more stoic, preferring to endure pain without complaint. Culture can have a direct bearing on many aspects of life functioning. Children of poor Vietnamese immigrants (in the USA) tend to perform better academically than better-off white children. Why? Because Vietnamese people place a higher value on education. Older siblings are expected to help younger siblings. The more siblings a child has, the better he or she is likely to do at school.

Most cultures incorporate wisdom about coping with adversity. This can be transmitted through stories, sayings, art and literature, and parental advice. Many children's stories contain hidden messages about coping with adversity. The story of Robin Hood is about a man who is suffering a great setback or loss. Robin Hood has to live in the wild after coming back from war to discover that the sheriff has killed his father and wants to kill him too. In this story the dark forest represents the unconscious—a place within that is mysterious to us. To defeat the sheriff, Robin has to first overcome the bully of the forest. The bully represents the obstacles that sometimes stand between us and taking action to overcome our problems. Sometimes we have to overcome something just to get started. You may never have thought of the story of Robin Hood in this way, but that is what it means. In this era of Internet and movies, story-telling has become a more public, less personalized affair. We may have to look for cultural wisdom in movies, books and TV shows rather than our grandparents.

ACTIVITY

Accessing cultural resources

Wherever you come from or live now, you are surrounded by culture. Whatever culture you most identify with contains within it wisdom about coping with adversity. Whether you like opera or watching movies, you can gain support from culture.

1   *Think about what cultural media you enjoy.* Books, music, sport, cinema, theatre, even the stories your father used to tell.
2   *Avail yourself of the cultural opportunities around you.* Go to the movies; talk to your grandfather or mentor; or read a book.
3   *Books.* Biographies are a great source of inspiration and lessons learned. There is nothing like reading about how someone else has coped with adversity. A few good reads are:

- Overcoming disability: *Reach for the Sky: The Story of Douglas Bader* by Paul Brickhill
- Finding meaning in adversity: *Man's Search for Meaning* by Victor Frankl
- Love/self-discovery: *The Little Prince* by Antoine de Saint Exupery
- Persistence: *The Pursuit of Happyness* by Chris Gardiner
- Resilience: *The Power of Resilience* by Robert Brooks and Sam Goldstein
- Surviving PTSD (rape): *Lucky* by Ann Siebold
- Surviving PTSD (combat): *Souled Out* by Michael S. Orban
- Surviving trauma (severe burns): *The Sun Farmer* by Michael McCarthy
- Surviving illness (cancer): *It's Not About the Bike* by Lance Armstrong
- Inspiration: *Prayers For healing: 365 Blessings, Poems & Meditations from Around the World* by Maggie Oman Shannon.

4 *Movies*. Psychologist John Hesley recommends movies to his patients as a way of helping them understand and learn how to cope with their problems. Hesley recommends the following:[4]

- PTSD: *Distant Thunder*; *Saving Private Ryan*.
- Chronic illness: *Terms of Endearment*; *Whose Life Is It Anyway?*
- Personal courage: *Life Is Beautiful*; *The Shawshank Redemption*
- Support: *City Slickers*; *Fried Green Tomatoes*
- Finding meaning: *Dead Poets Society*; *It's a Wonderful Life.*

As you can see, you don't have to be an opera lover to benefit from culture. Think about what other practical ways you can absorb cultural wisdom to help you in overcoming your pain, and make those ways a part of your life.

Community

As we have seen, one of the biggest contributing factors to stress and pain is isolation and lack of support. We spoke earlier about the importance of strong family relationships as a source of safety and support, and how feeling supported can lessen the impact of stress and pain. Another excellent source of support and resilience is community. The word community comes from the Latin *com-munis* which literally means "to fortify together". When people come together to support each other and share in one another's pain, adversity becomes easier to bear. For example, Puerto Rico is a collectivist society where the needs, values and goals of the community are valued over those of the individual. Puerto Ricans place a high value on giving and receiving support, both within and outside the family. Chronic pain sufferers are not held responsible for the existence and elimination of their pain. A person's suffering is seen as a problem for the whole community. Health care providers play a much more supportive role than would be expected in Anglo cultures, and 95 per cent of the population are covered by government insurance. Not surprisingly, the incidence of depression among chronic pain sufferers in Puerto Rico is significantly less than in other countries.[6]

A community is a group of people with a common interest. A community can be made up of people living together, such as a small town or neighbourhood, or people living at different locations but united by a common purpose or interest. Examples of communities include church groups, support groups, volunteer organizations, and interest groups. The best way to access community as a way of increasing your resilience is to join a community group or organization. Support groups can be found online or in directories of local community organizations.

ACTIVITY

Accessing community

Join a community. A community is a group of like-minded people such as fellow trauma survivors, fellow chronic pain sufferers, or even a church group. Your local community center or church is a good starting place. If you are unable to connect with a community group physically, you can join one online. Online communities exist for just about every human problem, interest or need imaginable. A few examples of online support communities are:

1   *Chronic pain*:
    • The Fibro Community <www.fmscommunity.org>
    • Chronic Life: <www.chroniclife.com>
    • National Pain Foundation <www.nationalpainfoundation.org>
    • Hope A-Z <www.hopeaz.com>
2   *Traumatic stress*:
    • www.support4hope.com
    • www.ptsdforum.org
    • www.giftfromwithin.org
    • www.traumasurvivorssupport.org

The above are just a small, select sample. If you search the Web you can find many more to suit your particular needs. Linking up on the Internet can also be a first step toward linking up physically, especially if you find a group in your area.

Play/humor

Another source of resilience and an increasingly popular antidote to stress and pain is play and laughter. As we've seen, stress, trauma and pain can take away your sense of fun and your motivation to be playful. Traumatized children have been found to lack the ability to play normally. Their games tend to be repetitive re-enactments of what happened to them. They often play alone, instead of interacting with other children. Traumatized adults are no different. They often abandon previously enjoyed activities, they become antisocial and withdrawn, or engage in self-destructive forms of "play" such as substance abuse, reckless relationships and other forms of risk-taking behavior. This inability to relax, play and laugh leaves you stuck in the past and unable to connect with life joyfully and spontaneously.

When you play, you stimulate the creative, intuitive side of your brain. In play, the frontal lobes win out over the reflexive responses of the emotional brain.[7] Play helps us learn to cope with reality by allowing us to experiment with simulated emergencies. Play is one of the few times when we are in charge of circumstances, which allows for the development of different responses. Play looks like an emergency, but it isn't; studies with dogs show that even though they are rushing around as if they're in extremity, there is actually no adrenaline pumping through their system. Human play can take the form of card-games, word-games, sport, or playing games on a computer. Computer games in particular allow us to deal with threats in an imaginary world, where we can generate creative responses without feeling overwhelmed by stress or anxiety.

How did Irish writer James Farrell cope with having to spend a lot of time in an iron lung because of breathing difficulties caused by polio? He wrote a black comedy called *The Lung* whose hero, also stricken by polio, had a craving for alcohol and women. Humor and laughter have been found to stimulate the production of endorphins and lower cortisol levels. In a now famous experiment, Norman Cousins found that daily laughter reduced the inflammation of his ankylosing spondylitis.[8] Laughter creates an emotional barrier between yourself and your problems. When you laugh, you cannot stay feeling stressed or helpless. Humor and laughter can also stimulate increased self-esteem and more positive thinking. David H. Rosen, a humor researcher, found that people who watched a humorous video were more hopeful compared with those who didn't.[9] Rosen feels that humor may inhibit negative thoughts and allow for more positive ones. Humor makes you look at things from a different, usually wider perspective.

Benefiting from humor requires more than just watching funny movies or telling jokes: it requires having a creative attitude toward adversity, so that you can see things in a different (less negative) light. Comic relief arises from the ironies and incongruities found in everyday life, experiences in which inhibitions are suppressed, allowing a natural flow of emotion. One of the most striking examples of this is in the movie *Life is Beautiful*, when the imprisoned protagonist deliberately misinterprets the German guards' commands to make his young son think they are in a holiday camp.

ACTIVITY

Learning to use humor

Having a sense of humor is another ingredient of resilience which can be cultivated. Developing a sense of humor requires learning to think differently, rather than learning lists of jokes or attending laughter classes. The best humor is free of sarcasm and put-downs. Here are a few tips for developing a sense of humor:

1 *Look out for the odd, bizarre and the funny.* Life is full of paradox, contradiction and absurdity. Why did your spouse put an empty jar of peanut butter back in the cupboard? Why does your telephone company send you a bill for 1 cent?

2 *Learn to pay attention to the little things.* This is the secret of Jerry Seinfield's comedy. In a recent interview, Jerry Seinfeld described how he could get a laugh out of nothing more unusual than finding a good cup of coffee or a car-parking space in New York City.

3 *Don't take yourself so seriously.* The next time something goes awry, try stepping back and laughing (gently) at yourself. Remember what John Lennon said: "Life is what happens to you while you're making plans."

4 *Don't take life too seriously.* As Shakespeare said, "All the world is but a stage."

5 *Read funny books; watch funny movies.*

6 *Try to find people who have a similar sense of humor to you.* Humor needs to be shared, but remember that everyone has a different sense of humor.

Faith

Faith is an element of religion. Having faith means believing in something greater than yourself. It could be faith in God, but it could equally be faith in another person, a set of values or your community. Christians learn to believe from an early age that there is someone looking over them—someone they can turn to in times of adversity, even when they feel that everyone has forsaken them. Christians are taught that suffering is inevitable but that it can also be transformative and that there is something beyond the present circumstances. Whatever you may think about religion, these teachings can be very helpful in times of stress. Religious faith has been found to help people maintain health and overcome adversity. Extensive research suggests that there is a strong relationship between religious faith and mental and physical health, and that religious faith can help in coping with illness and recovery from illness.[10–12] For example, a recent study of elderly people undergoing elective cardiac surgery showed that patients who didn't derive strength and comfort from religion were more likely to die during the first six months after surgery.[13]

From a purely psychological standpoint, it's not surprising that having faith increases your resilience. Believing in something or someone outside your self can be a great comfort in times of adversity. Having religious faith provides you with a direct emotional connection to thousands of years of wisdom about coping with suffering. Christians are reminded: "Fear not, for I am with you. Do not be dismayed. I am your God. I will strengthen you; I will help you; I will uphold you . . ." *Isaiah 41:10*. Christian mysticism teaches believers to let go of life's problems and hand over their worries to God, a concept which is central to practices such as mindfulness, and being able to detach one's self from pain.

Having faith can also mean believing that, in the grand scheme of things, the world is a good place and life remains worthwhile, regardless of what has happened. This is what Alice Walker had in mind in her novel *The Color Purple*. This sort of faithfulness reminds us that beauty and goodness can survive, despite evil and suffering. It's the appeal of ancient prayers such as the Desiderata.

> *You are a child of the universe no less than the trees and the stars; you have a right to be here. And whether or not it is clear to you, no doubt the universe is unfolding as it should. Therefore, be at peace with God, whatever you conceive him to be. And whatever your labours and aspirations, in the noisy confusion of life, keep peace in your soul. With all its sham, drudgery and broken dreams, it is still a beautiful world. Be cheerful. Strive to be happy.*

Knowing how to turn a problem into a strength

Another useful ability for building resilience is knowing how to turn a problem into a strength. The ability to turn tragedy into a triumph is a form of psychological alchemy wherein we transform something bad into something useful. Turning problems into strengths is more than just being able to find something positive in a negative situation; its about processing what's happened, absorbing change and moving on.

> Michael Weisskopf, a correspondent for *Time* magazine, lost his right hand when he picked up a grenade an Iraqi insurgent threw into the back of his vehicle. Prior to losing his hand, Weisskopf was a fearless, self-absorbed, career journalist. A separated father of two, he regarded fatherhood as a job "with little payoff". Weisskopf maintained an emotionally uncommitted relationship with his girlfriend of 12 months who didn't even know that he was still legally married.
>
> After losing his hand, the normally self-reliant Weisskopf found himself unable to make a peanut butter sandwich, and dependent on his children to tie his shoelaces.

How to turn a problem into a strength

Think about a negative situation or circumstance in your life—perhaps the problem that led you to pick up this book. Acknowledge that this problem has caused you pain, and put that aside for the moment. Ask yourself the following questions:

1   How have I survived despite this problem?

_____

_____

2   What have I learned from this problem?

_____

_____

3   What has my response to this problem taught me about myself?

_____

_____

4   What qualities have I had to develop as a result of this problem?

_____

_____

5   How has this problem made me a better person?

_____

_____

6   What does the way I have coped with this problem say about my ability to cope in future?

_____

_____

Note: Try to answer the above questions as fairly and objectively as possible. Avoid the temptation to answer them in the negative—these questions are not about that.

He also suffered an identity crisis—unable to work as a reporter, play tennis or even make love normally, he felt like a nobody. There was also the constant pain, as his amputated hand generated crushing, stabbing phantom limb pain. Weisskopf felt lost and depressed, and wondered whether life was worth living. Then, one day as he was watching his children sledding in the snow, hearing them shout "Watch this, daddy", Weisskopf suddenly found himself crying. With the clear insight that often only comes after an emotional cartharsis, Weisskopf suddenly realized how close he had come to never seeing his children again and that he really loved being a father.

After this incident, Weisskopf changed from being a self-absorbed loner into someone with a much greater capacity for intimacy and commitment. Weisskopf realized that people really loved him for who he was, not for what he did or how successful he was. He became a better father, a better partner (he married his girlfriend) and a more rounded human being. He vowed to never put his career ahead of his family again. Weisskopf's view of the accident also changed; instead of seeing losing his hand as a tragedy, he came to see it as a win-win situation with the prize being "the rest of my life".[14]

As Weisskopf's story demonstrates, turning a problem into a strength isn't easy, and often comes after significant emotional turmoil; but if you can find something useful in even the worst of times, you can transcend seemingly hopeless situations. Stress, injury and pain are destructive, but they can also be transformed into something useful. At the very least, pain means we have to accept our vulnerability, and stress means we need to review our priorities. If we can find some meaning beyond the loss and suffering, we can transform our pain and stress. Try the "How to turn a problem into a strength" exercise.

Conclusion

Resilience is a vital quality for overcoming physical and emotional pain. Resilience gives you a kind of immunity against stress and pain. Resilience is something you can develop—a mental exercise where the muscles you build are psychological. Building resilience involves connecting with activities, places and people that make you feel strong. In this chapter you have learned about a number of activities that can increase your resilience. The list is by no means comprehensive—resilience can also be enhanced through pets, Yoga or Pilates, being with nature, having a hobby, helping others, or just living an interesting life. Individual differences, cultural factors, personal interests and preferences, and education will determine what strategies are appropriate for you. As with any behavioral change, you will need to make a conscious effort to implement new routines. The more often you engage in these activities, the easier it becomes.

12

Overcoming pain with EMDR

Where "it" was, "I" shall come to be.
Sigmund Freud*

Painful memories are always stressful, regardless of whether the pain is physical or mental. We have seen how stress can lead to pain through its effects on the brain and nervous system. Post-traumatic stress is a unique type of stress wherein these symptoms are magnified through overwhelming anxiety, numbness and dissociation. Overcoming pain that is connected to trauma requires resolving the undigested sensory-emotional reactions that are maintaining the pain. As per the phase-oriented approach, the most effective way to overcome trauma is to combine safety and support, reconnecting with feelings, emotional regulation skills and changing thinking into a unified process. This allows a controlled "unfreezing" of painful sensations and emotions embodied in traumatic memories, and their integration into normal consciousness. Once a traumatic memory has been processed this way, it ceases to be a source of pain. Because of a good family background, or genetic inheritance, many people possess the sensory-emotional skills described in this book and can resolve trauma without ever needing to read a book like this or consult a therapist. But for those of us lacking in these skills, or just faced with something beyond our capabilities, professional help is necessary. This is where EMDR comes in.

---

* New Introductory Lectures on Psychoanalysis, vol. 22, lecture 31, "The Dissection of the Physical Personality", *Complete Works*, Standard Edition, eds. James Strachey and Anna Freud (1964).

EMDR is based on the premise that the human brain is designed to process information (sensations, feelings, images and thoughts) in a way that allows them to be understood and managed. The result is that life experiences get remembered and filed in an adaptive way—a way that enables them to be utilized later on. Francine Shapiro describes this natural processing capacity as "adaptive information processing" (AIP). Normally we will think about our experiences, talk or express feelings about them, and even dream about them. This natural processing of events involves combining the four sensory-emotional strategies described in the preceding chapters. Over time, this natural processing of painful memories leads to their being smoothed over and integrated into memory in a less distressing way. Remember how Aron worked through his feelings to overcome the trauma of being trapped by a rock in Chapter 2?

Traumatic experiences overload this innate information-processing capacity, leading to a failure to integrate sensory-emotional aspects of experience normally. The result is intrusive sensory-emotional fragments which persist long after the event that triggered them has ended. These can include numbness, flashbacks, increased physiological arousal, and physical pain. Where there is injury or pain, this can act as a trigger for the unresolved traumatic memories, leading to a vicious cycle of trauma and pain.

Resolving trauma and trauma-related pain requires reconciling the physical and emotional effects of unpleasant events and transforming them into something useful. The result is that normal adaptive information processing is enabled, and the elements of traumatic memories get integrated into consciousness in an adaptive way. For example, instead of tensing up and hurting every time you think of the accident/illness/combat trauma, etc., you can think, "It's over now and I survived." For the war veteran suffering from recurring headaches, this might mean being able to finally file away those awful images and stop the headaches. For the adult survivor of childhood abuse and fibromyalgia, it might mean being able to finally let go of those painful memories and stop hurting.

What is EMDR how can it heal pain?

The challenge for overcoming traumatic memories is overcoming the dissociative barrier which is keeping those memories compartmentalized, and managing the overwhelming emotions associated with them. This requires learning three core emotional skills:

1   how to tolerate negative feelings
2   how to control negative feelings
3   how to integrate negative feelings.

We have spent the last seven chapters looking at how to implement these skills to overcome physical and emotional pain, via a number of sensory-emotional processing skills. We have also seen how overcoming pain requires practicing these skills in a unified way; however, because of the intense emotion, avoidance and dissociation associated with traumatic pain, it not always possible for an individual to tie these skills into an integrated process unaided.

This is where EMDR comes in: EMDR involves a guided application of the four sensory-emotional processing skills, so that traumatic memories can be processed safely and effectively, and no longer cause us physical or emotional pain.

EMDR was born in 1989, following Francine Shapiro's fateful walk in the park (as described in Chapter 7). As a result of her fortuitous experience of feeling better following spontaneous eye-movements, Shapiro discovered that traumatic memories could be resolved rapidly through concentrating on the memory while concentrating on a bilateral stimulation—a procedure known as dual attention stimulus. In her ground-breaking initial scientific study of EMDR, Shapiro found that the method could stimulate significant reduction in physical and emotional distress associated with PTSD in just a few sessions.[1] Since then, dozens more studies have led to the general acceptance of EMDR as an effective treatment for PTSD.[2,3]

Because of the overlap between physical and emotional pain, clinicians soon saw the potential of EMDR as a treatment for chronic pain. A growing number of studies indicate that EMDR can be effective in the treatment of chronic pain and trauma-related pain.[4-7] Recipients of EMDR usually report feeling more relaxed, less distressed, and more able to distinguish between real and imagined threats. For example, Jenny, a chronic fatigue sufferer, lived in fear of the next pain flare-up and how she was going to cope. The anxiety that she felt about her pain caused tension, which added to her pain. Intellectually, Jenny "knew" that she was a strong person, but emotionally she didn't feel it. After EMDR treatment, which involved learning to soothe her pain using a combination of dual attention stimulus and healing imagery, Jenny felt more confident in her ability to cope, which made her feel less anxious and less vulnerable to pain flare-ups. Pain experts are excited by the promise of this method.[8] As described in Chapter 4, there is some evidence to suggest that EMDR changes brain activity associated with PTSD.

As the name suggests, EMDR works a little differently to traditional methods. Many traditional therapeutic approaches would involve re-telling the details of the trauma, with the expectation that this will eventually facilitate a sense of mastery over what happened. In EMDR you don't have to do this—in fact, it is actually possible to reprocess a trauma without telling the therapist any of the details of what happened. Let's say you have suffered a car accident where you were seriously injured. In EMDR the first thing you would be asked to consider is your safety—where do you feel safe and have you been able to access this place or person following your trauma? The aim of this is to create an emotional "anchor" to feelings of security, which provides stability while confronting the painful emotions associated with the trauma. The safety anchor is reinforced by holding it in mind while simultaneously concentrating on the bilateral stimulation, like the exercises in Chapter 7. Once safety has been established, trauma reprocessing can begin.

Processing trauma with EMDR begins with being asked to recall the trauma in terms of an image, and the negative thoughts and feelings that go with it, while simultaneously attending to a bilateral stimulation. The bilateral stimulation usually consists of tracking the therapist's horizontal hand movements, but auditory tones and tapping may also be employed. The effect of focusing on the bilateral stimulation, also known as dual attention stimulus (DAS) is to reduce the distress associated with the traumatic memory. Recipients of DAS typically report feeling calmer, less anxious and less pain, effects which can last anywhere from a few minutes to forever. Where further work is needed, the therapist simply keeps repeating the dual attention stimulus while the client focuses on whatever comes into their mind until they run out of material. The reprocessing ends with the client being asked to review their negative thoughts in relation to the trauma. For example, an accident victim might go from feeling helpless and thinking "I'm gonna die", to "I survived".

What happens in an EMDR session?

EMDR treatment involves a well-defined series of tasks. One of the first tasks of the treatment phase is to decide what the main problem is. By definition, traumatic pain involves unpleasant physical or emotional reactions which stem from a life-threatening or otherwise highly stressful event. The therapist will help you turn a wordless jumble of images and sensations into a structured unit of information, capable of being processed normally by your brain. This is accomplished via three questions, designed to separate out the physical, mental and emotional elements of the traumatic memory. The three questions go something like this:

1 When you think of the problem, what image do you get?
2 When you think of the problem, what thought do you have about yourself?
3 When you think of the problem, what feeling do you get?

These questions may also be varied in the treatment of chronic pain. For example, the negative cognition can be dispensed with in the desensitization phase of non-traumatic pain. The "image" in Question 1 often relates to the pain, rather than a traumatic memory, and has to be constructed out of your perceptions of the pain (e.g. what size, shape and color it has, etc.). Notice also how these questions set up a mental separation between the problem and how it makes you feel.

Note: The "thought" referred to in Question 2 refers to negative self-beliefs such as "I'm not good enough/weak/stupid", etc. These are often unconscious, but powerful influencing factors in terms of coping.

Clients are also asked whether their emotional reaction to the trauma reminds them of anything they have experienced before, particularly early life experiences. This associative linking up of present experience with earlier, dissociated memories often results in an "aha" moment.

> When Harvey's therapist asked him if the depression he was feeling as a result of his chronic pain reminded him of anything he'd felt before, Harvey remembered how alone and helpless he'd felt when his father abandoned his mother. As a sensitive nine-year-old, Harvey could see that his mother wasn't coping and that he would have to learn how to take care of himself. Harvey developed himself into someone who could fix any problem and who was always available to help others in need. His chronic pain had taken away this means of getting love. The therapist's question helped Harvey connect his current pain and depression with the trauma of being abandoned as a child.

Describing the trauma in this way helps the client access unconscious aspects of the problem, thereby overcoming the dissociation which maintains traumatic memories and making them available for normal mental processing. For example, once Harvey had made the connection between his current feelings and his childhood trauma, the therapist targeted his childhood trauma with EMDR desensitization and reprocessing. As Harvey focused on his feelings of abandonment while simultaneously attending to the bilateral stimulation, he felt his feelings of distress softening. Feeling less distressed enabled Harvey to think differently about this situation. Harvey realized that although he was alone *then*, he was not alone *now*—he had a wife and children who loved him very much. Although this realization did not cure Harvey's pain, it alleviated his depression, which helped him start taking a more active, positive approach to coping.

Another element of EMDR treatment is the creation of future templates. A future template is a resource for dealing with future episodes of physical or emotional pain. Future templates are useful for PTSD sufferers needing to deal with on-going post-traumatic symptoms, or chronic pain sufferers needing to deal with future pain flare-ups. For example, a PTSD sufferer might practice remembering a safe place as a way of buffering themselves against unwanted traumatic thoughts and feelings. A chronic pain sufferer might practice thinking of healing imagery to help cope with future episodes of pain. Leanne got an image of her pain shrinking from a large red ball to a small coin-sized object after she focused on her pain and bilateral stimulation. The trigger-word that she associated with this process was "relief". On several occasions, Leanne's therapist helped her practice focusing on her pain, together with the image of it shrinking and the word "relief". When Leanne returned home, she found that when she focused on her pain and the healing imagery while listening to a recording of bilateral sounds, she could control her pain. She also noticed that she felt less worried about the pain following EMDR, as though it just wasn't such a big problem. Leanne found having a therapist to guide her through this process indispensable.

Esther's story: healing accident-related pain and trauma

Perhaps the best way to understand how EMDR can help resolve trauma and pain is through the eyes of someone who has experienced it. Esther suffered from a combination of post-traumatic stress and chronic pain after a car accident during which she was trapped in the vehicle for several hours.

> Esther and her husband were nearing the end of an interstate trip to visit their daughter when another car veered onto the wrong side of the road and crashed into them. Esther could remember seeing the other car coming toward them, and realizing that they were going to collide, but there was nothing she could do. After that, there was a great "thump" followed by the sound of breaking glass, then silence.
>
> When Esther regained consciousness, she noticed a sharp, stabbing pain in her knees. "At least I'm alive," she thought. She tried to move, but she couldn't because her legs were jammed under the dashboard. She noticed her husband trying to open the passenger door to get to her, but it was jammed shut. Esther's relief at surviving turned to terror as she realized she couldn't get out of the wrecked car, which she feared could catch fire any minute. Esther's heart was racing, and the following hour (while she waited for emergency crews to arrive and cut her free) seemed like a lifetime. Esther went into shock and by the time the emergency crew prised her from the wrecked vehicle, she was shaking uncontrollably.
>
> Esther suffered various injuries as a result of the accident, including a shattered knee, a haematoma in her right breast, and abrasions on her legs and hands. Even after surgery and many months of rehabilitation, Esther's knee continued to be very painful and prevented her from doing many of the physical activities of everyday life. Equally distressing, whenever Esther had to travel by car, her heart would race and her palms would sweat. If other vehicles came too near, she would involuntarily press down hard on the floor of the car with her feet, as though she could somehow make it stop. She begged her husband to drive more slowly, even though he was not a reckless driver.
>
> Esther noticed that her pain and anxiety seemed to feed on each other; whenever her knee hurt really badly, she got flashbacks of the accident, and whenever she was reminded of the accident it seemed to intensify her pain. She also had sleeping problems and would often wake up feeling tired. All this made her feel weak and vulnerable. For a long time Esther resisted the idea of seeking professional help; she had always managed to cope by herself and she couldn't see any reason why she

shouldn't be able to deal with this accident by herself. But as the months wore on, Esther's anxiety did not get better and she began to feel increasingly frustrated and depressed. At her GP's suggestion, Esther finally agreed to see a psychologist who specialized in the treatment of trauma and pain.

To her surprise, Esther found the psychologist easy to talk to and she actually felt relieved to be able to express freely all the feelings that were inside her; up until then, Esther had kept a lot of her feelings to herself to avoid upsetting her husband. The therapist didn't just want to talk about the accident, he also asked Esther about her life in general, her marriage, and how she normally coped with stress. The therapist also asked Esther whether she had experienced any other trauma in her life. Esther had been sexually assaulted as a teenager, an event which had taken her many years to get over. She had no desire to re-open this wound, so with a forced smile she said, "No, nothing else bad has ever happened to me."

"OK," the therapist said, "now we are ready to start working on your problems." Esther felt a little confused by this statement; she had assumed that talking about what happened was the treatment. The therapist told Esther about trauma and how traumatic memories get stored in a way that prevents them from getting processed normally. Then he told her about EMDR, a method of treating trauma that works by activating the brain's innate capacity for information processing and healing. Although Esther had never thought about how her brain worked, the idea that processing her memories about the accident would help made sense; however, she was also curious as to how someone could artificially make this happen. The therapist explained the theory behind how EMDR works, how the bilateral stimulation stimulates the parts of the brain involved in maintaining traumatic memories, in a way that neutralizes brain activity associated with painful memories. The therapist admitted that a full understanding of how EMDR influences the brain was still some years away, and that the important thing was whether or not she found it effective.

Esther nodded appreciatively; she didn't really understand, but she liked the idea that the treatment she was about to receive had some basis in brain physiology. The therapist went on to explain the EMDR procedure to Esther: that she would be asked to think about her pain, the memory of the accident, and any negative thoughts associated with the accident, while simultaneously concentrating on a bilateral stimulation. The therapist advised Esther that once he commenced the bilateral stimulation, the important thing was for her to focus on how she felt in her body and "let whatever happens happen". Esther was so relieved that she didn't have to talk about the accident in order to feel better, that she was happy to give it a try.

"OK," said the therapist, "what would you like to work on first, the trauma or the pain?"

That was a hard question; the pain was really annoying, but Esther figured if she had to live with the pain, that would be easier than having to live with the trauma.

"The trauma," Esther said. "I'd really like to get rid of the trauma."

"OK," the therapist said, "so can you get a mental image of the worst aspect of the accident? Esther immediately got an image of herself trapped in the wrecked car.

"And when you think of that image, how does it make you feel?" asked the therapist. "Anxious," she replied. "And when you think of that image and that feeling, what does it make you think about yourself? "Helpless," she said. "It makes me feel helpless."

"OK, now I'd like you to think of being trapped in the car, the anxiety, and the thought 'I'm trapped' and watch my finger and just notice."

As the therapist started motioning his hand backwards and forwards in front of her face, Esther was initially aware of the image, her feelings and the negative belief. But almost as soon as she started concentrating on the therapist's hand movements, she noticed the image fading and her anxiety decreasing. Then suddenly her anxiety shot back up and she got an image of her childhood abuse. The feelings of helplessness she felt as a child were exactly the same as those she felt when she was trapped in the car.

After about 30 seconds or so, the therapist instructed her to "take a deep breath and relax". After a brief pause he asked her, "So what do you notice now?" "Really anxious," Esther replied. She didn't like this treatment. "OK," the therapist said, "have you ever experienced anything before that made you feel this way?" This time Esther felt that she needed to tell the therapist the truth. "Yes," she said, "it reminds me of how I felt when I was being sexually abused as a child." "Is that what you're thinking of now?" asked the therapist. "Yes," said Esther, a little nervously. "Do you feel okay to continue?" asked the therapist. "Yes," said Esther. "OK," said the therapist, "stay with that." And he resumed moving his finger backwards and forwards in front of her eyes. This time, Esther noticed that the image started fading and her anxiety also seemed to melt. The therapist again instructed her to take a deep breath, relax and check in with her feelings again. This time, she noticed that her mind was blank and her body felt completely relaxed.

"So how do you feel now?" the therapist asked. "Fine," Esther replied, a little confused. "I feel fine." Esther could not believe how differently she felt physically; she had not felt this calm in years. "OK," he said, "and what about the memory of the abuse, where's that now?" "Uh, it's not there," Esther replied. "Good," said the therapist, "and what about the car accident?" Esther looked for but could not find the image of this memory. "I can't think of that either," said Esther. "Good," he said. "So what are you thinking of right now?" "Nothing," Esther replied, "my mind's completely blank." "OK," said the therapist, "what if I ask you to think of the sexual abuse again now?" Esther paused a moment and then said, "Angry, I just feel angry—he stole my childhood." Esther noticed how good feeling angry felt; it was like she wasn't a victim anymore. "That sounds like a pretty normal way to feel about something like that," the therapist commented. Esther could only nod her head in silent agreement. After a short pause, the therapist asked Esther, "Is there anything else about that you would like to work on?" Esther felt tired and drained — she felt that she just needed some time to think about things. "Uh, no, I can't think of anything," Ester replied. "OK," said the therapist, "just to wrap things up I'd like you to think of the accident again, and how it feels now, and tell me what thought you get when you think of that now." Esther remembered how she felt before, and her earlier cognition "I'm helpless", but that no longer seemed right. "I survived," she said. That's what I realize now." "Great," said the therapist, "just think of that." And Esther again found herself tracking his hand backward and forward. After this last set, Esther felt more convinced than ever that what had happened to her was over, and left the therapy feeling a mixture of numbness and elation. Even her knee seemed to hurt less.

At the next session the therapist reviewed Esther's progress, and Esther was pleased to tell him how much more confident she had been feeling. Esther realized with surprise that she had hardly thought about the accident since the first treatment session. Esther also reported that she felt much less anxious when traveling by car, and that she was looking forward to her next trip to visit her daughter. "Great," said the therapist, "so what would you like to work on today?" "The pain," said Esther. The therapist then asked Esther to describe the pain in her knee in terms of how it felt: whether it felt hot or cold, what size it was, whether it had a color, and even whether it reminded her of anything else she had ever felt — for instance, like something was torn. The therapist then asked Esther to rate the intensity of her pain on a scale of 0 to 10, where 10 represented the worst possible pain and 0 represented no pain at all. Esther rated her pain as a 6 out of 10. Esther found it strangely helpful to talk about her pain in this way, almost as though it was a separate part of herself. She usually felt so *emotional* when she thought about her pain. The therapist then instructed Esther to concentrate on her pain while attending to his bilateral hand movements the same way she had before. Again Esther noticed a change in how she felt physically: the pain in her knee almost seemed to shrink to a tiny spot; it was very strange.

After no more than three rounds of dual attention stimulus, Esther's pain had disappeared. The therapist asked her to describe what it felt like now where the pain was before. It sounded crazy, but Esther could only liken it to a feeling of connectedness.

The therapist asked Esther to try to connect that feeling to something she had experienced before. Esther got an image of a round ball of light which seemed to radiate healing energy. The therapist asked her to think of a word that best described that image. "Healing," she replied. "I can heal." "Great," said the therapist, "just concentrate on the white ball and the words 'I can heal'." And again he commenced sweeping his hand backwards and forwards in front of Esther's eyes. This seemed to make the words almost go into Esther's body, and she felt a surge of warm energy. Her knee continued to be free of pain and felt completely normal. The therapist advised Esther that this relief could last anywhere from a few hours to several days. He also advised her that she could use this process herself whenever she felt pain, by thinking of the image of the white ball of healing light and the words "I can heal" while listening to a recording of bilateral stimulation.

Esther's pain relief lasted about a day. When the pain came back, it did not seem to have the same intensity as before. Esther remembered what the therapist had taught her, and she stopped what she was doing and sat down with her iPod set to the bilateral tones, while focusing on her knee pain and imagining the white ball of light. To Esther's amazement the pain started to disappear, the same way it had in the therapist's office. After no more than 10 minutes, Esther was able to get up and go about her daily business virtually pain free. That night her knee was hurting a bit, and she repeated the same procedure and was able to fall asleep without being bothered by the pain. Esther felt in control of her pain for the first time.

Over the coming months, Esther continued to practice and refine this technique with the help of her therapist. Esther's pain continued to decrease in intensity and importance. Esther's attitude to life changed; she started attending church again and re-connected with some old friends. Esther realized that although she loved her husband, there were some things he would just never understand. Life felt good, almost better than it had prior to the accident.

Esther's story demonstrates how chronic pain can be exacerbated by a combination of past and present trauma which the sufferer may not be aware of. It also demonstrates how processing trauma can overcome pain. Instead of just telling and re-telling her story, Esther *learned* how to feel differently through the combination of focused attention and dual attention stimulus in EMDR. With the assistance of a trained therapist, EMDR enabled Esther to harness the power of the four sensory-emotional steps for processing physical and emotional pain in a way that she could never have achieved on her own. Esther also found the EMDR treatment changed her; she felt less weighed down by her past, more connected with her self and more able to recognize and respond to her feelings in the present.

How you can benefit from EMDR

As Esther's story demonstrates, although many of the elements of EMDR can be learned (e.g. reconnecting with feelings, controlling negative feelings), applying them in a unified way to overcome trauma is often beyond the capabilities of the average individual. This is especially so where a present trauma comes on top of early childhood neglect or abuse. Complex, multiple trauma such as torture, or witnessing atrocities or emergency work also tend to be beyond the capacity of individual coping. Severely traumatized people may be at risk of uncontrolled emotional reactions and dissociation, which can be traumatic in themselves; but with the guidance of an EMDR therapist, you can learn and apply the sensory-emotional skills necessary for processing traumatic pain.

Deciding to seek professional help is not always easy. Many societies encourage self-reliance and independence. Victims of trauma may hold faulty cognitions that they should be strong and not need help. Even self-help books like this may seem to suggest that we should be able to overcome our problems on our own. But trying to cope on your own is unrealistic and unfair; who wouldn't need help if they were subject to physical or emotional abuse or neglect during their most fragile years? Who wouldn't need help if they had experienced a painful, life-threatening event wherein they felt helpless to save themselves? So never dismiss your feelings or deny yourself the right to be helped.

There are many different mental health professionals with different experience and methods. EMDR is one method which seems to fit with what we know about brain structure and functioning. Brain scans of EMDR patients suggest that the method can change brain activity associated with trauma and pain, but a lot more research is needed to confirm this. Despite its strange-sounding name and unusual methodology, EMDR contains many elements of traditional psychotherapeutic approaches. The advantage of EMDR is that it works with the sensory-emotional aspects of physical and emotional pain in a more effective, efficient way. Why take 50 hours to feel better if you can get the same result (or better) with 10? If this seems like a wild claim, consider that there are documented cases of PTSD being cured in two or three sessions of EMDR, phantom limb pain being cured in 10 sessions or less. If you feel the need to access additional professional help with an EMDR-trained therapist, see Appendix D. Don't worry if you are not sure whether EMDR can help; the therapist will help you determine whether this is an appropriate treatment for you. It's also important to feel confident in your therapist, that they have the knowledge and skills you need. Generally speaking, you should be able to notice changes within a few sessions, sometimes dramatic, sometimes more subtle. One of the most common and noticeable treatment effects of EMDR is a sense of distance from the painful feelings/memories. This can seem quite strange and magical. Many EMDR clients report feeling different in their bodies, as though their physical self has changed. Most EMDR clients report feeling more connected with their bodies, in a healthy way. There should be a sense of progression from session to session as the momentum of change builds. You should not have to work hard to maintain the changes that happen. You should feel different. Like the quote at the beginning of this chapter, you should feel like there is more of you in your life and less of "it", whatever it was.

Afterword

We have seen that pain is both a physical and an emotional problem, involving some combination of physical injury and emotional stress. We've reviewed the five main types and effects of stress that lead to pain, from negative emotions to structural and functional changes in the brain. We've also seen that pain is located as much in the brain as it is in the body. We've looked at how the brain works, and how it processes information. We've seen that the brain is designed to process information adaptively, but that this capacity can be damaged by severe stress. If chronic pain represents a kind of failure in information processing, overcoming pain requires re-programming our brains to process information more adaptively. Knowing that the brain is neuroplastic, and knowing how it processes information, has enabled us to develop strategies that work with the brain in terms of how it processes information. Knowing how the brain is affected by stress has also enabled us to develop specific strategies for reversing the sensory-emotional processes that maintain physical and emotional pain. Based on integrating EMDR with the phase-oriented approach to treating PTSD, these strategies involve learning new skills and new ways of manipulating feelings through focused attention, bilateral stimulation, detached awareness and cognitive monitoring. Through the exercises and audio CD, you should have learned how to feel differently by exposing yourself to sensory information that alters neurological aspects of your pain experience. Regular practice of these techniques should help you to learn how to feel better, naturally and effortlessly. You *can* "change your brain, change your pain". Unfortunately, sometimes, no matter how much we learn, we have to live with a certain amount of pain. This is where resilience comes in. Having a good attitude, goals, a flexible mind and a sense of belonging can all help protect us against the impact of pain. Focusing on these "quality of life" factors can make the unbearable bearable. There is also the option of seeking professional help. Since gaining professional acceptance as a treatment for PTSD, EMDR is increasingly recognized as a treatment for pain. Chapter 12 describes the EMDR treatment process and how EMDR can be helpful in overcoming trauma-related pain. As Esther's story illustrates, pain in the present is often connected to pain from the past, and it takes professional skills to make these connections safely and stimulate the necessary information processing. If your pain involves severe injury, stress or trauma, you may need to use this book as an adjunct to professional assistance. Whatever you decide to do from here, it is hoped that the information in these pages has inspired you to feel and think about your pain differently, and that you will continue to discover new ways of feelings better.

APPENDICES

Appendix A

Safety/negative beliefs worksheet[*]

Threatening event or situation	Feeling	Self-limiting negative attitude or belief
Example 1 Being injured and in pain	Stress	"I'm helpless." "It's all my fault."
Example 2 Being criticized by my spouse	Shame/anger	"I'm stupid." "I deserve to be punished."
Example 3 Being pressured at work to do more than I feel capable of	Anxiety	"I'm not good enough." "My needs don't count."

[*] Refers to Chapter 5, "Identifying negative attitudes or beliefs".

Appendix B

How to talk about pain*

Sharing our hurt with others is one of the most powerful ways of overcoming pain and stress. Even if it doesn't take the pain away, just expressing our feelings can relieve tension and make adversity easier to bear. Talking about pain can be difficult: the person with pain may not want to burden their family and friends; family and friends may not know what to say. Either way, not talking about pain only makes things worse, so here are some guidelines for how to talk about pain.

For the chronic pain sufferer:

1 *Tell someone how you are feeling.* Having chronic pain can make you feel guilty, anxious and depressed; these are normal feelings which must be acknowledged and expressed. Not expressing your feelings often leads to a build-up of frustration, depression and anger. Expressing your feelings relieves tension and improves coping. Obviously you should be careful about whom you tell and how; your feelings are personal and you do not want them to be mistreated by sharing them with the wrong person.

2 *Finding the words.* Sometimes it's hard to find the right words to describe pain and stress. If you are not accustomed to expressing your feelings, you may need to learn more words to describe how you are feeling. Some emotional intelligence websites or books have lists of "feeling" words, but this won't show you how to connect the words with the feelings. A better technique is to observe people you know who are good at expressing themselves, or to watch dramas or foreign movies. Being able to name what you are feeling is powerful: it leads to mastery over feelings.

3 *Know what you want.* Try to be conscious of what you want out of expressing your feelings. It is human to need to share our pain — to feel that someone else understands us. Remember though that perfect understanding between two human beings is rare — particularly when it comes to suffering. The important thing is that even if the person you express yourself to doesn't completely understand you, you have at least expressed yourself.

4 *Find the right balance.* Naturally, you don't need (or want) to talk about your pain all the time — that would be too depressing. The trick is to express your feelings enough to feel supported and not alone. This can be challenging, even for a good communicator; however, once you have built up an empathic relationship there will be many times when you won't need to say anything — just a look is often enough to convey how you are feeling.

* Refers to Chapter 5, "Opening up".

5 *Be patient.* Because pain is invisible, well people around you will sometimes "forget" that you are in pain and expect things of you that you cannot manage. Understand that it's hard for others to be mindful of your needs all the time and that you will have to remind them of your condition from time to time.

For family members:

1 *Learn to listen.* Listening is one of the most helpful things you can do for a person in pain. Listening involves more than just hearing what is being said; a good listener listens with their heart too. Notice where the words resonate in your own body—this will give you a direct, non-verbal connection with the person in pain.
Listening is hard. It may not feel like you are doing anything, but by being a good listener you create a space for the pain sufferers' feelings— sometimes a space that they are unable to give themselves. Listening is thus a very powerful communication tool.

2 *Pay attention.* Listening is a full-brain activity—you can't listen properly while you are doing something else. To listen properly, you must focus your attention completely on the person you are communicating with, listening with your whole heart and mind. Don't feign interest if your attention is really on something else; it's better to ask them to wait until you are finished with what you are doing.

3 *Have an open mind.* Don't assume you know what the chronic pain sufferer in your life feels or is going through. Their reality is probably very different to yours. Avoid judging: In general, people do not go around pretending they are in pain to get sympathy—research shows that exaggerating or malingering are actually rare. Remember: "Pain is **whatever** the experiencing person says it is, **wherever** the experiencing person says it is."

4 *Demonstrate that you understand—or are at least trying.* Repeating and summarizing what is said is a good way of showing that you are trying to understand. Just a simple "that sounds pretty frustrating" shows the other person that you have listened and are in tune with their feelings.

5 *Only ever offer advice when asked.* It's tempting to offer advice and solutions to people with chronic pain—you want to help, and offering advice can seem like a practical thing to do. Although well-intentioned, this often just gets in the way of good listening and empathy when this is most needed. If they really need you to tell them how to manage their pain, they will ask.

6 *Be patient.* Communicating with a chronic pain sufferer can be challenging at times. They may not always tell you directly what they are feeling or want. They may be irritable, changeable and contradictory. Remember that they are going through a very stressful experience and that it is probably not you that they are really angry with most of the time.

Appendix C

Self-help CDs based on EMDR*

Calm and Confident based on EMDR

Designed for people affected by severe stress, trauma and pain, this CD consists of two 30-minute relaxation sessions incorporating a powerful blend of positive suggestions, soothing music and bilateral stimulation. This CD will help you feel more relaxed, sleep better and also feel more connected with yourself emotionally.

The most effective relaxation training I have heard from any audio library.

Dr Scott Borelli, London

Pain Control based on EMDR

Designed for chronic pain sufferers, this CD consists of two 30-minute pain-control sessions incorporating a powerful blend of pain-relieving suggestions, soothing music and bilateral stimulation. This CD will help you to experience your pain differently by altering the way your nervous system reproduces your pain.

I bought this second CD because the first one was remarkable. The first time I used it I felt my body relax for the first time in a VERY long time. I never expected any relief but at the end of listening, the pain was so much more bearable. Thanks so, so much.

Susan

These CDs are available from:

Canada	**TherapistResources** www.emdrresources.com	*Australasia*	**Open Leaves Bookshop** www.openleaves.com
USA	**Mentor Books** www.mentorbooks.com		**Mark Grant** www.overcomingpain.com
		UK	**Karnac Books** www.karnacbooks.com

* Refers to Chapter 7, "How to change your pain".

Appendix D

How to find an EMDR-trained therapist

If you think EMDR treatment might be helpful for you and would like to consult with a therapist trained in this method, the following information will help.

The easiest way to find an EMDR-trained therapist is to look on the website of your national EMDR association. These are listed below.

Canada	www.emdrcanada.org Look under "Members".	*Australia*	www.emdraa.org Look under "Practitioners".
USA	www.emdria.org	*Europe*	www.emdrassociation.org.uk www.emdr-europe.org

As the associations' websites mostly only list therapists who have joined an association, there may be EMDR therapists in your area who are not listed here. Another method is to type in "EMDR" and the name of the town or city where you live—this will sometimes bring up the name of an EMDR therapist who may not appear on any of the above sites. You can also ring around therapists in your area and ask them if they are EMDR-trained.

REFERENCES

Prologue

1 Trivedi, M.H. (2004). The link between depression and physical symptoms. *Primary Care Companion to The Journal of Clinical Psychiatry, 6*[suppl 1], 12–16.

Chapter 1

1 Maguire, E.A., Gadian, D.G., Johnsrude, I.S., et al. (1999). Navigation-related structural change in the hippocampi of taxi drivers. *Proceedings of the National Academy of Sciences*, Apr 11, 2000, *97*(8), 4401–4403.

2 Woon, Fu L., & Hedges, D.W. (2008). Hippocampal and amygdala volumes in children and adults with childhood maltreatment-related posttraumatic stress disorder: A meta-analysis. *Hippocampus, 18*(8), 729–736.

3 Felitti, V.J., Anda, R.F., Nordenberg, D., et al. Relationship of childhood abuse and household dysfunction to many of the leading causes of death in adults. The Adverse Childhood Experiences (ACE) Study. *American Journal of Preventive Medicine*, May 1998, *14*(4), 245–258.

4 Taal, L.A., & Faber, A.W. (1998). Post-traumatic stress, pain and anxiety in adult burn victims. *Burns, 23*, No. 7/8, 545–549.

5 Dionne, C.E. (2005). Psychological distress confirmed as predictor of long-term back-related functional limitations in primary care settings. *Journal of Clinical Epidemiology, 58*(7), 714–718.

6 Sansone, R. A., Pole, M., Dakroub, H., & Butler, M. (2006). Childhood trauma, borderline personality symptomatology and psychophysiological and pain disorders in adulthood. *Psychosomatics, 47*(2), 158–162.

7 Cohen, S. (2005). Keynote presentation at the Eighth International Congress of Behavioral Medicine: The Pittsburg common cold studies: Psychosocial predictors of susceptibility in respiratory infectious illness. *International Journal of Behavioral Medicine, 12*(3), 123–131.

8 Sullivan, R., Wilson, D.A., Feldon, J., Yee, B.K., Meyer. U., Richter-Levin, G., Avi, A., Michael, T., Gruss, M., Bock, J., Helmeke, C., & Braun, K. (2006). The international society for developmental psychobiology annual meeting symposium: Impact of early life experiences on brain and behavioral development. *Developmental Psychobiology*, Nov, *48*(7), 583–602.

9 Sternberg, W.F., Scorr, L., Smith, L.D., Ridgway, C.G., & Stout, M. (2005). Long-term effects of neonatal surgery on adulthood pain behavior. *Pain*, Feb, *113*(3), 347–353.

10 Walker, E.A., Katon, W.J., Roy-Byrne, P.P., Jemelka, R.P., & Russo, J. (1993). Histories of sexual victimization in patients with irritable bowel syndrome or inflammatory bowel disease. *American Journal of Psychiatry, 150*(10), 1502–1506.

11 Hallberg, L.R., & Carlsson, S.G. (1998). Psychosocial vulnerability and maintaining forces related to fibromyalgia. In-depth interviews with twenty-two female patients. *Scandinavian Journal of Caring Sciences, 12*(2), 95–103.

12 Romans, S., Belaise, C., Martin, J., Morris, E., & Raffi, A. (2002). Childhood abuse and later medical disorders in women: An epidemiological study. *Psychotherapy and Psychosomatics*, Basel, May–Jun 2002, 141–149.

13 Jaspers, J.P.C. (1998). Whiplash and post-traumatic stress disorder. *Disability & Rehabilitation*, Nov 1998, *20*(11), 397–404.

14 Walker, A.M., Harris, G., Baker, A., Kelly, D., & Houghton, J. (1999). Post-traumatic stress responses following liver transplantation in older children. *Journal of Child Psychology and Psychiatry*, Mar 1999, *40*(3), 363–374.

15 Cordova, M.J., Cunningham, L.L., Carlson, C.R., & Andrykowski, M.A. (2001). Posttraumatic growth following breast cancer: A controlled comparison study. *Health Psychology*, May 2001, *20*(3), 176–185.

16 Rue, V.M., Coleman, P.K., Rue, J.J, & Reardon, D.C. (2004). Induced abortion and traumatic stress: A preliminary comparison of American and Russian women. *Medical Science Monitor*, Oct 2004, *10*(10), SR5-16. Epub Sep 23, 2004.

17 Beckham, J.C., Crawford, A.L., Feldman, M.E., Kirby, A.C., Hertzberg, M.A., Davidson, J.R.T., & Moore, S.D. (1989). Chronic posttraumatic stress disorder and chronic pain in Vietnam veterans. *Journal of Psychosomatic Research, 43*(4), 379–389.

18 Eisenman, D.P., Gelberg, L., Liu, H., & Shapiro, M.F. (2003). Mental health and health-related quality of life among adult Latino primary care patients living in the United States with previous exposure to political violence. *JAMA*, 2003, *290*, 627–634.

19 Arguelles, L.M., Afari, N., Buchwald, D.S., Clauw, D.J., Furner, S., & Goldberg, J. (2006). A twin study of posttraumatic stress disorder symptoms and chronic widespread pain. *Pain*, May 13, 2006. Epub ahead of print. Downloaded July 4, 2006. www.ncbi.nlm.nih.gov/entrez

20 Romans, S., Belaise, C., Martin, J., Morris, E., & Raffi, A. (2002). Childhood abuse and later medical disorders in women: An epidemiological study. *Psychotherapy and Psychosomatics*, Basel, May–Jun 2002, 141–149.

21 National Center for PTSD Fact Sheet. Based on: Kessler, R.C., et al., Posttraumatic stress disorder in the National Comorbidity Survey. *Archives of General Psychiatry*, Dec 1995, *52*(12), 1048–1060.

22 de Leeuw, R., Schmidt, J.E., & Carlson, C.R. (2005). Traumatic stressors and post-traumatic stress disorder symptoms in headache patients. *Headache*, Nov–Dec 2005, *45*(10), 1365–1374.

23 Fortin, A., & Chamberlain, C. (1995). Preventing the psychological maltreatment of children. *Journal of Interpersonal Violence, 10*, 275–295.

24 Janet, P. (1889). *L'automatisme psychologique*. Paris: Felix Alcan. Reprint. Reprint: Societe Pierre Janet, Paris, 1990.

25 Freud, S. (1962). On the psychical mechanism of hysterical phenomena: A lecture. In J. Strachey (Ed. and trans.), *The Standard Edition of the Complete Psychological Works of Sigmund Freud* (Vol. 3, pp. 25–39). London: Hogarth Press. (Original work published 1893.)

Chapter 2

1 Cosmides, L., & Tooby, J. (2000). Evolutionary psychology and the emotions. In *Handbook of Emotions*. M. Lewis, & J.M. Haviland-Jones (Eds). NewYork: Guilford Press.
Strain, J.J. (1979). Psychological reactions to chronic medical illness. *Psychiatric Quarterly*, *52*(3), Fall, 173–183.

2 Kubler-Ross, E. (1967). *On Death & Dying*.

3 Polatin, P.B., Kinney, R.K., Gatchel, R.J., Lillo, E., & Mayer, T.G. (1993). Psychiatric illness and chronic low-back pain. The mind and the spine— which goes first? *Spine, 18*, 66–71.

4 Burton, K., Polatin, P.B., & Gatchel, R.J. Psychosocial factors and the rehabilitation of patients with chronic work-related upper extremity disorders. *Journal of Occupational Rehabilitation* 1997, *7*, 139–153.

5 Sapolsky, R. (2003). Taming stress. *Scientific American*, September 2003, 87–95.

6 Fernandez, E., & Turk, D.C. (1995). The scope and significance of anger in the experience of chronic pain. *Pain, 61*, 165–175.

7 Gülec, H., Sayar, K., Topbas, M., Karkucak, M., & Ak, I. (2004). Alexithymia and anger in women with fibromyalgia syndrome. *Türk Psikiyatri Derg*, Fall, *15*(3), 191–198.

8 Engel, G.L. (1959). "Psychogenic" pain and the pain-prone patient. *American Journal of Medicine, 26*, 899–918.

9 Carson, J.W., Keefe, F.J., Goli, V., Fras, A.M., Lynch, T.R., Thorp, S.R., & Buechler, J.L. (2005). Forgiveness and chronic low back pain: A preliminary study examining the relationship of forgiveness to pain, anger, and psychological distress. *The Journal of Pain*, Feb, *6*(2), 84–91.

10 McCracken, L.M., & Eccleston, C. (2005). Coping or acceptance: What to do about chronic pain? *Pain*, *105*, 197–204.

11 Ralston, A. (2004). *Between a rock and a hard place*. New York: Atria Books.

Chapter 3

1 Craig, A.D. (2002). How do you feel? Interoception: The sense of the physiological condition of the body. *Nature Reviews Neuroscience*, *3*, 655–666.

2 Rutledge, T., Reis, S.E., Olson, M., et al. (2004). Social networks are associated with lower mortality rates among women with suspected coronary disease: The National Heart, Lung, and Blood Institute-Sponsored Women's Ischemia Syndrome Evaluation Study. *Psychosomatic Medicine*, Nov–Dec, *66*(6), 882–888.

3 Evers, A.W., Kraaimaat, F.W., Geenen, R., Jacobs, J.W., & Bijlsma, J.W. (2003). Stress-vulnerability factors as long-term predictors of disease activity in early rheumatoid arthritis. *Journal of Psychosomatic Research*, Oct, *55*(4), 303–304.

4 Baca, B.E., Cabanas, A.M.L., Perez-Rodriguez, M.M., & Baca-Garcia, E. (2004). Mental disorders in victims of terrorism and their families. *Medicina Clínica (Barc)*, May 15, *122*(18), 681–685.

5 DeVane, C.L. (2001). Substance P: A new era, a new role. *Pharmacotherapy,* Sep 2001, *21*(9), 1061–1069.

6 Woon, Fu L., & Hedges, D.W. (2008). Hippocampal and amygdala volumes in children and adults with childhood maltreatment-related posttraumatic stress disorder: A meta-analysis. *Hippocampus*, *18*(8), 729–736.

7 Teicher, M.H., Samson, J.A., Tomoda, A., Ashy, M., & Anderson, S.L. (2006). Neurobiological and behavioral consequences of exposure to childhood traumatic stress. In Arnetz, B.B., & Ekman, R., *Stress in health and disease*, 190–205. Wiley-VCH. Verlag GmbH & Co. (available online).

8 Kuchinad, A., Schweinhardt, P., Seminowicz, D., et al. (2007). Accelerated brain gray matter loss in fibromyalgia patients: Premature aging of the brain? *The Journal of Neuroscience*, Apr 11, 2007, *27*(15), 4004–4007.

9 Pilowsky, I., Crittenden, I., & Townley, M. (1985) Sleep disturbance in pain clinic patients. *Pain*, *23*, 27–33.

10 Guzman-Marin, R., Bashir, T., Suntsova, N., et al (2007). Adult hippocampal neurogenesis is reduced by sleep fragmentation in the adult rat. *Neuroscience,* Aug 10, 2007, *148*(1), 325–333.

11 Nicassio, P.M., Moxham, E.G., Schuman, C.E., & Gevirtz, R.N. (2002). The contribution of pain, reported sleep quality, and depressive symptoms to fatigue in fibromyalgia. *Pain*, Dec, *100*(3), 271–279.

12 Dotto, L. (1990). *Losing sleep: How your sleeping habits affect your life.* New York: Morrow.

13 Schmidt, N.B., & Cook, J.H. (1999). Effects of anxiety sensitivity on anxiety and pain during a cold pressor challenge in patients with panic disorder. *Behaviour Research and Therapy*, *37*, 313–323.

14 Waldenström, U. (2004). Why do some women change their opinion about childbirth over time? *Birth*, Jun, *31*(2), 102–107.

15 Ohayon, M.M., & Schatzberg, A.F. (2003). Using chronic pain to predict depressive morbidity in the general population. *Archives of General Psychiatry*, Jan, *60*(1), 39–47.

16 Lepine, J.P., & Briley, M. (2004). The epidemiology of pain in depression. *Human Psychopharmacology: Clinical and Experimental*, Oct, *19* Suppl 1, 53–77.

17 Dersh, J., Gatchel, R.J., Mayer, T., Polatin, P., & Temple, O.R. (2006). Prevalence of psychiatric disorders in patients with chronic disabling occupational spinal disorders. *Spine*, May 1, *31*(10), 1156–1162.

18 Ford, D.E. (2003). Depression, trauma and cardiovascular health. In Paula P. Schnurr and Bonnie L. Green (Eds), *Trauma and health: Physical health consequences of exposure to extreme stress.* American Psychological Association, 2003.

19 Marano, Hara Estroff (2002). When depression hurts. *Psychology Today*, Jul–Aug 2002.

20 Gregory, R.J., MD, & Berry, S.L., BS (1999). Measuring counterdependency in patients with chronic pain. *Psychosomatic Medicine*, *61*, 341–345.

21 Barsky, A.J. (1989). Somatoform disorders. In Kaplan, H.I., & Sadock, B.J. (Eds), *Comprehensive textbook of psychiatry*, Vol 1 (5th ed.). (pp. 1009–1027). Baltimore: Williams & Wilkins.

22 Grabe, H.J., MD, Spitzer, C., MD, & Freyberger, H.J., MD (2004). Alexithymia and personality in relation to dimensions of psychopathology. *American Journal of Psychiatry*, July 2004, *161*, 1299–1301.

23 Marchesi, C., Brusamonti, E., & Maggini, C. (2000). Are alexithymia, depression, and anxiety distinct constructs in affective disorders? *Journal of Psychosomatic Research*, *49*(1), 43–49.

24 Taylor, G.J., Parker, J.D.A., Bagby, R.M., & Acklin, M.W. (1992). Alexithymia and somatic complaints in psychiatric out-patients. *Journal of Psychosomatic Research*, *36*, 417–424.

25 Martin, J.B., & Pihl, R.O. (1986). Influence of alexithymic characteristics on physiological and subjective stress responses in normal individuals. *Psychotherapy and Psychosomatics, 45*(2), 66–77.

26 Cox, B.J., Kuch, K., Parker, J.D., Shulman, I.D., & Evans, R.J. (1994). Alexithymia in somatoform disorder patients with chronic pain. *Journal of Psychosomatic Research*, 1994, *38*(6), 523–527.

27 Lumley, M.A., Smith, J.A., & Longo, D.J. (2001). The relationship of alexithymia to pain severity and impairment among patients with chronic myofascial pain: Comparisons with self-efficacy, catastrophizing, and depression. *Journal of Psychosomatic Research,* 2002, *53*(3), 823–830.

28 Lumley, M.A., Stetner, L., & Wehmer, F. (1996). How are alexithymia and physical illness linked? A review and critique of pathways. *Journal of Psychosomatic Research*, Dec 1996, *41*(6), 508–518.

29 Teicher, M.H., Samson, J.A., Tomoda, A., Ashy, M., & Anderson, S.L. (2006). Neurobiological and behavioral consequences of exposure to childhood traumatic stress. In Arnetz, B.B., & Ekman, R., *Stress in health and disease* (pp.190–205). Wiley-VCH. Verlag GmbH & Co. (available online).

30 Calof, D.L. (1995). Dissociation: Nature's tincture of numbing and forgetting. *Treating Abuse Today*, May–Jun, *5*(3), 5–8.

31 Nijenhuis, E.R.S, Van Dyck, R., Ter Kuile, M., Mourits, M., Spinhoven, P., & Van der Hart, O. (1999). Evidence for associations among somatoform dissociation, psychological dissociation and reported trauma in pelvic pain patients. In ERS Nijenhuis, *Somatoform dissociation: Phenomena, measurement and theoretical issues* (pp.146–160). Assen, The Netherlands: Van Gorcum.

32 Krystal, H. (1988). *Integration and self-healing: Affect—Trauma—Alexithymia.* Hillsdale, NJ: Analytic Press. pp.114–115.

33 Putnam, F.W. (1995). Developmental pathways of sexually abused girls. Paper presented at the Harvard Trauma Conference, Boston, MA, USA.

34 Bryant, R.A., Marosszeky, J.E., Crooks, J.J., Baguley, I.J., & Gurka, J.A. (1999). Interaction of posttraumatic stress disorder and chronic pain following traumatic brain injury. *Journal of Head Trauma Rehabilitation,* Dec, *14*(6), 588–594.

35 Maaranen, P., Tanskanen, A., Honkalampi, K., Haatainen, K., Hintikka, J., & Viinamäki, H. (2005) Factors associated with pathological dissociation in the general population. *Australian and New Zealand Journal of Psychiatry*, May, *39*(5), 387–394.

36 Lumley, M.A., Smith, J.A., & Longo, D.J. (2002). The relationship of alexithymia to pain severity and impairment among patients with chronic

myofascial pain: Comparisons with self-efficacy, catastrophizing and depression. *Journal of Psychosomatic Research*, Sep 2002, *53*(3), 823–830.

37 Peterson, C., Seligman, M., Yurko, K., Martin, L., & Friedman, H. (1998). Catastrophizing and untimely death. *Psychological Science*, Mar, *9*(2), 127–132.

38 Scaer, R.C. (2001). The neurophysiology of dissociation and chronic disease. *Applied Psychophysiology and Biofeedback*, *26*(1), 73–91.

39 Staud, R. (2000). *Abnormal pain memory helps to explain fibromyalgia*. Downloaded from www.sciencedaily.com/releases/2000/10/001030082926.htm

Chapter 4

1 Rome, H.P., & Rome, J. Jr (2000). Limbically augmented pain syndrome (LAPS): Kindling, corticolimbic sensitization, and the convergence of affective and sensory symptoms in chronic pain disorders. *Pain Medicine*, 2000, *1*(1), 7–23.

2 Ray, A.L., & Zbik, A. (2001). Cognitive behavioral therapies and beyond. In C.D. Tollison, J.R. Satterthwaite & J.W. Tollison (Eds), *Practical pain management, third edition*. Philadelphia: Lippincott Williams & Wilkins.

3 Craig, A.D. (2002). How do you feel? Interoception: The sense of the physiological condition of the body. *Nature Reviews Neuroscience 3*, 655–666.

4 Castrén, E. (2005). Is mood chemistry? *Nature Reviews Neuroscience*, Mar 2005, *6*(3), 241–246.

5 deCharms, R.C., Maeda, F., Glover, G.H., et al. (2005). Control over brain activation and pain learned by using real-time functional MRI. *Proceedings of National Academy of Sciences*, Dec 20, 2005, 18626–18631.

6 Brown, D., Scheflin, A., & Hammond, D. (1998). *Memory, Trauma Treatment and the Law*. New York: Norton.

7 Servan-Schreiber, D. (2004). *Healing without Freud or Prozac*. London: Rodale Ltd.

8 van der Kolk, B. (2002). Beyond the talking cure: Somatic experience and subcortical imprints in the treatment of trauma. In Francine Shapiro (Ed.), *EMDR as an integrative psychotherapy approach*. American Psychological Association. Washington DC, USA.

9 Siegel, D.J. (2002). The developing mind and the resolution of trauma: Some ideas about information processing and an interpersonal neurobiology of psychotherapy. In Francine Shapiro (Ed.), *EMDR as an integrative psychotherapy approach*. American Psychological Association. Washington DC, USA.

10 Glaser, J.L., Brind, J.L., Vogelman, J.H., Eisner, M.J., Dillbeck, M.C., Wallace, R.K., Chopra, D., & Orentreich, N. (1990). Studies with long-term participants of the Transcendental Meditation and TM-Sidhi program. *Journal of Psychology, 124*(2), 177–197.

11 Foa, E.B., Keane, T.M., & Friedman M.J., et al. (2008). *Effective treatments for PTSD: Practice guidelines from International Society for Traumatic Situations* 2nd ed. The Guilford Press.

12 Elofsson, U.O., von Scheele, B., Theorell, T., & Sondergaard, H.P. (2007). Physiological correlates of eye movement desensitization and reprocessing. *Journal of Anxiety Disorders*, June 3, Epub ahead of print.

13 Levin, P., Lazrove, S., & van der Kolk, B. (1999). What psychological testing and neuroimaging tell us about the treatment of posttraumatic stress disorder by eye movement desensitization and reprocessing. *Journal of Anxiety Disorders*, Jan–Apr, *13*(1–2), 159–172.

14 van der Kolk, B., Burbridge, J., & Suzuki, J. (1997). The psychobiology of traumatic memory: Clinical implications of neuroimaging studies. *Annals of the New York Academy of Sciences*, *821*, 99–113.

15 Elofsson, U.O., von Scheele, B., Theorell, T., & Sondergaard, H.P. (2007). Physiological correlates of eye movement desensitization and reprocessing. *Journal of Anxiety Disorders*, Jun 3, Epub ahead of print.

16 Bagby, R.M., Taylor, G.J., & Parker, J.D.A (1994). The twenty-item Toronto alexithymia scale — II: Convergent, discriminant, and concurrent validity. *Journal of Psychosomatic Research*, *38*(1), 33–40.

Chapter 5

1 Baca, B.E., Cabanas, A.M.L., Perez-Rodriguez, M.M., & Baca-Garcia, E. (2004). Mental disorders in victims of terrorism and their families. *Medicina Clínica (Barc)*, May 15, *122*(18), 681–685.

2 Evers, A.W., Kraaimaat, F.W., Geenen, R., Jacobs, J.W., & Bijlsma, J.W. (2003). Stress-vulnerability factors as long-term predictors of disease activity in early rheumatoid arthritis. *Journal of Psychosomatic Research*, Oct, *55*(4), 303–304.

3 Thieme, K., et al. (2005). Predictors of pain behaviors in fibromyalgia syndrome. *Arthritis and Rheumatism*, *53*(3), 343–350.

4 Rutledge, T., Reis, S.E., Olson, M., et al. (2004). Social networks are associated with lower mortality rates among women with suspected coronary disease: The National Heart, Lung, and Blood Institute-Sponsored Women's Ischemia Syndrome Evaluation study. *Psychosomatic Medicine*, Nov–Dec, *66*(6), 882–888.

5 Hawkley, L.C., & Cacioppo, J.T. (2003). Loneliness and pathways to disease. *Brain Behavior and Immunology*, Feb, *17* Suppl 1, S98–105.

6 Cyrulnik, B. (2005). *The whispering of ghosts: Trauma and resilience.* New York: Other Press.

7 Usher, R. (2001). The sunnier, southern side of the street. *Time*, p. 87, November 12, 2001.

8 Kleinman, A. (1988). *The illness narratives: Suffering, healing, and the human condition*. New York: Basic Books Inc.

9 Cozolino, L. (2002). *The neuroscience of psychotherapy: Building and rebuilding the human brain*. New York: W. W. Norton & Co.

10 Pennebaker, J.W. (1990). *Opening up: The healing power of expressing emotions*. New York: Guilford Press.

11 Solano, L., Donati, V., Pecci, F., Persichetti, S., & Colaci, A. (2003). Postoperative course after papilloma resection: Effects of written disclosure of the experience in subjects with different alexithymia levels. *Psychosomatic Medicine, 65*, 477–484.

Chapter 6

1 Siegel, D.J. (1999). *The developing mind*. New York: Guilford Press.

2 Damasio, Antonio (1999). *The feeling of what happens: Body, emotion and the making of consciousness*. London: Heinemann.

3 Connelly, M., Keefe, F.J., Affleck, G., et al. (2007). Effects of day-to-day affect regulation on the pain experience of patients with rheumatoid arthritis. *Pain*, Sep 2007, *131*(1–2), 162–170.

4 Greenspan, S.I., & Shanker, S.G. (2004). *The First Idea*. Da Capo Press. Chapters 1 and 2.

5 Furnham, A., & Petrides, K.V. (2003). Trait emotional intelligence and happiness. *Social Behaviour and Personality, 31*(8), 815–824.

6 Paquet, C., Kergoat, M.J., & Dubé, L. (2005). The role of everyday emotion regulation on pain in hospitalized elderly: Insights from a prospective within-day assessment. *Pain*, Jun, *115*(3), 355–363.

7 Goleman, D. (1995). *Emotional intelligence: Why it can matter more than IQ*. New York: Bantam Books.

8 Linehan, M.M. (1993). *Skills training manual for treating borderline personality disorder*. New York: Guilford Press.

9 Mar, R.A., Oatley, K., Hirsh, J., de la Paz, J., Peterson, J.B. (2006). Bookworms versus nerds: Exposure to fiction versus non-fiction, divergent associations with social ability, and the simulation of fictional social worlds. *Journal of Research in Personality, 40*, 694–712.

Chapter 7

1 Connelly, M., Keefe, F.J., Affleck, G., et al. (2007). Effects of day-to-day affect regulation on the pain experience of patients with rheumatoid arthritis. *Pain*, 2007, Sep, *131*(1–2); 162–170.

2 Paquet, C., Kergoat, M.J., & Dubé, L. (2005). The role of everyday emotion regulation on pain in hospitalized elderly: Insights from a prospective within-day assessment. *Pain*, Jun, *115*(3), 355–363.

3 Shapiro, F. (1989). Efficacy of the eye movement desensitization procedure in the treatment of traumatic memories. *Journal of Traumatic Stress*, 2, 199–223.

4 Kabat-Zinn, J. (1990). *Full Catastrophe Living*. New York: Delta Books.

5 Grossman, P., Niemann, L., Schmidt, S., & Walach, H. (2004). Mindfulness-based stress reduction and health benefits: A meta-analysis. *Journal of Psychosomatic Research,* Jul, *57*(1), 35–43.

6 Lazar, S.W., Kerr, C.E.M., Wasserman, R.H., et al. (2006). Meditation experience is associated with increased cortical thickness. *Neuroreport*, Nov 28, 2005, *16*(17), 1893–1897.

7 Siegal, D.J. (2007). *The mindful brain: Reflection and attunement in the cultivation of well-being.* USA: W.W. Norton & Co.

8 Elofsson, U.O., von Scheele, B., Theorell, T., & Sondergaard, H.P. (2007). Physiological correlates of eye movement desensitization and reprocessing. *Journal of Anxiety Disorders*, Jun 3, Epub ahead of print.

9 Levin, P., Lazrove, S., & van der Kolk, B. (1999). What psychological testing and neuroimaging tell us about the treatment of posttraumatic stress disorder by eye movement desensitization and reprocessing. *Journal of Anxiety Disorders*, Jan–Apr, *13*(1–2), 159–172.

10 Lansing, K.M., Amen, D.G., & Klindt, E.C. (2000, November). *Tracking the neurological impact of CBT and EMDR in the treatment of PTSD.* Paper presented at the annual meeting of the Association for the Advancement for Behavior Therapy, New Orleans, LA, USA.

11 van der Kolk, B., Burbridge, J., & Suzuki, J. (1997). The psychobiology of traumatic memory: Clinical implications of neuroimaging studies. *Annals of the New York Academy of Sciences*, *821*, 99–113.

Chapter 8

1 Warburton, D.E., Nicol, C.W., & Bredin, S.S. (2006). Health benefits of physical activity: The evidence. *CMAJ*, *174*(6), 801–809.

2 Trivedi, M.H., Greer, T.L., Grannemann, B.D., Chambliss, H.O., & Jordan, A.N. (2006). Exercise as an augmentation strategy for treatment of major depression. *Journal of Psychiatric Practice*, *12*(4), 205–213.

3 Ratey, J. (2008). *Spark: The revolutionary new science of exercise and the brain.* New York: Little Brown & Co.

4 Hayden, J.A., van Tulder, M.W., Malmivaara, A., & Koes, B.W. (2005). Meta-analysis: Exercise therapy for nonspecific low back pain. *Annals of Internal Medicine*, 2005, May 3, *142*(9), 765–775.

5 Smith, T.P., Kennedy, S.L., Smith, M., Orent, S., & Fleshner, M. (2006). Physiological improvements and health benefits during an exercise-based comprehensive rehabilitation program in medically complex patients. *Exercise Immunology Review, 12,* 86–96.

Chapter 9

1 Ancoli-Israel, S. (2001). "Sleep is not tangible" or What the Hebrew tradition has to say about sleep. *Psychosomatic Medicine, 63,* 778–787.

2 Davis, G.C. (2003). Improved sleep may reduce arthritis pain. *Holistic Nursing Practice,* May–Jun, 128–135.

3 Hartman, K., & Pivik, R.T. (1995). Sleep variations in motor and EEG activities in chronic low back pain subjects: Relationship to sleep quality. *Sleep Research, 24,* 393.

4 Haack, M., & Mullington, J.M. (2005). Sustained sleep restriction reduces emotional and physical well-being. *Pain,* Dec 15, *119*(1–3), 56–64, Epub Nov 16.

5 Killgore, W.D., Kahn-Greene, E.T.T., Lipizzi, E.L., Newman, R.A., Kamimori, G.H., & Balkin, T.J. (2007). Sleep deprivation reduces perceived emotional intelligence and constructive thinking skills. *Sleep Medicine,* Aug 30, Epub ahead of print.

6 Older, S.A., Battafarano, D.F., Danning, C.L., et al. (2005). Delta wave sleep interruption and fibromyalgia symptoms in healthy subjects. [Abstract] *Journal of Musculoskeletal Pain, 3*(Suppl 1), 159.

7 Bader, K., Schafer, V., Schenkel, M., Nissen, L., & Schwander, J. (2007). Adverse childhood experiences associated with sleep in primary insomnia. *Journal of Sleep Research,* Sep, *16*(3), 285–296.

8 Brody, J.E. (2000). New respect for the nap, a pause that refreshes. *Science Times,* Jan 4, 2000.

9 Howard, P.J. (2000). *The owner's manual for the brain.* Bard Press, pp. 127–154.

10 Miaskowski, C., & Lee, K. (1999). Pain, fatigue, and sleep disturbances in oncology outpatients receiving radiation therapy for bone metastasis: A pilot study. *Journal of Pain and Symptom Management,* May, *17*(5), 320–332.

11 Wozniak, P. (2000). Good sleep, good learning, good life. Downloaded March 3, 2008. http://supermemo.com/articles/sleep.htm# Siesta%20and%20catnapping

12 Malhotra, S., Sawhney, G., Pandhi, P. (2004). The therapeutic potential of melatonin: A review of the science. *Medscape General Medicine, 6*(2), 46. Downloaded May 25, 2007. www.medscape.com/viewarticle/47238

Chapter 10

1 Young, J.E. (1999). *Cognitive therapy for personality disorders: A schema-focused approach (revised edition)*. Sarasota, Florida: Professional Resource Press.

2 Peterson, C., & Seligman, M.E.P. (1984). Causal explanations as a risk factor for depression: Theory and evidence. *Psychological Review, 91*, 347–374.

3 Peterson, C., & Bossio, L.M. (1991). *Health and optimism*. New York: Free Press.

4 de Charms, R.C., Fumiko, M., Glover, G.H., et al (2005). Control over brain activation and pain learned by using real-time functional MRI. *Proceedings of the National Academy of Sciences of the United States of America*. Dec 20, 2005. *102*(51), 18626–18631.

5 Roffman, J. (2005). How does psychotherapy change the brain: What neuroimaging has taught us about psychotherapy. *Curbside Consultant, 4*(2), Jun–Jul 2005.

6 Lyubomirsky, S., Souza, L., & Dickerhoof, R. (2006). The costs and benefits of writing, talking, and thinking about life's triumphs and defeats. *Journal of Personality and Social Psychology, 90*, 692–708.

Chapter 11

1 Davidson, R.J. (2000). Affective style, psychopathology, and resilience: Brain mechanisms and plasticity. *American Psychologist, 55*, 1196–1214.

2 Urry, H.L., Nitschke, J.B., Dolski, I., et al. (2004). Making a life worth living: Neural correlates of well-being. *Psychological Science, 15*(6), 367–372.

3 Kluger, Jeffery (2009). The biology of belief. *Time*, Feb 23, 2009, pp. 32–36.

4 Rosen, S. (1982). *My voice will go with you: The teaching tales of Milton H. Erickson*. New York: W.W. Norton & Co., pp. 47–52.

5 Hesley, J. (2001). *Rent two films and let's talk in the morning*. New York: John Wiley & Sons Inc.

6 Bates, M.S., Rankin-Hill, L., Sanchez-Ayendez, M. (1997). The effects of the cultural context of health care on treatment and response to chronic pain and illness. *Social Science & Medicine, 45*(9), 1433–1447.

7 Marano, H.E. (1999). The power of play: Psychological benefits of play. *Psychology Today*, Jul 1999.

8 Cousins, N. (1976). *Anatomy of an illness*. New York: W.W. Norton.

9 Laughter best medicine for hope. *Medical Research News*, Apr 11, 2005. Downloaded Apr 17, 2006. www.news-medical.net/

10 Matthews, D.A., McCullough, M.E., Larson, D.B., Koenig, H.G., Swyers, J.P., & Milano, M.G. (1998). Religious commitment and health status. *Archives of Family Medicine*, *7*, 118–124.

11 Larson, D.B., Sherill, K.A., Lyons, J.S., Craigie, F.C., Thielman, S.B., Greenwold, M.A., et al. (1992). Associations between dimensions of religious commitment and mental health reported in the American Journal of Psychiatry and Archives of General Psychiatry: 1978–1989. *American Journal of Psychiatry*, *149*, 557–559.

12 Levin, J.S., Larson, D.B., & Puchalski, C.M. (1997). Religion and spirituality in medicine: Research and education. *Journal of the American Medical Association*, *278*, 792–793.

13 Oxman, T.E., Freeman, D.H., & Manheimer, E.D. (1995). Lack of social participation or religious strength and comfort as risk factors for death after cardiac surgery in the elderly. *Psychosomatic Medicine*, *57*, 5–15.

14 Weisskopf, M. (2007). *Blood brothers*. New York: Henry Holt & Company.

Chapter 12

1 Shapiro, F. (1989). Eye movement desensitization: A new treatment for post-traumatic stress disorder. *Journal of Behavior Therapy & Experimental Psychiatry*, *20*(3), pp. 211–217.

2 Wilson, S.A., Becker, L.A., & Tinker, R.H. (1997). Fifteen-month follow-up of eye movement desensitization and reprocessing (EMDR) treatment for PTSD and psychological trauma. *Journal of Consulting and Clinical Psychology*, 65, 1047–1056.

3 Shapiro, F. (2002). Appendix A: Evaluations of EMDR. In *EMDR as an integrative psychotherapy approach*. American Psychological Association, Washington DC, USA.

4 Grant, M., & Threlfo, C. (2002). EMDR in the treatment of chronic pain. *Journal of Clinical and Consulting Psychology*, *58*(12), 1–16.

5 de Roos, C.J.A.M., Veenstra, A.C., den Hollander-Gijsman, M.E., van der Wee, N.J.A., de Jongh, A., Zitman, F.G., & van Rood, R.Y. (2006). Eye movement desensitization and reprocessing (EMDR) for chronic phantom limb pain (PLP): A preliminary study of 10 cases. *Pain* (in press).

6 Schneider, J., Hofmann, A., Rost, C., & Shapiro, F. (2006). EMDR in the treatment of chronic phantom limb pain. *Pain Medicine* (in press).

7 Wilson, S.A., Becker, L.A., & Tinker, R.H. (1997). EMDR treatment of phantom limb pain. Conference report regarding EMDR treatment of 6 patients with phantom limb pain. *EMDR International Conference, 1997,* San Francisco, USA.

8 Ray, A.R., & Zbik, A. (2002). Cognitive behavioral therapies and beyond. In Tollison, C.D., Sattherwaite, J.R., & Tollison, J.W. (Eds). *Practical Pain Management*, pp. 189–207. Philadelphia: Lippincott Williams & Wilkins.

INDEX

Made in the USA